Ideology and Christian Freedom

A theo-political reading of Shusaku Endo's 'Silence'

Matthew A. Stanley

Samsara Diagnostics

CONTENTS

This book is dedicated to my son, Judah, whose smile greeted me each morning after my writing session.
I pray that he grows into a man who walks with God — strong, free, wise, and full of love.

FOREWORD

Ever since I first watched Martin Scorsese's adaptation of *Silence* during my junior year at Wheaton College, Endo Shusaku's work has been something of a gordian knot for me — his text ties together the inextricable questions of faith, philosophy, and culture which have come to captivate my attention.

I have not stopped returning to this story year after year. Every time I do, my mind is again flooded with a torrent of questions. It reminds me afresh of the profound complexity of the situation we find ourselves in as finite creatures.

Setting aside for a moment the techniques of story craft which Endo wields so masterfully, the hold this novel exercises over me derives from how it unites a specific constellation of problems — Christianity, Buddhism, power, culture, freedom, psychology, faith... the list could go on.

In this text, the three pillars of my own inquiry — Christian theology, Western philosophy, and Japanese Buddhism — all come together to dialogue with (and complicate!) each other. The story told in *Silence* provides a way into this web, and facilitates a path to start in one problem and travel by way of the text to any other node in the network.

This book was born from traveling these paths again and again, and now I am attempting to knit them back together again.

My hope for this text is that readers would enjoy each chapter alongside Endo's novel, and that each one would illuminate a perhaps previously unseen thread operating in that text. More than anything, this work is a success only in so far as it serves to drive the reader's deeper wrestling and engagement with Endo's story.

***

I would like to thank two people specifically who were so kind and supportive to me in college when I was intensely working on these questions — Dr. Miho Nonaka and Dr. Hanmee Kim. You both provided me an opportunity in your classes to re-read *Silence*, to question the story anew, and to read the text within all the difficulties and ambiguities of its context. I'm grateful for your instruction and for the care you showed me as a student.

I also need to thank all of the people who pre-ordered this book. You all gave me the support that I needed to know that others wanted to hear what I had to say, and the promise that I made to you carried me at many points in the writing process. Thank you, Michael Sawyer, Thad and Nancy Stanley, Sandy Coffee, Bill Harley, Nick Gallo, Daniel Pessoa, Steven Reitz, Paul Bedore, Michael Contrares, Eric Taggart, and Lucas Berry.

Finally, I could not have completed this work without the support of my loving wife, Bethany. She sacrificed to give me the time and space to write, and she provided me with the clarity and encouragement I needed when the going got hard. The way that she loves our son with such a high level of consistent care makes me love and respect her immensely. I'm thankful to call her my wife, my teammate, my friend. I love you, honey.

I'm immensely thankful that you, dear reader, would consider taking the time to read my work. I offer it up to you unsure if it will help anyone on their journey, but I have hope that it will find the right people at the right time. *Silence* was that text for me, and it's an honor to offer something back to the book which has given me so much.

Soli Deo Gloria

INTRODUCTION

By way of introduction

Endo Shusaku's novel *Silence* still remains largely unknown to the public, even despite the tailwinds from a recent paperback re-publication and an acclaimed film adaptation by Martin Scorsese. I found as I was writing this book that when I asked people if they had heard of the novel or the movie, the majority would shake their heads. However, I also found that many would return to me weeks or months later saying that they had watched the movie and found it captivating. Frankly, I've never met anyone who has interacted with the work without it also have a powerful effect upon them.

The Japanese-Catholic writer Endo Shusaku (1923-1996) published *Silence* (*Chinmoku*) in the year 1966, and the English translation appeared a mere three years later. The novel was received with acclaim by the literary community, even winning the prestigious Tanizaki Prize in the year it was released. The book has since received three film adaptions — Japanese (1971), Portuguese (1996), English (2016) — and Endo even penned a stage adaptation called *The Golden Country*.

Silence tells the story of two young Jesuit priests who travel to Japan during the early half of the 17th century in order to locate one of their old mentors who, they have heard reports, has apostatized under the

Tokugawa regime's brutal persecution of the Christian Church. Their arrival in Japan immerses them in a world of squalid poverty, brutal violence, and complex spiritual conflict, all of which begins to break up their old conceptions of self, casting them on a journey where their relationship to God and others is irrevocably transformed. The two priests arrive at starkly different conclusions, and the text provides its readers with no final answers.

I was attending Wheaton College (IL) at the time when the school announced that the novel *Silence* would serve as the cornerstone of the newly developed "common core curriculum." Every freshman had to read the book in one of their core seminars, while I, as a senior, would go on to read (and re-read) the novel in two of my upper division courses the following year. This challenging text has been a constant companion to me ever since I first encountered it. I can still recall how the book and its themes suffused my college campus, creating a collective atmosphere of wrestling. Moments like these remain rare in our age of virulent social atomism.

I carried all of this — the text, the movie, my questions, and our collective wrestling — with me as I graduated from college. When I found myself on my own for the first time, caught in the sweltering heat of a Chicago summer, I turned for solace to the books which I knew so well. The only things I had known how to do well to that point in my life was to think and to write, so think and write was precisely what I did. On my evenings and weekends I feverishly typed on my laptop, crammed into tiny coffee shops huddled under the towering monstrosities of the endless Chicago sprawl. The seeds of this book were being planted just as autumn gave way to those short and frigid winter days on the shores of Lake Michigan.

This project finds its formal genesis in a conference presentation that never was. Near the end of 2018, I was accepted to present a paper at the Society of Christianity & Literature's conference in Denver that following spring. My proposed talk had as its subject a reading of *Silence* which drew on ideas from Karl Barth and Slavoj Žižek in order to portray Fr. Rodriguez' decision as a radically counter-intuitive act of faith.

However, things would turn out differently. On a cold winter's night in early March, the apartment abutting mine caught fire, leaving my own apartment uninhabitable, and landing me on friends' couches for the next month. Add in being handed an exceptionally demanding and time-sensitive project at work, and I found myself in over my head. I had to regretfully withdraw the presentation. In many ways, this book is an attempt to complete what I had begun then. However, it also represents an evolution of that original vision. I look back with thankfulness that God gave me more time to think, to grow, and to re-consider. This book might not have existed if my life had continued on the path I thought I was following at the time.

This book's mission

This book carries a simple burden — to investigate how to live in the freedom at the heart of Jesus' teaching.

In order to accomplish that mission, this book serves as an intervention at three different levels of discourse. First, on the face of it, this text provides the reader with an orientation to the historical context and conflicts which run through Endo's novel *Silence*. By then placing the characters and their experiences into this historical context, we will venture some analysis and judgments about their decisions. Please be aware that this does mean I will be discussing spoilers — this book is best read after having read *Silence*, or at least after having watched Scorsese's film adaptation. This book's theoretical intervention at the level of literary and historical discourse aims to enrich the reader's own wrestling with Endo's novel by intensifying the conflicts which run like deep currents through the text, and thus it serves to supplement the reading process.

However, as I've started to indicate already, this book speaks to our own moment as well. It also operates at the level of contemporary Christian discourse by attempting to address a context in which conversations about the relationship between Christianity and the nation-state have returned with a renewed force.

This book has in mind both the Christian Nationalism which has taken root in conservative Christian communities and the forms of progressivism, social justice activism, and intersectionality which have been taken up by many on the Christian Left. Against the revival of Christian Nationalism on the Right, this book contends that Christianity has always been disruptive to any nationalist project because it identifies with whichever element in the social body is excluded in order to achieve the formation of the unified fiction called the "nation-state." The forces of love and liberation at work in the work of Jesus in and through His Spirit community the Church cannot find a place within the striated structure and ideological stasis of the nationalist project. They are thus constantly undermining and resisting the homogenizing forces of nationalism because the freedom in which the Spirit community lives cannot be fully represented or co-opted for the sake of the utility of the whole political community. It always threatens to become a doorway for the radical in-breaking of God's apocalyptic change.

This picture of Christianity demands that we rehabilitate a liberation theology for our moment. However, any contemporary re-formulation of a liberation theology must also take into account its historical and material context. As the Christian Left has increasingly

taken onboard the discourse, norms, and practices of progressive ideologies which are generated by the governing apparatus of our society,
they have become captured and neutered for the project of liberation.
The alliance between the bio-political state and the global forces of
capital continually stir up a maelstrom of speech about identity and
rights, but these words pose no threat to the ruling order. One cries
in the street for absolute control over the pronouns which refer to
them, while they nonetheless obliviously endure the debasement of
their money, the servitude of wage-labor, the poisoning of their food,
and the disabling effects of metastasizing state bureaucracy.

Thus, we are lead to the third level at which this text attempts to
intervene into our context. In our haste to resist the dehumanizing
forces of this alliance between the bio-political state and the inhuman
operation of capital, we must not lose sight of the very mechanism of
that freedom — our ability to become a *subject* which can intervene in
the world, surpassing the mere passivity of being an object. How can
the human being act outside of this seamless fabric of physical, chem-
ical, and biological processes? What is the grounds for the human's
freedom?

Archimedes famously said "Give me a lever long enough and a fulcrum on which to place it, and I shall move the world." The lever is the
easy part of this experiment — the question is where he would place
the fulcrum. Without a fulcrum, there is no leverage, and so too with
the human's experience in their world. Without a fulcrum to provide
a leverage point, a creature cannot interrupt the continual flow of
reality in order to introduce a cut or a break. The animal continuously
produces behaviors under the conditions of its environment, but the
human being has acquired this ability to resist, to stop, and to re-direct
— this standpoint of freedom is called subjectivity.

The place from which the subject acts constitutes the terrifying abyss which threatens every stable arrangement, whether natural or human. This is not only because the work of freedom cannot necessarily be determined from the outset, but also because the human who is free is not completely in control of the event which is emerging through our experience of freedom. Slavoj Žižek describes this experience beautifully in his *Freedom: A Disease without Cure* where he characterizes the highest experience of freedom as that of *compulsion.* At the moment when we are most free, we find that we cannot *not* be free. We find ourselves at the disposal of some*thing* else, as though freedom is actualizing itself *through* us![1] As human beings, we cannot escape our freedom, but rather remain responsible for our freedom at all times. This is why we cannot absolve the Nazi guard who was "just following orders." Nonetheless, this experience of freedom also reveals that we are not a unified whole in possession of a self-identity. The place where we act from in our freedom is a standpoint which is, somehow, *outside of us* while simultaneously remaining the source of our most intimate, personal, and radically singular experiences.

What is in this book?

We will travel through Endo's text to an exploration of human freedom as such. At each point in this text, its words can be heard in any of these discursive registers, but since I have nonetheless been forced by necessity to decide on a definite structure for this book — the chapters will proceed in the following way:

---

1. Slavoj Žižek, *Freedom: A Disease without Cure* (London: Bloomsbury, 2023), 8-9.

Chapter one introduces the reader to what I call "the Missing Prologue" of *Silence* — the history of the Japanese people in their encounter with Christianity, and especially the anomalous event we now called the Shimabara Rebellion. Although Endo's novel places the reader near the end of the Christianity century in Japan (1549 to 1650), he does not supply us with much context for these violent persecutions. Thus, this book attempts to provide a streamlined introduction to the history of Christianity in Japan. As Christianity enters a few centuries of twilight in Japan during Endo's narrative, we have to ask ourselves how it came to this, what role all the involved parties had to play, and whether things could have turned out differently. This will set the stage for our investigations in subsequent chapters.

The second chapter expands and re-examines the historical account of the Japanese people, this time looking at the story from the political perspective of the Tokugawa regime and their nationalistic project to forge a unified Japan. What central problem was the Tokugawa regime trying to solve in their persecutions, and thus what threat did they perceive Christianity as posing to the people of Japan? This chapter contextualizes the story of Christianity within the broader story of the Japanese people, and especially the island of Kyushu where Endo's novel takes place. We will see how Kyushu represents the 'outside' which constantly intrudes into the attempted production of an 'inside' to the Yamato imperial line (and later, the Tokugawa regime). We will also take a look at the methods of violence, social control, and ideology which the Tokugawa regime used to achieve this fictional construction of a Japanese "people" and a truly Japanese "nation."

The third chapter asks the question of the role of Buddhism in Japanese history, and especially its failure to produce substantive political resistance or to mobilize the peasantry. The reader will be introduced to how Buddhism was imported and implemented in Japan, its entanglement with the political establishment, transformations during the Kamakura period, and the changes it underwent during the times of the three warlords who were unifying Japan during Christianity's growth in Japan. The reader will also be introduced to the critiques of Fukansai Habian, a former Zen monk and Japanese-Christian apologist who wrote the *Myotei Mondo*, an extended dialogue in which a Christian nun expounds and engages with the major schools of Buddhism to advance an ethical critique of Japanese religion. Habian argues that Buddhism ultimately dead-ends into a nihilistic ethical vision, and that only Christian furnishes the resources to live according to right and wrong in this life.

Having traveled through a comprehensive investigation of the historical context and its conflicts, the text takes a theoretical turn to begin considering the psychological experience of Rodriguez. Chapter four dives deep into the strategy which the Inquisitor Inoue uses to extract apostasy from Fr. Rodriguez. To understand Inoue's psychological stratagems, we turn to Friedrich Nietzsche's critique of pity to perceive the unique ways which compassion and victimhood can be used for coercion. As a priest, Fr. Rodriguez finds himself especially vulnerable to the peculiar dangers of being in a helping relationship to others, and thus he is uniquely susceptible to the strategy which Inoue uses to gaslight him, break down his self-structure, and enable the discovery and enactment of a new way of being which is more in line with power's demands.

Chapter five moves to clearly articulate the centrality of freedom in our understanding of the good news of Christianity. We focus on what Jesus said that he came to do, how it resonates with core themes in the Old Testament, and the radical way that Paul picks up these motifs in his own work. Along the way, we try to formulate a liberation theology which opposes itself both to the nationalist project but also the progressive cooptation of liberation discourse. We focus instead on how liberation theology follows Jesus in attempting to side with the contradiction in society, for as we saw in chapter two, every whole is established through the rejection of some despised element. Jesus makes himself this rejected part which founds the whole, and thus the message of Jesus compels his followers to identify with the scapegoat as well in our struggle to live into the freedom of God-in-Christ.

Chapter six rounds out the text with an exploration of contemporary subjectivity alongside a reading of Rodriguez and his decision to step on the *fumi-e*. We will investigate the pervasive role of cynicism in the condition of modernity, and how the explosion of interest in meditation, drugs, Stoicism, and other personal regimes are symptomatic of this cynicism which survives through an intense attachment to the ego. This stance of "Western Buddhism" as Žižek calls it allows one to accommodate themselves to the daily experience of structural violence and oppression, all in order to posture as an individual or find some deeper meaning without affecting any material changes. Rodriguez's decision to give power what it demands — compliance — in exchange for his private and ineffectual faith. Our attempts to cast Rodriguez's choice to step on the *fumi-e* as brave or indicative of some deeper spiritual insight obscures the structural effects and material location of Rodriguez's decision. When we overlook the material network of signs and objects which make up the process of mean-ing, we prepare ourselves to accept power's dangerous deal where we can enjoy meaning in our hearts while nonetheless remaining in deep complicity with oppression.

Finally, the Conclusion will explicitly engage in some analysis of the contemporary revival of nationalism, especially the Christian variant, in order to alert us to what we are in danger of losing through a full-throated return to nationalist or patriotic projects. A central

contention of this book will be that Christianity inherently under-
mines the project of nation-building, that it de-stabilizes ideological
formations, and that it radicalizes selfs into subjects who act towards
liberation and the experience of God's freedom. Any attempts to
develop a Christian nationalism must necessarily file these elements
down in the Gospel message. Nonetheless, both sides of the political
spectrum suffer from the Western Buddhist stance exemplified by Fr.
Rodriguez in *Silence*, which means that we must renew our labor
of being in relationship with others and working towards concrete
liberation, especially for the poor and the downtrodden who are so
precious in the eyes of God.

The imperative to surrender to the winepress

I want to clarify at the outset — while this book is critical of Fr. Rodriguez's actions, we are not overly harsh or excessively fault-finding.
We merely wish to move one layer deeper than the moralistic discourse
of youth pastors and apologists who would make of Endo's novel a
moral fable in which the hero falls by blatantly transgressing God's
command. This text ventures beyond the facile debate of whether it
was morally right or wrong for Rodriguez to apostatize, and instead
charts a course into the choppier waters of the manifold complexities
of moral psychology. Why did Rodriguez make his choice, what did
he really do, what did it really mean, and how can we find ourselves
implicated in this story as well?

Life is a *situation*, and we must endeavor to treat it as such, for
Endo's novel invites us to see *ourselves* in Rodriguez, and in this maneuver we discover that all of his temptations are our own. We find
ourselves, just like Fr. Rodriguez, riven by contradictory senses of
duty, compassion, and self-reproach, discovering ourselves already in

the midst of a complex terrain of power struggles whose histories and outlines we can hardly trace. The siren song of inner peace and outer conformity offers us an end to the conflict, but in the process they transform each one of us into a mendacious agent who betrays the kingdom which God in Christ is bringing into the world.

A word of warning — to read *Silence* well, we must first rid ourselves of the belief that we are better than any person in the text. Rodriguez's internal grandiosity and final apostasy, Kichijiro's craven conformity and incessant groveling, Inoue's ruthless calculations and political persecutions, Ferreira's pitiless collaboration and despairing resignation— none of these are below any of us. They crouch at our side as an ever-present possibility. We must resist at any cost the temptation to indulge in feelings of self-righteousness which exalts ourselves over these characters, for not only did Jesus tirelessly decry such a stance as deceptive and misleading, but also because it will hinder us from fully engaging with the possibilities inherent in this text.

What would we have done in the messy situations which Endo paints for us, and how do we know whether we are as strong as we believe? We can ask these questions because Endo more than anyone else seems to be asking *himself* precisely these same questions through the people and events in his novel. We must enter into Endo's relentless questioning in order to understand how this text can transform us. In order to evaluate Fr. Rodriguez's actions, we must first make the effort to surrender ourselves to the *vice grip* in which he found himself, and thereby give ourselves over to be trampled in the winepress just as he was. Without placing ourselves in the maw of power's ruthless cunning or stepping into the jaw of life's contradictions, we cannot see how Fr. Rodriguez's decisions are so uncomfortably *close* to our mundane lives.

We rob ourselves when we blunt the razor edge of Endo's novel. As long as we approach Fr. Rodriguez as an other — an apostate, a moral degenerate, or an irredeemable fool — we will never be forced to confront how his pretensions and compromises mirror our own. All our strategies to insulate ourselves from him must be stripped away for us to encounter this story in the way that Endo hopes that we will. The questions which swirl in Rodriguez's mind in this book — have not all of us found these same words on our lips in prayer? Are we not creatures caught in a web of painful contradictions and unrelenting struggle? We find spread before us a buffet in which there are only bad decisions to choose from.

While one might object that we cannot know the answer to the question of 'what would I have done in that scenario' in a definitive sense, I would reply that we nonetheless cannot turn aside from the task. The indeterminacy of knowing who we would be under such circumstances acts as a catalyst to find — rather, *forge* — a new answer for ourselves. For only through this wrestling will we find that we have been changed. We cannot absolve ourselves of the questions of faith and doubt, hate and forgiveness, love and evil, and every grey shadow which haunts the in-between. These are the liminal phenomena and thorny questions which haunt the story of *Silence*, and towards which this book presently turns its attention.

The personal and the political in the work of interpretation

A question still remains for this introduction to address — why write a book *about* a book? Especially a lesser known Japanese novel? Isn't a book about a book excessively abstract?

I'll admit that it's a risky endeavor. Even as I've written this book, I've wondered myself about how this format will connect with readers. However, I've concluded from my wrestling that I cannot sever my connection with Endo's text, because the reflections here were born out of my engagement with it, and thus are intimately tied up with the events, characters, and conflicts encountered in *Silence*.

To extract these ideas from their textual origin would be to lose something of inestimable value, and would also foreclose the path of their emergence such that the reader would not be able to re-trace my own steps in their discovery. Thus, this book is also my vulnerable invitation to you to taste and to see whether you also can believe that the things I've said here are true and salient.

Having said that, I also want to be clear that this book serves not only as a source of philosophical and theological speculation, but also as a textual supplement to Endo's novel. In these pages I labor to situate the story of *Silence* in the broader historical trends and perennial political challenges present in the history of the people of Japan, and thereby to lay bear what is *at stake* in these profoundly personal moments which Endo makes us privy to.

While Endo's novel is a work of fiction, it is also self-consciously *historical* fiction, which I take to be an invitation on Endo's part to wrestle not only with the existential and theological dimensions of the text, but to grapple with them in their historical context rather than as pure abstractions without relation to the events in which they took place. This book's approach takes *Silence*'s genre as *historical* fiction quite literally, and thus attempts to articulate what these characters' actions mean as though they really did unfold historically in the time and place that Endo sets his narrative.

In what follows I will unfold a structural-political reading of the text of *Silence*, an interpretive approach which opposes itself to the

mostly ethical-existential readings which abound. Whereas these ethical-existential readings tend to prioritize the intentions and personal meanings which characters attach to events, a structural analysis
concerns itself more with the meaning of the effects and outcomes
which the agent's actions (intentional or otherwise) cause in the state
of affairs in which they find themselves.

As we begin to sketch an agent's actions within their context, we
ask questions like — How does this decision shift who has the advantage in a given situation? How does it empower or harm allies?
What role does self-deception play? In what ways have they worked
against their own explicit aims? What are the gaps between what they
think is happening and what is actually happening? In this way, we
are interested in both the resonance and the incongruence between a
character's interpretation of an event and the objective circumstances
of that event.

To be explicit on this point, the analysis in this book assumes
that *(1) we can pass judgment about the meaning of others' actions* and *(2) that these judgments can be valid or invalid.* This is not to
say that these determinations are always so clear-cut as to be patently
obvious, but rather to say that the validity of another's actions can
be the legitimate object of reasoned debate. The meaning of one's
actions are not so inward and ineffable as to preclude at the outset any
possibility of making judgments about them in their context.

Further, this books also contends that *(3) the validity of a judgment
about the meaning of a subject's action must derive primarily from
a structural analysis of the context in which that subject's actions take
place,* and thus our work must proceed first from the social, symbolic,
economic, and political relations which not only provide the shape
of the situation in which the subject acts, but perhaps even more

crucially, the set of options which the agent has at their disposal to choose when they act.

Far from an exercise in making excuses, we are looking at how we can adjudicate claims about the meaning of decisions in a way which could potentially differ from the agent's own self-explanation about the situation. In this approach, we actually discover new ways to blame, even where the agent would try to excuse themselves.

This structural-political approach has as one of its primary strengths that it does not eliminate the ethical-existential reading, but rather *includes* it. The private meaning of subjects are unequivocally active components within the context in which those agents act, and thus must be included in any analysis, but a structural-political reading makes these intentions *non-authoritative* and *non-exhaustive* for the analysis of the subject's actions. This is to say that *the meaning of an agent's actions is determined primarily but not comprehensively by the political and symbolic context in which the agent's action takes place*, not purely on the basis of the intention which the subject privately imputes to their own actions. In fact, a central part of this book's analysis will be to examine the ways in which the private interpretation of meaning serves precisely as a *screen* which the subject uses to occlude or mystify their own actions to themselves.

The author is dead but we are present to the text

In closing, and before we embark on this journey together, I want to briefly comment on the role of authorial intent in interpretation — this book does not claim to know what Shusaku Endo personally believed or intended for any particular character, words, motifs, or scenes in *Silence* to mean. Any comments I will make in this book about Endo's meanings or intention for this story are conjectures based on my encounter with his text, which is an artifact inevitably marked by the traces of his own intense struggle with God, himself, and his world. We are caught in the conundrum that, while we cannot immediately access Endo's mind, yet we cannot defer making an attempt at an interpretation of his work. We must risk the hermeneutic task nonetheless.

However, having said that, it's clear that the text also serves as a palimpsest in which Endo attempts to erase and self-efface himself such that his characters may come to possess, through the power of his words, lives which are now animated independently of his own. This is the point of writing a novel — to give life to beings who are different from us, and thus who can address us from another standpoint. A story demands to be encountered as something distinct from its author. Against more classical hermeneutical theories, this book does not take authorial intent (whatever that may mean) to be definitive or exhaustive of a text's meaning, but rather, sees meaning arising through the dynamic interaction of the reader with the text in so far as the text serves as an artifact which makes the author's own experience present in a symbolic way to the reader. Thus, the process of interpretation involves a coming to a mutual understanding of the reader and the text.

The text includes us in the activity of its story-telling, because we bring ourselves to the act of reading, interpreting, and changing. The only way the text can transform us if we are present to the text, affecting and being affected by Endo's work. We work with the text as the text works with us, and I offer this work in that same spirit.

1

---·---

THE MISSING PROLOGUE

Introduction

The Missing Prologue

In the story *Silence*, we encounter the Christian community in Kyushu beleaguered and barely hanging on, but with almost no explanation as to why or how. Endo does not provide his readers with anything by way of the historical context for his narrative, leaving us only to infer the barest of details from the oblique references made within the story itself. The only historical data we are provided concerns the two priests and their mentor, Ferreira, the relationship which will generate the catalyst for the rest of the tale.

The prologue to *Silence* informs us that the story concerns an apostate priest named Cristóvão Ferreira, and that it relates the experiences of his students Francisco Garrpe and Sebastian Rodriguez who go to Japan in search of their teacher to confirm his apostasy. This character Ferreira was, in fact, based on a real person. The name Sawano Chu'an, which the ex-Father Ferreira takes to himself in *Silence*, was the adopted name of the real Cristóvão Ferreira, a Jesuit priest in Japan who famously apostatized in 1633[1]. He was hung over the pit to be tortured for his faith — it is said that he apostatized after 5 hours.[2] The world was shocked, for he had been appointed to an interim leadership role over the mission to Japan only a year earlier.[3]

The infamous pit torture (anat-surushi) endured by Cristovão Ferreira and the Japanese-Christians.

The character of Fr. Sebastian Rodriguez — whose letters, the preface informs us, compose the text of the novel — also has his roots in a historical person, one named Giuseppe di Chiara, an Italian Jesuit missionary who traveled to Japan in the early 17th century after hearing reports of Cristóvão Ferreira's apostasy. Just like the character Fr. Rodriguez, Chiara also entered Japan illegally during a time of intense persecution of Christians, and was arrested by the Japanese authorities in 1643. He eventually apostatized in prison, and took the Japanese name Okamoto San'emon, living out the rest of his days in Edo.[4]

However, the omission of any substantive historical background to the story of *Silence* should strike us as all the more surprising when we consider that the largest and bloodiest peasant uprising in Japanese history has just taken place not far from where the story takes place. We learn of the terrible inquisition which is taking place, but we do not hear any specific reason

---

4. Giuseppe Chiara," Wikimedia Foundation, July 15, 2023, https://en.wikipedia.org/wiki/Giuseppe_Chiara.

why the Tokugawa regime has resorted to such cruel measures against its own people. The Shimabara Rebellion reveals a "missing prologue" which sheds crucial light on what is *at stake* in the events of *Silence*. This chapter brings the story of the Shimabara Rebellion, and the history preceding it, to the reader's full attention in order that we might engage more deeply with the full range and complexity of the situation in which Endo's characters find themselves entangled.

Japan, the Swamp

We will start our investigation with a naive question — *why is the Inquisitor Inoue persecuting Japanese Christians?*

Inoue carries out his persecution under the direct orders of the Tokugawa Shogunate (*bakufu* or military government), but what is the Tokugawa regime's reasoning behind this brutal inquisition? The Inquisitor provides different answers at different points in the story, but when we compare these answers with each other we begin to see that his ostensive reasons for the persecution seem to exhibit some inconsistencies.

During an interrogation early in his imprisonment, a Japanese official openly questions the existence of universal truth to Fr. Rodriguez, pointing out that some plants may die and wither when they are transplanted to different soil.[5] Later, the apostate Ferriera re-states this perspective again in even starker terms — "Japan is a swamp."[6] This metaphor recurs throughout the dialogues in the novel, and it conveys Inoue's assessment that Japan's religious and cultural character makes

---

5. Shusaku Endo, *Silence* (New York: Picador, 1969), 117.

6. Ibid., 158.

it particularly inhospitable to the Christian religion. By likening Japan to a swamp, Inoue wants to persuade Rodriguez that his efforts to proselytize the Japanese will be fruitless, and that Christians should abandon any hope of Christianity taking root in Japan. "Nothing grows in a swamp," he explains. This new religion is not adapted for the Japanese way of life.

However, this metaphor of Japan as a swamp raises more questions than it puts to rest. After all, if Japan is a swamp, why persecute Christians? If Japan is really the swamp that Inoue claims that it is, the regime should be able to safely ignore Christianity while it simply withers away from lack of interest on the part of the population. If what he says is true, why unleash the most violent religious persecution in Japanese history? This passive metaphor of "the swamp" doesn't explain enough.

Inoue's claims seem even more inconsistent upon a cursory investigation of the condition of the Christian church in Japan prior to the regime's persecutions. Both Ferreira and Rodriguez allude to this "golden age" of Christianity in Japan flourishing after Francis Xavier's arrival in 1549. Especially under the work of Xavier's successor, Alessandro Valignano, the numbers of Japanese-Christians increased exponentially, rising to as many as 240,000 Christians in 1590.[7] Valignano labored tirelessly to adapt the Christian mission in Japan to the customs and ways of the Japanese people. To that end, he invested heavily in training local leaders in order to raise up a self-sustained and self-perpetuating Japanese church. He was also

---

7. Kazuo Kasahara, *A History of Japanese Religion* (Tokyo: Kosei Publishing Co., 2001), 431.

not afraid to cultivate relationships with Japanese leaders to secure friendly regions to safely plant and grow churches.

The Japanese island of Kyushu, where the first Christian missionaries arrived, had historically offered particularly fertile ground for foreign encounters, new ideas, and dissident movements. Kyushu may actually be a swamp, but not in the sense that Inoue means — the diversity of its ecosystem, both biological and ideological, has historically been unrivaled anywhere else in Japan. As the threshold between Japan and the rest of the world, the island of Kyushu has played the crucial role of the "outside" to the comparatively homogenous geographic "interior" of the Imperial court in Kyoto and, during the story of *Silence*, the Shogunate ruling from Edo.

Kyushu served as the wild borderlands of Japan, but also the gateway to the rest of the world, and as such it provided an unusually open climate for cultural exchange. The seeds of Christianity could have found no better conditions in all of Japan. The warlords in Kyushu tended to be particularly idiosyncratic and difficult for the regime to control, and the people of the island had long developed their way of life far away from the watchful eye of the centers of political power in the east. The regime's political and ideological grip on the leaders and peasants in the region was exceptionally weak, and this was a crucial problem which the Tokugawa regime had to set about solving very early on.

Rather than describing an empirical reality then, we can see how Inoue's swamp analogy reflects an aspirational sentiment of the Tokugawa regime about the type of unified and ideologically aligned nation they hoped to build through their social control and religious purges. Instead of expressing the reality as it might be observed on the ground amongst the diverse communities of actual Japanese folk, the Tokugawa regime had already decided what vision of national character will be most advantageous for them. They will have to force the populace into line with this ideal by insisting that this has *always* been who the Japanese people are. Anyone wishing to craft such a national character for a disorganized people group must retroactively posit this new conception of Japanese identity as always having been there already in order to effectively conjure this fictional nation into reality.

Inoue's explanation for the persecutions thus serves to obscure the true nature of the current situation. The idea that "Japan is a swamp" attempts to justify the regime's actions by positing an unchanging reality to an abstract entity called "Japan" which by its very definition excludes Christianity. This not only blatantly ignores the ways that the Japanese people have borrowed significantly from neighboring nations throughout their history (including their importation of Buddhism!), but it also shifts the responsibility for the violent persecutions from the regime to "Japan" conceived as an imaginary social whole, all while perversely disavowing the elite's self-interested motivations for pursuing this specific program of violence against Christians.

The Japanese regime cannot escape their responsibility for the violence and cruelty perpetrated on both Japanese-Christians and foreign missionaries, but we must understand these persecutions first and foremost as *political* in their nature, not necessarily religious. Having said that, the question still remains as to the nature of the political threat the Japanese regime took Christianity to represent to their project of establishing sovereignty over Japan and its people. How and why did Christianity attract the ire of the Shogunate, drawing out from the Japanese the most violent persecution in their nation's history?

This chapter begins to answer this question through taking recourse to the history of Christianity's introduction and growth in

Japan. We will give special attention to two landmark events in this history— (1) the *San Felipe* Incident and (2) the Shimabara Rebellion. While the history of Christianity in Japan covers over a century, and exhibits all the complexity one would expect, these two events provide anchors for our narrative in order to present the dense knot of conflicts which were playing themselves out through the fraught encounters amongst European missionaries, Japanese-Christians, and the Tokugawa regime.

European-Christians and the *San Felipe* Incident

The arrival and growth of Christianity in Japan

Christianity arrived in Japan, briefly flourished, and then was largely eradicated, all within the span of about 100 years. However, this particular century was also a crucial time of transition in Japanese society. This chapter and the next will explore this claim in some detail, but we will come to see how the actions of the three unifiers — Oda Nobunaga, Toyotomi Hideyoshi, and Tokugawa Ieyasu — during the "Christian century" from 1549 to 1650 radically altered the landscape of the Japanese people, and laid the foundations for what Japan would become today. As Europeans began to arrive in Japan for the first time, they brought both trade and new ideas with them, all of which shifted the political calculus of the regime. Whether it was how to deploy guns in battle, studying European astronomy, or navigating the reality of Japanese-Christians within the network of elites, the government of Japan was never the same after these transformative encounters which began right as the Japanese people were emerging from the century long Ōnin War into the peace which these three unifiers were attempting to forge.

Francis Xavier of the Society of Jesus (Jesuits) lead the first group of missionaries who brought Christianity to Japan. Xavier was returning from Indonesia to the Portuguese province of Goa when he encountered some escaped Japanese criminals who informed him about the state of affairs in Japan. At hearing this news, he resolved to bring the Gospel to Japan. Upon returning to Goa, Xavier immediately began to make preparations for a trip to Japan, and he eventually managed to arrive in the port city of Kagoshima on August 15, 1549, along with two other padres, the now-converted Japanese criminals, and two servants.[8]

Based on the reports of the situation that he had received from the ex-criminal Yajiro and his Christian compatriots, Xavier had high hopes for the Japanese reception of the Gospel, as they seemed to exhibit a strong sense of honor, habitual politeness to all, and a sharp intellect. They struck him as possessing many of the natural virtues which Christianity already taught, which would presumably lower the barrier to introducing them to Jesus Christ and the manner of living which he taught. When the whole party was received with warmth and respect, this only heightened Xavier's positive expectations.[9] Xavier always retained a soft spot for the Japanese, even calling them "the

---

8. Joseph Jennes, *History of the Catholic Church in Japan, from its beginnings to the early Meiji period (1549-1873); a short handbook* (Tokyo: Committee of the Apostolate, 1959), 8.

9. C. R. Boxer, *The Christian Century in Japan 1549-1650* (Berkeley: University of California Press, 1967), 37.

delight of his heart," often extolling them over his fellow Europeans in certain respects.[10]

Francis Xavier departed Japan in 1551, leaving behind about a thousand active converts,[11] which appears quite impressive in retrospect when one considers that Xavier and his fellow padres had no understanding of the Japanese language whatsoever. They had to learn Japanese from scratch, as well as rely on the translation services of the recently converted Yajiro who spoke only some broken Portuguese. While Xavier would never again return to Japan — he died suddenly of a fever on December 3, 1552 while waiting off the coast of China for a boat to make the return voyage to Goa[12] — the seed he planted would continue to grow. The two associates he had brought with him, Fr. Cosme de Torres and brother Juan Fernandez, continued the work which Xavier had pioneered. They also saw success, doubling the community within a span of about 7 years, as well as winning over a number of monks from the Zen sect in the area.[13] However, their work was severely hindered by a lack of leaders — between 1552 and 1564 there were never more than four priests in the entire Japanese

---

10. Boxer, 40.

11. Ibid., 39.

12. Henry James Coleridge, *The Life and Letters of Francis Xavier, Volume 3* (London: Burns and Oates, 1872), 571-572.

13. Richard Henry Drummond, *A History of Christianity in Japan* (Grand Rapids, MI: W.B. Eerdmans Publishing Company, 1971), 45.

mission, and between 1565 and 1570 there were no more than six.[14] This meant that many parishes had to make do with only an occasional visit from a priest, and consequently some promising mission fields (such as Kagoshima[15]) were never able to be nurtured the way that they really needed.

The Jesuits primarily pursued a strategy of targeting the local warlords and their samurai for conversion.[16] These were the elite of Japanese society, and the expectation was that the conversion of local leaders and their respected warriors would normalize Christianity amongst the masses. However, this strategy was also motivated by practical necessity in that the Christian church was highly vulnerable to the constant political change and warfare, and thus they needed daimyos to provide safety and legal protection so they could carry out the work of evangelism and training Japanese converts. While Christianity's first forays into politics were thus born from the necessity to secure a stable base of operations, these political maneuvers were often initiated by the daimyos themselves. Many of the leaders in the region were intrigued by the Jesuits, and wanting to establish a relationship with them, would invite them for an audience and guarantee the safety of the Christian church within the realm.[17]

This goodwill towards the Christians rarely sprang from a purely religious motivation though. The presence of Jesuits often prepared

---

14. Ibid., 46.

15. Jennes, 18.

16. Ibid., 21.

17. Ibid., 21-24.

the way for the arrival of Portuguese merchant ships and their goods, which were a boon to the local economy.[18] The benefits which accrued to daimyos who were friendly to Christians can be seen most clearly in the example of the first Christian daimyo, Ōmura Sumitada. Ōmura first came into contact with the Jesuits as part of a negotiation process to open up his port Yokoseura to Portuguese trade in return for guaranteeing the protection of the Church in his domain. He was baptized a Christian only a few months later in 1563. However, it seems that Ōmura was a bit too zealous in persecuting Buddhism within his domain though, because a revolt broke out in Yokoseura, which caused the Portuguese to shift their commercial operations to another port city within Ōmura's domain — Nagasaki.[19] In fact, Ōmura even turned the ownership and management of the city over to the Jesuits outright in 1580. Nagasaki would eventually grow to be a vital and international port city, largely because it took on this role of the institutional and cultural hub of Christianity in Japan.[20]

The conversion of Ōmura set off a chain reaction in which more daimyos approached the Jesuits, with nearby Arima Yoshisada and two other lords in the Amakusa islands receiving baptism in the following years, although one daimyo quickly apostatized when Portuguese ships did not start visiting his ports.[21] The conversion of a daimyo

---

18. Ibid.

19. Ibid., 22.

20. Andrew Cobbing, *Kyushu: Gateway to Japan – A Concise History* (Kent, UK: Global Oriental LTD, 2009), 151.

21. Jennes, 23.

would mean that his entire domain would become *de facto* Christian, leading to his subjects receiving baptism *en masse,* as well as the establishment of new churches and monasteries for training both lay people and leadership alike. While this obviously added numbers to the mission, it also created its own unique set of problems. Numbers of converts were desperately needed so that the mission could report back to Europe to receive more funding and resources, but adding so many new converts at once put a massive strain on the existing infrastructure to serve the Church. Further, the conversion of the daimyos embroiled Christianity further in the pre-existing conflicts amongst the daimyos in Kyushu and beyond.

Alessandro Valignano[22] was handed leadership of the Jesuit mission in Japan in 1579, taking the place of Francisco Cabral, who had served as the leader over the mission since 1570. Cabral had been relieved of his duty and transferred to Macau. Despite the growth of the Christian community to as much as 100,000 in the 30 years since Xavier's arrival, it was suspected that Cabral's leadership was responsible for a lull in the mission's effectiveness. Valignano and

---

22. Valignano is a fascinating character who deserves an in-depth study, but that would need to be another book entirely. I think that his unique perspective as a leader came from his background — he spent time in jail before joining the Jesuits. He reformed his life and went on to become a one of the most influential leaders in the evangelism of Asia. Matthew Ricci would eventually call Valignano the founder "of the Church in China." See: Jack Hoey III, "Alessandro Valignano and the Restructuring of the Jesuit Mission in Japan, 1579-1582" *Eleutheria* 1, no.1 (October 2010), 24.

Cabral subscribed to very different philosophies of how missionary priests should comport themselves amongst and engage with native believers, with Cabral emphasizing European superiority, inflexibility in regards to local customs, and disdain for the Japanese in general.[23] After a thorough tour and inspection of the mission, Valignano identified these prejudices as a serious issue, and he poured his efforts into reversing course. He put strict regulations in place which forced the Jesuits to master the Japanese language, clean themselves regularly, eat the same things the Japanese do, comport themselves with the same dignity as Buddhist monks did, and much much more. His immovable conviction was that the Jesuits *must* adapt to the Japanese people as much as physically possible.[24]

Only a few years into his leadership, Valignano's census of the Japanese mission indicates that there were about 150,000 Christian converts in Japan, amounting to a quarter of all the estimated number of Christians in Asia at the time.[25] Also, as Valignano was quick to point out, Japan was the Christian mission which had shown the most success in Asia on at least two important fronts, namely, making inroads with the elites and persuading people to convert for intellec-

---

23. Otis Cary, *A History of Christianity in Japan: Roman Catholic, Orthodox, and Protestant Missions* (Tokyo: Charles E. Tuttle Company, 1976), 92. Also, Jennes, 47.

24. Hoey III, 27.

25. Boxer, 78.

tual or disinterested motives.[26] Christians had not come under any persecution by this time, save for petty clashes with various Buddhist schools, and they were seeing success converting daimyos, samurai, and even some Buddhist monks (we will meet one monk in chapter 3 of this book). Further, the warlord Oda Nobunaga was so focused on the unification of Japan and the suppression of the Buddhist temples at this tie that Christianity had been no more than an after-thought for him, and thus many Christians had found themselves into powerful roles by the time that Toyotomi Hideyoshi came to occupy Oda Nobunaga's position immediately after Nobuanga's defeat at Honno-ji in 1582.

A number of faithful Christians were counted amongst Hideyoshi's faithful prior to and during his reign as Shogun,[27] including the commander of Hideyoshi's fleet, Konishi Yukinaga, and Kuroda Yoshitaka, a general of the cavalry. The governors of the cities of Osaka and Sakai were Christians at this time, and there were still many prominent Christian daimyos in Kyushu who were sup-

---

26. Boxer, 78. Many missions elsewhere in Asia primarily converted through the provision of material benefits, creating a phenomenon referred to as "rice Christians." While many in Japan converted because of their daimyo, there were also many of the elite and the clergy who converted because they were persuaded of its truth. Further, the Jesuits seemed to report that the average Japanese convert tended to be more devout and pious than the average convert of other missions.

27. Boxer, 139.

portive of Hideyoshi.[28] An especially important Christian daimyo named Takayama Ukon had shown himself faithful to Hideyoshi in the past, and in turn received larger and more important lands upon Hideyoshi's ascension to power.[29] Hideyoshi is even said to have told the Jesuits that the only thing preventing him from becoming a Christian is the prohibition against multiple wives, and that he would convert if they would let him fudge on this single precept.[30] For this reason and others, many Christians believed that Hideyoshi's regime would take a favorable stance towards them.

Initially, this expectation seemed to bear itself out. Hideyoshi backed Takayama Ukon when he expelled the Buddhist priests and their idols from his newly acquired domain. Hideyoshi fully endorsed Takayama's right to govern the lands however he saw fit,[31] which boded well for Christian daimyos who wanted to make their territories a safe haven for Christians. In 1586, Hideyoshi signed two documents which granted the Jesuits a wide jurisdiction to preach their religion, including exempting them from having to house Japanese soldiers or obey certain obligations from feudal lords. The agreements Hideyoshi signed granted even more privilege to the Christians than Buddhist clergy were enjoying at the time. He even expressed that he wanted the

---

28. Cary, 98.

29. Ibid., 99.

30. Boxer, 139-140.

31. Ibid., 99.

documents sent to Europe so that the Christian kings there could see how favorable a view he had of Christianity.[32]

These favorable proclamations were secured by Gaspar Coelho, the vice-provincial who ran the Jesuit mission in Valignano's absence, however, it's believed that Coelho made a massive blunder during the series of interviews on his visit to Hideyoshi in Osaka which ultimately secured these generous provisions for the Jesuit mission. It was during these conferences that Coelho made promises to Hideyoshi that he could help secure troops for Hideyoshi's invasion of Korea, and also that he would secure an alliance of Kyushu's Christian daimyos to ally with Hideyoshi against the Satsuma clan which still was holding out against him.[33] These comments were a red flag for Hideyoshi, because they indicated that this man Coelho could command foreign legions and even exercise influence over the Christian daimyos. How could he be sure that this influence would not be turned against him?

These questions must have gnawed at Hideyoshi, for when he did finally sweep through Kyushu in 1587 to put down the remaining bastions of resistance, Hideyoshi showed had another run-in with Coelho. Coelho entertained Hideyoshi on a Portuguese ship moored at Hakata, when it appears that one of Hideyoshi's advisors who was an opponent of Christianity began a line of discussion which enraged Hideyoshi. The story goes that Hideyoshi sent a messenger to Takayama Ukon demanding that he renounce his faith or be relieved of his fiefdom, to which Takayama promptly refused to apostatize. At

---

32. Ibid., 101.

33. Boxer, 141.

receiving this refusal, Hideyoshi angrily sent for Coelho to be woken up and brought before him for questioning.[34]

Much ink has been spilled speculating on Hideyoshi's motivations for his erratic behavior towards Christians, but apparently Hideyoshi must have been dissatisfied with the answers which Coelho attempted to proffer in the middle of the night,[35] for he suddenly turned on the Christians in Japan — the next day, on July 25, 1587 Hideyoshi issued an edict giving the missionaries twenty days to leave Japan or to be imprisoned and punished.[36] It was also at this time that the city of Nagasaki was revoked from Jesuit control, becoming government property within just a few years, and ruled over by a governor appointed by the Shogun.[37]

Coelho was distraught by this turn of events and reportedly even looked into violent means to resisting it, but Hideyoshi did not ultimately end up enforcing any of his anti-Christian proclamations.

---

34. Boxer, 145-146.

35. The historical accounts relays that Hideyoshi had four specific questions for Coelho — (1) why are the Padres so desirous to make converts, and why do they use force on occasion? (2) Why do they destroy Shinto and Buddhist temples, and persecute bonzes (Buddhist priests/monks) instead of compromising with them? (3) Why do they eat useful and valuable animals like horses and cows? (4) Why do the Portuguese buy many Japanese and export them from their native land as slaves?

36. Boxer, 147. Also, Jennes, 64.

37. Jennes, 67.

Hideyoshi ordered all the Jesuits, both European and Japanese, to be transported to Nagasaki to be deported upon the arrival of the first Portuguese ship, although only three ended up actually departing the country,[38] with the rest simply quietly dispersing to friendly domains. Hideyoshi also banned all Christian symbols, and ordered all Japanese-Christians to de-convert or be punished, but these orders too were never followed up on.[39]

The Padres simply kept a low profile until Valignano received diplomatic permission from Hideyoshi to arrive in 1590, at which point Valignano immediately engaged in negotiations with with him. Over a dinner party, Valignao secured the necessary assurances from Hideyoshi, and promised in return more modest behavior from the missionaries, including discouraging the destruction of Buddhist and Shinto temples.[40] Coelho passed away in 1590, and thanks to Valignano's cool-head and diplomatic prowess, it seemed like the debacle had been buttoned up. Unfortunately, this was not the end of the trouble for the Jesuit mission.

The *San Felipe* Incident (1596)

At one point in Endo's novel, the Inquisitor Inoue shares a parable with Fr. Rodriguez[41] — he tells a story of a king with four foreign

---

38. Jennes, 66.

39. Boxer, 148-149.

40. Boxer, 153.

41. This exchange can be found on pages 129-132.

brides who all squabble with each other. Inoue puts the question to Rodriguez first — what should this king do? Rodriguez astutely perceives that more is going in this tale than meets the eye. We can intuit that these "four foreign brides" are actually the four European nations — Portugal, Spain, Netherlands, and England — who all want a piece of Japan's commercial activity. Rodriguez responds that the king should forego his polygamous ways and instead choose only one wife and be faithful to her alone — this bride would be the Church of Jesus Christ.

Inoue will have none of it. He sneers, and proposes his own solution — the king should banish these meddlesome wives and marry a woman from amongst his own people instead. Inoue's proposed solution contains all of the ideological ambiguity which we have been exploring and will continue to unpack in this book. Rodriguez suggests that the king reject the warring political powers to pledge himself to a religion, a spiritual kingdom made manifest on earth. In an interesting twist, Inoue's response seems to concede this subtle shift in the metaphor wherein the quarrelsome wives represent political powers whereas the solution involves a monogamous commitment to some religious or spiritual power.

The next chapter will paint a fuller picture of the discourse which was emerging in Japanese society at this time around how to synthesize Buddhism, Confucianism, and the diverse panoply of superstitions which fell under the general label 'Shinto.' However, suffice to say that the idea that the king would be picking a bride from among his people is a gross ideological construction. The religious options on offer in Japan at the time included various sects of Buddhism, Confucianism, and Christianity — all of which are foreign! — as well as a synthetic product called "Shinto" which was emerging from a patchwork of superstitions, local cults, syncretic Buddhist doctrines, and Japanese folklore all brought together into a single incoherent "tradition."

However, taking a step back, we can appreciate that the very nature of the parable which Inoue raises to Rodriguez indicates something of the dilemma in which the Japanese regime understands itself to have become ensnared. They consider the present situation primarily as a political problem, not a religious one. Spiritual practice and metaphysical claims all play a subservient role to the general pragmatic interests of the Japanese elite as they attempt to maneuver in the global political terrain shaped by the forces of the European states' imperialism. To properly understand the persecution of Japanese-Christians then, we have to contextualize them into this political struggle which is unfolding on a grander scale than their mundane lives.

Japan is both emerging from a long period of warfare and political fragmentation, while also simultaneously coming into contact with new and highly advanced political powers, all of whom are exerting pressure on them to increase the level of commercial intercourse. The solution which the Tokugawa regime would eventually settled on was a total lockdown of the nation against all foreign travel and trade, a policy which would later be called *sakoku* ("locked country"). However, this result was not inevitable, and it was arrived at only after a century of continual struggle, both intellectual, social, and political. Other possible futures for Japan existed.

The *San Felipe* Incident (1596) stands as a highly symbolic event in this bloody history in which Christians in Japan find themselves caught in a broader battle for political hegemony in the late 1500's and early 1600's. "One shipwreck leads to another" might be an appropriate way to describe this event in which a Spanish ship called the *San Felipe* finds itself wrecked by unfavorable winds against the southern shores of Shikoku. The local daimyo takes advantage of the situation by taking the captain and his crew hostage and seizing the valuable goods which could be recovered. Ultimately, the captain ends up in Hideyoshi's court to explain the situation, and his comments end up having an unexpectedly profound impact on Hideyoshi's actions.

To understand the significance of this event, we have to bear in mind how the European powers had divided up the world at this point in history. European Colonialism was in full swing, which meant that the predominant Christian groups in those countries were finally able to access the commercial networks and resources of those nations. However, because these different Catholic orders and societies were getting too competitive, the Pope had to restrain them by designating exclusive rights for certain groups to evangelize particular nations. *Ex pastorali officio* which was promulgated by Gregory XIII in 1585 prohibited all orders except for the Jesuits to undertake evangelistic works in Japan.[42] This meant that the Spanish Franciscans who had established a base in the Philippines at Manila had to respect this exclusive charter which the Jesuits possessed from the Pope to establish a mission in Japan. They were not pleased about this, for obvious reasons, and thus were constantly trying to find ways to enter the country of Japan to establish their own mission work.

Nonetheless, the Franciscans did manage to find a foothold in the country prior to the *San Felipe* Incident taking place. When Hideyoshi attempted to establish diplomatic ties with the Philippines by sending a threatening letter in 1593, the Franciscans seized upon this as a chance to go to Japan by acting in the capacity of intermediaries. Upon arrival in Japan, they were forced to remain in the capital city Kyoto while they awaited a reply to the report which they sent back to the

---

42. Jennes, 75.

Philippines. During this time as something of political prisoners, they acquired houses in Kyoto and built a church.[43] As they became more bold in their proselytizing efforts, Kyoto became the base from which the Spanish Franciscans started building their mission in Japan in defiance of the Pope's edict (and Hideyoshi's command not to evangelize).

Not only do we see internecine conflict amongst ecclesial factions, but also jostling amongst kingdoms are vying for access to the commercial markets of Japan. As we noted, the four brides in Inoue's parable represent Spain, Portugal, England, and the Netherlands. Two of these countries were Protestant, which only exacerbated the competition between them. The Protestants did not establish a mission in Japan,[44] but the Catholic-Protestant rivalry intensified the animosity between these different groups, likely even contributing to the ways

43. Cary, 119-121

44. Drummond, 89-90.

that Protestants opposed Catholic work in Japan at crucial momen ts.[45] Ultimately, it would be the ability of the Shogunate to rely on Protestant commercial ties which emboldened them to turn against the Portuguese Jesuits and the Spanish Franciscans, confident that they could maintain the flow of goods from Europe through English and Dutch channels if they eradicated the Catholic mission in their territory.[46]

The *San Felipe* Incident brought all of these conflicts to the fore, throwing them in Hideyoshi's face, confirming all of his suspicions and making it impossible for him to ignore any longer. When the captain of the *San Felipe,* was taken in by the Shogunate, he showed them a map of the Spanish empire's holdings, and he confirmed for them

---

45. The English navigator and pilot William Adams played a crucial role in this struggle between the Protestant nations and the Catholic nations after the times of Hideyoshi. Adams was an Englishman who arrived in Japan on a Dutch Trading Company ship, the last surviving ship in a fleet of six which had attempted to make it to Japan on a commercial expedition. Adams would end up staying the rest of his life in Japan acting as a trusted advisor to the Shoguns. He advised on matters related to trade deals and European shipbuilding techniques, but also seems to have spoken ill of the Roman Catholic missionaries thus imparting a bad impression of them with Ieyasu in particular. He portrayed the Roman Catholics as unwanted agitators in some European kingdoms, thus providing Ieyasu with more ideological ammunition for his persecutions.

46. Cobbing, 179.

that missionaries were sent into a country prior to Spanish conquest .[47] Naturally, this enraged Hideyoshi to hear, for as he looked around, he noticed that the Spanish Franciscans were spreading Christianity in the capital city against his orders. The Franciscans, both Spanish and Japanese, were rounded up by the authorities, transported to Nagasaki, and on February 5th, 1597, the 26 Martyrs of Nagasaki[48] were publicly crucified — a group composed of twenty Japanese-Christians and six Spanish. The whole group was composed of Franciscans, except for three Jesuits of Japanese birth.

The martyrdom at Nagasaki

Following the widely publicized execution of the 26 Martyrs of Nagasaki, Hideyoshi intensified his persecution efforts, first by forbidding any daimyos from becoming Christians,[49] and then by intimidating local daimyos to carry out persecution on the Christians in Kyushu. In 1598, one hundred and thirty-seven churches, the college in Amakusa, and the seminar in Arima were all destroyed. Priests were also rounded up and sent to Nagasaki for deportation.[50] However, Hideyoshi died later that year, bringing an end to the intense perse-

---

49. Cary, 129.

50. Ibid., 130.

cution at his hands. Japanese-Christians rejoiced to finally experience a respite from Hideyoshi's fury.

What immediately followed was a succession struggle in which Tokugawa Ieyasu moved to supplant Hideyoshi's six year old son who had previously been named his successor. In the two years from Hideyoshi's death to Tokugawa Ieyasu's total subjugation of the opposition the Christian Church took advantage of the lack of clear leadership in Japan to advance the mission. Valignano recorded 40,000 adult baptisms in 1599, with an additional 30,000 added by October of 1600, however many of these conversions came through Konishi Yukinaga's work to convert the territories over which he ruled.[51] By the end of 1600, the Christian Church could claim 300,000 adherents, many nobles, and at least 14 daimyos. [52]

Tokugawa Ieyasu's accession to the Shogunate was not necessarily a defeat for Christianity in Japan, considering that there were Christian leaders on both side of the conflict, but many of the Christian leaders who had supported Hideyoshi had their fiefdoms taken away or re-arranged after Tokugawa took power. This closed off new mission fields in Japan, but also put formerly Christian lands under the rule of anti-Christian rulers, such as Kato Kiyomasa, when those lands were given as spoils of war to Tokugawa's faithful vassals. In the case of Kiyomasa, he would subsequently unleash a persecution which would

---

51. João Paulo Oliveira e Costa, "Tokugawa Ieyasu and the Christian Daimyō during the crisis of 1600," *Bulletin for Japanese Portuguese Studies* 7 (2003): 51, 54.

52. Ibid., 56.

leave only a few thousand Christians left in a region which had tens of thousands only a few years early.[53]

However, the biggest change which the Christian Church underwent, and for which it likely was not prepared, was the shifting landscape in light of Japan's newly unified ideological and political landscape. Whereas in the past the Christian mission could constantly triangulated itself in relation to multiple warring parties, taking advantage of divided loyalties and the relative autonomy of particular leaders, the ascension of Tokugawa Ieyasu to complete power brought a level of political stability and centralized authority which gave Christianity fewer opportunities to build alliances or hide from antagonistic elites.[54] Further, as we will explore in the next chapter, the vision which Tokugawa Ieyasu was developing for a unified Japan and Japanese people would emphasize Confucian social ethics, Buddhist piety, and indigenous religions instead of Christianity. Persecution was already brewing within the Tokugawa regime.

The next chapter will explore in-depth the significance of Tokugawa Ieyasu's unification of Japan, the new mechanisms of social control for generating a unified Japanese consciousness, and the way that he would employ religion to support these social and political ends. In the decades subsequent to Tokugawa Ieyasu's rise to power, he would increasingly turn against Christianity, ultimately taking a hard line and moving to completely eradicate it from the country. Daimyos would be forbidden from converting, everyone would be made to register at their local Buddhist temple, and regular tests would be administered where people had to step on the fumi-e (a bronze image of Christ)

---

53. Ibid., 66.

54. Ibid.

to prove that they were not a Christian. The padres especially would come under intense persecution, as Endo so masterfully dramatizes in his novel. It was during these brutal decades when Christianity was systematically uprooted and the spiritual fields of Kyushu were salted.

However, near the end of the 1630's, indigenous Japanese-Christians would make themselves heard one final time in a most unexpected way.

The Shimabara Rebellion (1637-38)

When we read the history of Christianity in Japan, it's hard to avoid the painful conclusion that intra-European rivalry based on religious differences and squabbling over commercial profits ultimately created the mess which motivated the Tokugawa regime to persecute Christianity and its adherents. This sordid history should be sobering to the Church. From Cabral's mindset of superiority over the Japanese to the ways that the Jesuits and Franciscans actively worked against each other in their evangelistic missions, we encounter many examples of the ways that the Christian faith was caught in the crossfire of battles for economic and ecclesial victories, ultimately to the shame and detriment of the message of Jesus. Japanese daimyos who were both Christians killed each other in clan conflicts, the Protestant English spread tales about the Catholics, and, as we shall see in a moment, the Protestant Dutch even fired their guns on Japanese-Christians to suppress a peasant revolt. We can't overlook how this history contributed to the Shogunate's decision to remove these foreign conflicts from their borders entirely by simply closing the country down.

However, this book also carries a burden to extricate the revolutionary strand which runs through this entire historical state of affairs. Although the actions of Catholics and Protestants obscure this strand with their greed and rivalry, we can identify a much more radical thread which weaves it way through the story of Christianity in Japan. I think that the Shimabara Rebellion stands as a testament to this darker, almost apocalyptic, gesture with which religious claims can intervene into society.

Beyond the loyalties to clan or purely utilitarian considerations of profit, the message of Jesus can also stir up an alternative perspective which catalyzes resistance against oppression. This Christianity seems to disrupt the smooth functioning of the social machine in highly inconvenient and idiosyncratic ways. These Christians refuse to change their ways, they refuse to recant their confessions of one God who rules over all, and their wills cannot be broken by any torture or coercion. They go happily to their deaths, singing hymns as they are crucified. How can people such as these have a place in Japanese society, or any society for that matter?

The Shimabara Rebellion (1637-1638) was a peasant uprising which took place on the Shimabara peninsula,[55] about 40 kilometers east of Nagasaki. The rebellion lasted into spring of the next year before Matsudaira Tadamasa finally put down the rebels on April 14th. They had been holding out in Hara Castle since before the New Year, and when Matsudaira finally breached their defenses, he massacred every man, woman, and child inside the castle.[56] It remains to this day the largest and most violent peasant uprising in Japanese history. It was also bathed in the imagery of Christianity.

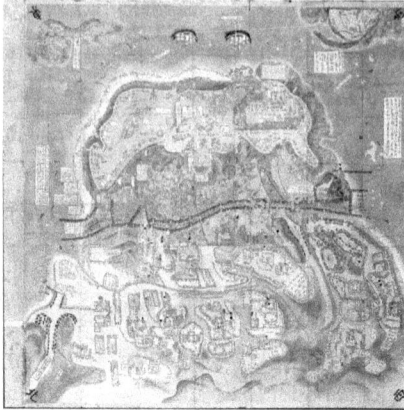

A map depicting the Amakusa /
Shimabara Rebellion centered on Hara
Castle. This map is known to be the most
accurate of the many drawings depicting
the Shimabara Rebellion. Source: Wiki-
media

The rebel forces which rose up against the local daimyos mostly consisted of peasants and farmers from the Shimabara peninsula and the neighboring island Amakusa, forming a force numbering about 37,000 strong. These mostly inexperienced peasants were led by a handful of master-less samurai, some of whom were former vassals under the Christian daimyo Konishi Yukinaga.[57] However, it was a young and charismatic Christian teenager referred to as Amakusa Shiro who stood as the figurehead of their movement, seemingly in fulfillment of a prophecy left by a fleeing missionary decades earlier, saying that "a remarkable youth will appear' in which 'multitudes shall bear the cross on their helmets' and 'white flags shall float over sea

---

57. Cobbing, 181-182.

and river, mountain and plain' [58] The prophecy also foretold the sky turning red and flowers blossoming out of season, all of which seemed to take place during the year of 1637, which saw an unusually dry winter.[59] Together, the peasants took up their farming implements and the old samurai dusted off their swords to rally under Amakusa Shiro's banner displaying the Eucharistic bread and cup with two angels praying on either side.

The banner of Amakusa Shiro

They say that the rebellion started when an enraged man slew the perpetrators who forced him to witness his daughter undergoing the dreadful *mino* dance, a torture method developed at this time under the neighboring daimyos in which the victim was wrapped in a coat of straw or grass and lit on fire.[60] In Endo's novel, this is the fate which Kichijiro's family undergoes, and from which he alone escapes by his apostasy, ultimately becoming a traumatic memory which he circles

---

58. Cobbing, 181.

59. Boxer, 378.

60. Boxer, 377.

back to again and again. This horrible punishment was used to strike fear into the populace in order to compel them to pay the exorbitant taxes which the local leaders had levied on the local people.

A letter from a Dutchman in Nagasaki at the time relates that the taxes which were imposed by the leaders in Arima and Amakusa were so extreme as to be impossible for them to pay.[61] The opulent young daimyos in the region financed their lifestyle by continually raising taxes on the poor, even during times of famine. It's said that they would even collect retroactive taxes to account for prior years when the peasants could not pay.[62] The daimyo Matsukura Shigemasa in particular seems to have harbored ambitions grander than the backwater Shimabara could contain, so he had devoted himself to building a new and grander castle at Shimabara, and this expensive endeavor would have to be shouldered by the people.[63] Little did he know that the very castle he had disliked and abandoned would become the site where thousands of rebels would make their last stand against the Shogunate a couple decades later.

While historians today seem to favor the interpretation that the rebellion was primarily about economic and political issues rather than religious ones,[64] official Japanese accounts have always seen it

---

61. Cary, 221.

62. Jonathan Clements, *Christ's Samurai: The True Story of the Shimabara Rebellion* (London: Robinson, 2016), Chapter 4: The Latter Days of the Law.

63. Clements, Chapter 3: The Mouths of Hell.

64. Sansom, 37-38.

differently.[65] The line between politics and religion can rarely be drawn so cleanly, especially in this region of Japan where Christianity had put down roots for so long. Japanese history emphatically records this as a *Christian* rebellion, and not without good reason. The Shimabara peninsula had originally been within the jurisdiction of the Christian daimyo Arima Harunobu, thus serving as a haven for Japanese-Christians. The Jesuits had established their seminary and the printing press in the district of Arima, and the region had provided refuge to many priests and missionaries during times of persecution.[66] This had been one of the great strongholds of Christianity in Japan, and many Christians continued to practice the faith in these islands long after it had been outlawed.

The people began to suffer religious persecution and to languish under the heavy taxation of Arima's apostate son, Naozumi, after Arima Harunobu passed away. This state of affairs continued when the land passed into the hands of Matsukura Shigemasa in 1614, and then again when his son Shigetsugu succeeded him in 1630.[67] Across the strait in Amakusa, the situation was not so different. While Amakusa had been under the rule of Konishi Yukinaga, it had served as a haven for Christians. However, Konishi was dispossessed by Hideyoshi and his lands were entrusted to Terazawa Hirotaka in 1592. Terazawa wanted to drive Christianity out of the domain, but he quickly realized that he would depopulate the entire island if he did so. Instead, he made a show of closing some churches, but then largely

---

65. Boxer, 378.

66. Boxer, 376.

67. Cary, 221.

left his subjects alone.[68] This changed under his son, Hatataka, who heavily taxed the people and punished them brutally when they did not comply — including forcing them to undergo the dreaded *mino* dance.

What began as pockets of local resistance to tax collectors, as well as some raids on granaries, had escalated into an all-out rebellion by December of 1637.[69] With the help from some *kinobushi* (samurai who had returned to working the land), the people had begun to gather around a Christian youth named Amakusa Shiro, regarding him as a quasi-messianic figure. They claimed that he was extremely learned without every studying, that he could perform miracles, and that his personal charisma bordered on hypnotic. We know very little about Amakusa Shiro, because the only accounts we have of him are embellished tales, hit pieces which demonize him, or an account given by his mother under interrogation.[70]

Who he really was will have to remain lost to the ages, but the effect which he had upon the mind of the rebels seems to have been profound. His appearance was hailed as the fulfillment of a folk prophecy which had circled amongst the local Christian communities since the departure of the padres in 1612, and the initial successes which this peasant army experienced only seemed to confirm this impression. His presence in battle seems to have brought hope and a reckless courage to this downtrodden people resisting their cruel masters. His fiery

---

68. Boxer, 376.

69. Cary, 222-223.

70. Clements, Chapter 4: The Latter Days of the Law.

sermons about sin and heaven, which he delivered twice a week, would enthrall his listeners.[71]

As both forces from the Shimabara peninsula and the Amakusa islands across the strait united, they made the decision to repair Mastukura's deserted castle at Hara, about twenty miles from Shimabara. The castle was impregnable from at least three sides which were built on bluffs which sloped down to the shoreline, and in additional to having two deep moats, the fourth side was partially protected by sw amp.[72] The force of 26,000 soldiers which arrived under Itakura was repulsed repeatedly by the occupants of the castle, ultimately resulting in Itakura's death, and the command of the siege passed to Matsudaira Tadamasa. Matsudaira took a different approach than his predecessor — he decided to hold off on attacking and instead simply wait for the rebels to run out of food and supplies.

Historical accounts report that it was during the siege of Hara castle that the Dutch enlisted to help suppress the rebels, which they did by sending a ship, the *De Ryp*, to fire cannons on the Shimabara rebels.[73] However, after a little over two weeks of the bombardment, the Dutch were told to withdraw, likely at the objection of other Japanese commanders who felt it was dishonorable to rely on foreigners to put down a rebellion in their own country.[74] While some historians suspect

---

71. Clements, Chapter 4: The Latter Days of the Law.

72. Cary, 223-224.

73. Drummond, 107. Accounts record that they fired over 400 shots during the course of two weeks.

74. Cary, 225-226.

that the Dutch's compliance was likely reluctant,[75] they nonetheless chose to ally with the Shogunate against Christian peasants, probably with the understanding that disobedience could compromise valuable economic ties with Japan. In the end, as is the way of human beings, the profit motive won out.

Painting of the 'De Ryp,' a Dutch ship which fired on the Christian peasants at Hara Castle in 1638.

On April 14, 1638, Matsudaira launched a series of assaults once he felt confident that the conditions in the castle had sufficiently worsened, and although it took to the third assault to break through the outer of the rebel's three lines of defense,[76] the forces loyal to the Shogunate managed to gain entrance to the castle. It took two whole days to completely put down the last of the resistance, at which point every rebel had been killed. With this gruesome defeat, the legends

---

75. Drummond, 107.

76. Drummond, 107.

of Amakusa Shiro, the Shimabara rebels, and Christianity in Kyushu come to a dramatic close.

The Shimabara Rebellion has only been quelled a few years prior to the narrative in *Silence* (Rodriguez mentions this briefly in passing[77]). Thus, the wounds would have still been fresh, both for the Tokugawa regime and for the Japanese-Christians. In many ways, the defeat at Shimabara would spell the final blow to Christianity in Japan, as well as the relationship which Japan will have with the outside world.[78] Following the suppression of the Shimabara Rebellion, the Tokugawa regime finally shut the country to foreigners by issuing that next year what would become the final exclusion order.[79] While a Portuguese diplomatic party would arrive the following year in a desperate attempt to re-establish relations with Japan, they would be executed without appeal upon their refusal to recant their Christian faith.[80] Once the Dutch were subsequently confined to the artificial island Dejima constructed off the shore of Nagasaki, this would mark

---

77. *Silence*, page 33.

78. Interestingly enough, it was their armies' defeat at the hands of a rabble of peasants on the Shimabara peninsula that likely caused the Tokugawa Shogunate to abort their plans to invade Luzon (Philippines). Boxer, 382. Without the Shimabara Rebellion, there may have been alternate timelines where Japan ruled over the Philippines, or conversely, was so weakened by their foreign adventures that the Edo period never happened.

79. Boxer, 38.

80. Boxer, 385.

the extent of foreign involvement in Japan and the high water of its isolation until the treaty of Kanagawa in 1854.

Conclusion

This opening chapter has only begun to scratch the surface of the historical and political complexity that marked the "Christian century" in Japan (1550-1650). While the next chapter delves deeper into the forces which shaped this crucial moment in Japanese history, the overarching theme we want to take from this historical narrative is the open and *contested* nature of what it would mean to be Japanese and to be a Japanese people. We are confronted by this even in Endo's book — what it means to *be Japanese* is not yet settled, despite many peoples' belief and insistence to the contrary. There are many groups, religions, ideas, and practices which are competing with one another to define how the people of Kyushu understand themselves and live together as a community. The people of Japan have not reached a consensus yet.

Just as with other cultures and ideas before, the Japanese who encountered Christianity appropriated it and cultivated it within their particular historical and psychological milieu. In the Church in Japan, Christianity was becoming other-than-European, mutating into a unique expression of discipleship to Christ, and struggling to bring forth a new vision of what it looks like for human beings to walk with God. The European-Christians appeared as a threat to the Tokugawa regime because they brought Christianity with them, but the real threat was what Christianity would *become* if it was embraced by the Japanese people.

In the Shimabara Rebellion, we witness a glimpse of this threat, which appears amongst us in the form of an apocalyptic demand which confronts the powers and principalities of this world. Men, women, and children resisting the gratuitous violence and wanton cruelty of their rulers, calling instead for the appearance of God's justice on the face of the earth, all under the banner of Christ their King. Their loyalty to a King who lives and reigns beyond the reach of the earthly powers ultimately introduces into every human community the terror of freedom — what we will be has not appeared yet, thus nothing can be taken for granted.

This book does not idolize Japanese-Christians or argue that theirs was a "purer" form of Christianity. Rather, it was an endeavor to walk with God-in-Christ right where they found themselves, and in the process, transform who they were. As they learned about Christ's sacrifice, the forgiveness of sins, the love of the neighbor, and the hope of heaven, the Japanese-Christian accessed a new standpoint from which they could see their history and culture such that they could ask again about its meaning and value. In light of Christ, what should we make of our former superstitions? What should we make of our social structure or who should lead the community? What art should we make and how should we care for one another? What should we *worship?*

One of the most glaring omissions in this book is the lack of direct material from the mouths of ordinary Japanese-Christians. While chapter 3 takes an in-depth look at a rare specimen of an apologetic dialogue composed by a learned Japanese-Christian convert, this type of document remains highly exceptional. The records of the practice of the *kurishitan* are few and far between, and even what we do have concerning the *kurishitan* comes to us only as anecdotes which re-surfaced with the re-appearance of the *kurishitan* community during the Meiji period, meaning these ideas and practices were already refracted through centuries of secrecy. Endo's novel does a beautiful job of imaginatively bringing us into the experience of ordinary Japanese-Christians, helping us to see what they would be concerned about and the ways that they would have practiced their faith. More work remains to be done in this area though, and as a Western Christian I'm at most qualified to work from what exists or find new material. Above all, I'm learning and wrestling, realizing that this story both is and is not about me. Even so, it cannot help but speak to me. Each of these chapters aims to help the book speak more deeply to you as well.

2

THE BIRTH OF TOKUGAWA NATIONALISM

Introduction

We teach history to elementary schoolers by using stories — this happened, then that happened, and then so-and-so did such and so forth. However, even adults sometimes struggle to rise above this facile level of understanding in which history marches on as a string of names, places, and dates, all following each other in a seemingly necessary succession. We forget that history was created, for even the moment you are in right now will be history some day.

So, tell me, what does it feel like to be part of history? To me, it feels like whatever comes next is not entirely pre-determined. What is happening in the world at this moment is, to an important extent, still open to our influence. If we are in history, then we are making history by our actions in this moment. What will be remains highly ambiguous because it depends on what we do next. We must not forget that every day we wake up and decide what world to make together.

The events which we live in and which will become history feel vital and unpredictable, like an untamed animal. They are driven forward by the pressing problems which present themselves to us, and history emerges from the actions we take to provide a provisional answer to the question which each moment puts to us, both as individuals and as a group. This means that we do well to read history first and foremost as a series of open experiments in which each event presents for us an attempt which our ancestors undertook under conditions of uncertainty. Each of these historical moments is an intervention which a person or some people inserted into the ever-growing chain of events, all with the aim of rising to the challenge which the world posed to them and their community.

How do you keep your offspring alive this winter? How do you kill this large animal? How do you find water today? How do you recover from this illness? These are the conundrums which afflict the human community at its most rudimentary levels. They are what push the community forward to search, strive, and wrestle with the world. But, having established adequate answer to these questions within our context, we can begin to ask ourselves higher order questions which were not available to us previously. How do we create beautiful things? Is there a higher purpose we should devote our lives to? What new stories can we devise? How can we organize ourselves towards flourishing? With such questions, we move from surviving to *becoming*.

To ask the question of what could be higher than mere survival is already to ask a strange question which no animal has ever really asked before the human animal raised it long ago. This transition from surviving to becoming thus carries with it certain dangers, because in asking these questions we introduce the notion of the *transcendent*. We find ourselves inexorably treading on *religious* ground. After we have removed our sandals, we must move forward with a heightened awareness of the incredible violence and horror which can accompany transcendence, for that which breaks into the world from the beyond is not all joy and light but also the darkness and destruction which re-makes the world.[1]

Endo's novel *Silence* takes place at a pivotal time in the history of the Japanese people. and as such, it also harbors an immense violence. In the hundred years from 1550-1650, the people of the Japanese archipelago were taking their next step in the process of *becoming*. This was a moment of surprising openness – the future timeline could have traveled in any number of directions. The Japanese people were beginning to reach beyond their previous level of civilization which was torn apart continually by political upheaval, heavily dependent on borrowing culture and technology from other kingdoms, and unable to make significant progress towards any larger projects. Japan had been stuck at the same level for over half a millennium. The life of a peasant in 800 AD and a peasant in 1500 AD would have been largely indistinguishable from each other, and quality of life was perhaps even marginally worse for the latter.

Because this process of becoming necessarily involves the question of transcendence — what will we love? what will we worship? for what will we die? — it also threatens an immense potential for violence. In the last chapter, we saw the Shimabara Rebellion as a representative moment in this history of violence which marks the transition that Japanese society was experiencing at all levels. These waves of violence speak to the changes which were taking place in this period

---

1. This is why the Prophets in the Old Testament always mixed such violent metaphors into their visions — they saw the double-sided aspect of God's coming. When God comes, He upends every-thing, which is a cause of rejoicing for some and a great calamity for others.

of social, political, and cultural transformation, but also to the birth pangs which inevitably accompany the birth of a new possibility for the Japanese people. We do not turn away from these things, nor do we write them off as ancillary to what was *"really"* going on, but rather we must read them as symptomatic of this moment, testifying to the field of possibilities which were working themselves out in the world.

To understand then the tortures of Rodriguez (including the Jesuits more generally), the suffering of the Japanese-Christians, and the zeal of the Tokugawa regime, we need to understand the central problem which the people of Japan were trying to solve at this volatile moment in history. What drastic and violent steps were needed to overcome the old state of affairs in order to forge a new and enduring social synthesis? The Japanese social field was highly contested because many possibilities were vying for an opportunity to come to fruition. What was this conflict of possible futures, and how does it illuminate the questions in Endo's book? These are the question we turn to in this chapter as we explore the history of the Japanese people from a political perspective, and the transformations which took place under the Tokugawa regime.

How do you solve a problem like sovereignty?

Today we know Japan as a liberal European-style democracy with a president, a parliament, and regular public elections. However, like many other contemporary democracies, Japan still retains an emperor. This seemingly superfluous vestige of the archaic kingship structure speaks to the tectonic plates which shift deep beneath the surface of Japanese civilization, testifying to centuries of military conflict and political intrigue.

While the emperors of Japan have shed their ideology of divinity in the wake of the nation's defeat in World War II, the imperial lineage of the Yamato clan nonetheless remains essentially unbroken for the past 1500 years. Today the position of the current emperor Naruhito resembles his other imperial ancestors in a number of ways, and, in some crucial respects, *more so* than his infamous grandfather Hirohito (Emperor Showa) who presided over Japan's imperial expansion in the early 20th century. The Japanese emperor and his imperial government have historically been quite weak in terms of absolute power, making Emperor Showa a notable anomaly in this respect.

The reasons for this imperial weakness fluctuated throughout different moments in Japanese history, but they usually involved some combination of struggling to control warring elite factions, weak or decadent emperors, and difficulty collecting sufficient tax revenue to support a standing army. Consequently, throughout its history, Japan has been ruled by a revolving door of martial governments which exercise political power while propping up the emperor in his formal role. This perpetual functional impotence of the imperial Yamato court has served as one of the defining factors of the narrative of the Japanese people.

Thus, the primary political struggle which has defined the Japanese archipelago for the past 1,500 years has been the question of how to establish a ruling and durable government which could effectively generate, sustain, and re-produce a stable political and ideological order across all four of the primary Japanese islands. This problem of re-producing a stable political situation supplies the driving force behind many of the events in Japanese history, and this book proposes to read the history of Japan as a series of attempts for various parties to solve this problem with more or less success at different times. The narrative of the Yamato imperial court and its ongoing struggle with various warlords and military governments presents us with a series of experiments in which they endeavor to solve in their historical moment the perennial challenges which every human government faces in their endeavor to establish sovereignty over a people and its territory.

As we looked at in the last chapter, the history of Christianity in Japan finds itself inextricably caught up in the central conflicts of the Japanese people, and it enters the Japanese story at precisely the point where Hideyoshi and his successor Tokugawa Ieyasu are forging the most enduring answer to this problem that Japanese history had seen up to that point. To understand the question to which the Tokugawa regime's actions constitute an attempted answer, this chapter will return to the first settling of Japan to consider the broad sweep of the history of the Japanese islands as a whole, and specifically the role that the island of Kyushu plays in this drama. Then, the second half of the chapter sketches for the reader the contours of the answer which the Tokugawa regime implemented to solve the problem of sovereignty, including sweeping social changes and the production of a new Japanese identity.

The fragmented origins of the Japanese people

The geographical and geological features of the Japanese islands present unique challenges to any governing body seeking to project and exercise sovereignty in its region. The four islands which make up the Japanese archipelago today — Kyushu, Shikoku, Honshu, Hokkaido — are positioned on the the Pacific rim's "Ring of Fire," and thus are volcanically active and largely mountainous. In fact, mountains compose 80% of the Japanese islands' land area.[2] This rocky landscape poses a number of challenges for its inhabitants, most notably — difficult overland travel, delayed communication by land, rocky and acidic soil not conducive to farming, sparse arable land, lack of thick and diverse biomass to replenish soil nutrients, deleterious effects of smoke and ash from volcanos, a rough monsoon season, and a reliance on monsoons for the island's total moisture and annual rainfall.[3]

When we consider the challenge which the Yamato clan and their elite competitors have faced throughout the history of the Japanese people, we want to keep in mind the ways that the environmental factors listed above would pose problems for a human organization which wanted to establish a well-nourished and well-managed growing population of people settled on patches of land which they work commercially, be it rice paddies, fruit orchards, or timber stands. This is the end goal of a regime — a compliant, productive, settled, and (ideally) growing population. If a regime cannot secure these econom-

---

2. William Wayne Farris, *Japan to 1600: A Social and Economic History* (Honolulu: University of Hawai'i Press, 2009), 1-3.

3. Ibid., 3.

ic and social outcomes, it will fail, typically by being overthrown from within or being conquered from without.[4]

The first people who settled Japan likely walked over from the north via the Sakhalin islands (Russian islands north of Hokkaido) when waters were lower and frozen, sometime around 35,000 BC.[5] These migrants were hunter-gatherers who did not practice any form of what we would call agriculture today. They moved around based on the seasons and the availability of resources — fishing and collecting marine life during the summer, collecting nuts and roots during the autumn, hunting larger mammals (deer, rabbits, etc) during the winter, and then returning to diving and fishing in the spring when the waters started to warm back up.[6]

Around 1,500 BC, the archaeological record seems to indicate some signifiant innovations, such as pottery, bow and arrow, the use of nets, and the arrival of dogs.[7] The people of this time, which historians now call the Jomon period, continued to forage, hunt, and gather on a

---

4. As Japan was isolated from the rest of East Asia by virtue of being on an island, the threat of foreign invasion remained negligible in most political calculus through Japan's history, and thus the vast majority of conflict tended to be internal to the people and the island itself. Famously, the Mongols who attempted to invade Japan in the 13th century failed, their fleet being destroyed by typhoons.

5. Ibid., 4.

6. Ibid.

7. Ibid., 6.

seasonal basis like their ancestors, but the invention of pottery allowed them to store more food for longer periods of time. Nonetheless, human life was short during this time — probably only an average of 34 years for men, and less for women.[8] Further, people tended to be small — men averaging only about 5 foot, 2 inches — and their bones indicate that most suffered from malnutrition throughout their lives.[9]

While rice farming had been developed in the river valleys of China thousands of years prior, these agricultural techniques did not begin to arrive on the Japanese islands until the second major wave of migration arrived in the archipelago.[10] This second and distinctively different wave of settlement seems to have unfolded from roughly 900 BC-250 AD. This second wave of settlement is now referred to as the Yayoi period, a broad term which denotes a heterogenous influx of peoples who arrived mostly in Kyushu by way of island hopping from various points across East Asia and the Pacific islands.[11] Because of this, the Yayoi settlement process was extremely diverse both racially, culturally, and linguistically. However, once these groups arrived on Kyushu, they began to create co-existing settlements and engage in inter-marriage, thus forging new connections and alliances amongst themselves.

---

8. Ibid.

9. Ibid.

10. Ibid., 10.

11. Cobbing, 7.

Towards the later half of the Yayoi period, we see significant population growth, but also increasing wealth disparities. The first written accounts of Japan from China already indicate the existence of squatting or bowing for superiors, a reverential practice which continues today, and seems to signal that strong hierarchy was present in Japanese society even from these early times.[12] Iron-smelting, better irrigation techniques, and continued population growth in agricultural settlements seems to have produced a society composed of a patchwork of micro-kingdoms.[13] We also begin to see large burial mounds (*kohun* □□) being constructed during this period,[14] many of which can be visited even today. These massive earthworks would have required an immense amount of human labor to construct, and thus they provide us with further indication of the disparities in wealth and power between the rulers and the peasants who made up each individual community.

The existence of the large tomb mounds, accompanied by other archaeological evidence such as pottery, bells, and weaponry, indicates that a larger cultural sphere was forming, but it remains undetermined to what extent this also coincided with a political sphere.[15] Communities were still highly federated, albeit with groups on the plains of

---

12. Farris, 21.

13. Ibid.

14. Farris, 15.

15. Gina L. Barnes, *Protohistoric Yamato: The Archaeology of the First Japanese State* (Ann Arbor, MI: The University of Michigan Center for Japanese Studies, 1988), 12.

southern Honshu (referred to in the literature as Eastern Seto) finding themselves in opposition to Kyushu, constituting the Western Seto region.[16] Archaeological evidence shows that these regions had distinctively different cultural connections and practices, with Kyushu (Western Seto) mirroring much of the culture on the Korean peninsula at the time, and even participating early on in sending tribute and emissaries to China.[17] Eastern Seto, by contrast, does not see a heavy presence of foreign goods, and much of their bronze was smelted down to form other cultural artifacts.[18]

The earliest historical picture we receive of one of these kingdoms belongs to the mysterious but legendary Queen Himiko,[19] who, the Chinese account of the *Wei zhi* (compiled between 223 and 297) reports, ruled over an influential kingdom called the Yamatai.[20] Scholars have tried to identify the Yamatai with the Yamato, but there is still no consensus on this question. Others have theorized that the Yamatai and Yamato were distinct kingdoms and lineages who inhabited the same cultural sphere, and that this opposition between Kyushu and Eastern Seto may have catalyzed an increasing unification of the king-

---

16. Ibid., 16.

17. Ibid., 2-4.

18. Ibid.

19. Cobbing, 27. Also, 35-36.

20. Barnes, 4. Also, Cobbing 37-42 for a discussion of debates about where Himiko ruled.

doms in southern Honshu, eventually forming the Yamato kingdom which began to extend its rule from Eastern Seto into Western Seto.[21]

Kyushu remained a vital touchstone for this unfolding drama, as we will explore in greater depth in the next section. The first people who walked over to Japan from Asia were migratory, and it was their progeny who eventually began to settle in small communities during the Jomon period. With the arrival of the Yayoi migration waves, Kyushu became a melting pot of various cultures, and the interactions and intermixing between the Jomon people and the Yayoi peoples eventually produced the Japanese population which inhabits the islands today. Each region began to develop its own sphere of influence, distinct practices, and even dialects. The political situation also remained fragmented, with kingdoms being highly federated affairs rather than "states" in the sense that we understand them today.

In the opposition between the kingdoms of Eastern Seto and the kingdoms of Kyushu, we also find a racial dimension present, with some scholars even arguing that Yamato expansion produced group cohesion in regions where it might have been looser previously, primarily through a process of resisting Yamato hegemony.[22] The Kumaso and the Hayato from Kyushu prove notable examples in this respect, with the Hayato in particular constituting an alternative lineage who were not fully subjugated by the Yamato until 721.[23] The Yamato made an early attempt to break up the Hayato's opposition by forcibly

---

21. Barnes, 16.

22. Mark J. Hudson, *Ruins of Identity: Ethnogenesis in the Japanese Islands*, (Honolulu: University of Hawai'i Press, 1999), 196.

23. Ibid., 195.

moving them from Kyushu across the straits of Shimonoseki to the Kinai peninsula, and also pressed their most elite warriors into service as palace guards, forming something of an exoticized elite unit which was confined to the palace.[24]

Yamato expansion produced not only resistance in Kyushu, but also to the north as their armies came into contact with the Emishi who inhabited Tohoku (northern Honshu). The Emishi were fierce riders known for their exceptional horseback riding skills, so much so that the Yamato attempted to ban horse trading with the Emishi on multiple occasions.[25] However, the Yamato campaign to subjugate the Emishi continued into the ninth century, and was accompanied by a corresponding consciousness of cultural difference between the two groups. Even today the Tohoku region maintains a distinct identity, such as its famous Matagi hunters who have deeply Ainu origins.

Speaking of the Ainu, some groups in the archipelago never really became "Japanese." The Ainu people inhabited Hokkaido for thousands of years without assimilating into the Yamato kingdom. The Ainu are related to those who walked over to Japan from the Sakhalin islands, and their people's footprint historically spans Hokkaido and the Sakhalin islands, extending even to the tip of the Kamchatka peninsula. While the Ainu experienced subjugation at the hands of the Japanese during various periods throughout the history of the archipelago, Hokkaido was not officially annexed until 1869. The Japanese violently dispossessed the Ainu of their land, and while they are today recognized as an indigenous people in Japan, many of them have been

---

24. Ibid., 195.

25. Ibid., 199.

so absorbed into Japanese society that the Japanese government estimates there are only 25,000 Ainu left.[26]

Thus, while Japan appears to be a highly homogenous society today, an investigation of the origins of the people and kingdoms of the Japanese archipelago reveals that it was diverse in its ethnic origin and highly fragmented politically from the very beginning. Much of the early political fragmentation stemmed from the patchwork and diverse nature of these settlement waves, but also the sheer difficulty of overland travel on the volcanic islands played a significant role. For the most part, power was both developed and exercised locally rather than with empire-building ambition, although great mound tombs continued to be built for leaders. The rise of the Yamato kingdom and its imperial line then marked a decisive transition in the Japanese archipelago, but as with all great changes, the future arrived unevenly. Kyushu took a while to subdue and incorporate into this Yamato cultural center, and as history would show, that assimilation always remained tenuous.

Kyushu's outside to Kyoto's inside

Kyushu's seminal importance to the Japanese archipelago and its people cannot be overstated — this southernmost island unites all of the various contradictions which a straightforward history of "a Japanese people" must intentionally obscure in its quest for narrative unity. When Westerners think of Japan today, we picture the streets of Kyoto, the Shinto shrines nestled in the hills, or the bright and flashing

---

26. https://archive.org/details/ainuofjapan00pois/page/4/mode/2up

lights of Tokyo. But the origin of the Japanese people we know today lies far to the southwest on the island of Kyushu where the Yayoi settlers landed and began to forge new relationships of interdependence and loyalty.

If we picture Japan from West to East, we can see how Kyushu as the Western most island serves as the gateway to the rest of the world, and thus it came to serve as the contact barrier where the outside world enjoyed its congress with Japan. Just as the Yayoi arrived on its shores centuries before, Kyushu also became the place where foreign dignitaries and Chinese and Korean merchants would dock their ships to trade with the mysterious country of Wa (as it was referred to in Chinese chronicles).[27] It was Kyushu as well where the first Europeans arrived, on the tiny island of Tanegashima (immediately introducing guns to the Japanese people, in typical European fashion[28]), and then European merchants and missionaries soon found their way into the port cities on the far Western edge of Kyushu.

As the birth place of the Japanese people, Kyushu directly embodies all of the dynamic forces which generated the nation we know today. The land itself is extremely volcanically active, and even the most active volcano in Japan, Mt. Aso, calls Kyushu its home. This geologic volcanism also reflects the ethnic and cultural dynamism which was suppressed and lost in the ensuing battles for Yamato hegemony in the archipelago around the 5th century AD. For, while the Yamato clan did not ultimately establish the seat of their power in Kyushu (they settled further east on the Nara), it was nonetheless the mythical land of their origin — Ninigi, the grandson of the Sun Goddess Amat-

---

27. Cobbing, 27. Also see Farris, 21.

28. Drummond, 29.

erasu, first descended to earth at Takachico in southern Kyushu, and from this story the Yamato chronicles stake their claim as a "heavenly race."[29] The *Kojiki* records the first (likely mythical) emperor in the Yamato line descended from Amaterasu, Jinmu, as having traveled from Kyushu to where the Yamato kingdom was established.[30]

However, Kyushu was also called home by rival clans and ancient kingdoms who were only ever partially subjugated. We modern humans with our access to phones and internet forget just how difficult it was to carry out surveillance over large distances, making the exercise of political sovereignty weaker and weaker the further one goes from major cities of influence. Leaders and the populace in sufficiently distant regions could often enjoy a significant level of practical autonomy prior to modern communication methods like the telegraph, especially in a mountainous archipelago like Japan. The growth and development of communication technology in modern times has struck a significant blow to the ability of a general populace to act in subversive or uncooperative ways.

Kyushu's displacement, both in geographical and mythical space, from the larger unifying forces which were at work far away on Honshu — first near Nara, then Kyoto, and even later in Edo (now Tokyo) — enables it to therefore take on this dynamic identity as both a backwater and a gateway of cultural exchange. Precisely what made this island so susceptible to political agitation — acting as a counter-balance to the central Honshu regime — is also what facilitated the constant inflow of foreign objects, dignitaries, and ideas. This westernmost lo-

---

29. Cobbing, 1-3.

30. Barnes, 10.

cation and geographic remove from the imperial Court in Nara (later, Kyoto) made Kyushu the "outside" to the Yamato's "inside."[31]

In the year 609, the Yamato court established a special outpost of their authority at Dazaifu (just outside Fukuoka) to act as a direct representative of the Imperial court in receiving foreign dignitaries and quelling the local lords and people. Generals posted in this command often had the sense of having been placed on the frontier in a strange and dangerous land, almost as if they had found themselves in a foreign country. Although the actual distance from Kyoto to Dazaifu is only around 380 miles (less than the distance from Boston to DC), the mental distance traversed was vast. In terms of the imaginary coordinates of the Japanese empire, they had been placed far away from the source of power, culture, and religion.

So drastic was this distance that the role at Dazaifu could at times be characterized as a political death-sentence — a functional exile — and many political leaders were anxious to move on from the role in order to return to the imperial court in Nara. Nonetheless, some leaders saw it as an opportunity to arrogate to themselves autonomous power away from the watchful eye of the Yamato state. Fujiwara Hirotsugu was appointed to Dazaifu in 739, but famine, disease, and frustrations with the imperial court motivated him to raise an army of 15,000, including drawing on the remaining Hayato population in Kyushu.[32] He was defeated in a three month campaign by the superior Yamato

---

31. Cobbing, xvii.

32. Cobbing, 79-80.

army, but this was the first major time that an internal leader had marshaled violent resistance from within the Yamato political structure.[33]

Throughout Japanese history Kyushu has continued to play this role of the contact barrier with the outside world. Cities in Kyushu have served as merchant hubs for other Asian nations to trade with Japan, as well as the meeting places where European traders arrived and shared knowledge from Europe. The island also provided a launching pad for bands of Japanese pirates (*wako*) to attack and raid the East Asian coastline routinely.[34] As we saw in the last chapter too, Kyushu was the bastion of the last remaining resistance to Toyotomi Hideyoshi, which he did not successfully put down until 1587. Ultimately, Kyushu never wained in its ability to provide fertile soil for new ideas and political agitation, for it was also from Kyushu that the disaffected samurai (the Satsuma-Choshu alliance) emerged who spear-headed the Meiji Restoration, bringing an end to 250 years of Tokugawa rule in 1868, thus ending the Edo period as we mark it today.[35]

This was the land and the history that Francis Xavier stepped into when the Jesuit mission arrived in Kyushu in 1549. Like a new planet coming into the orbit of a solar system, the gravitational pull of these new forces began to subtly shift and warp the future of the Japanese people. New challenges would arise, old problems would return in new guises, and unexpected horizons would begin to dawn. The old powers could not ignore these new possibilities which were working

---

33. Cobbing, 80.

34. Ibid.

35. See Cobbing's account on pages 220-225.

themselves out in the life of the Japanese people. Any calculus going forward would have to reckon with the new questions and possible futures which the encounter with Christianity as it was facilitated by its European evangelists. At a crucial moment in the history of the Japanese people, the news of Jesus arrived on their shores to introduce a strange new possibility into the contested field of their social and individual lives.

Ideology and Social Transformation under Tokugawa Ieyasu

Christianity appeared in Japan two decades before Oda Nobunaga marched on Kyoto (1568), sparking the unification campaign which his successors Toyotomi Hideyoshi and Tokugawa Ieyasu would bring to completion three decades later. Finally crushing his opposition at the Battle of Sekigahara in October 1600, Tokugawa Ieyasu would usher in the most enduring political stability the Japanese archipelago had known to that point in its history, a period presided over by military governors (*shogun*) from the Tokugawa clan, and lasting until the Meiji Restoration in 1867. This means that this foreign religion Christianity appeared precisely at the historical moment when powerful warlords were crafting a new vision for what the Japanese nation could be in the wake of centuries of chaos.

The birth of this newly unified Japanese nation demanded also the appearance of a Japanese "people" who understood themselves as "Japanese." This new consciousness which needed to emerge would have to find a way to bring political, social, and psychological unification to a heterogenous populace which was geographically fragmented, diverse in its folkways, and used to pragmatically navigating life with a revolving door of leaders telling them what to do. For a united Japanese state to emerge and endure, both the peasantry and the elite needed to assume a universal identity which would supersede their old loyalties to their clan, family, and region. If this new Japanese consciousness could not be born, the internecine conflicts of ages past would remain interminable.

Benedict Anderson in his *Imaginary Communities* points out that various nationalisms started to emerge in history at the moment when traditional religious and social structures were breaking down in unprecedented ways,[36] leaving people unmoored in their social location and self-understanding. As the context of the village or the fiefdom broke down, this was replaced by a new, more abstract context of the people and the nation. This is precisely what was happening in the transition from the feudal Sengoku era (1467-1568) to the long peace of the Edo period (1603-1869). The Tokugawa military regime brought not only political stability to the country, but also radical social change which rapidly stabilized into a long period of ideological stagnation. This forging of a new national ideology and a new Japanese identity had to accompany the construction of the unified political structure under the Tokugawa *bakufu* (military government), otherwise the old cycle of violence would start afresh. Stricter social transformation was required to ensure that Japan did not return to its centuries of war and violence.

The Tokugawa regime undertook this project with all the seriousness which it demanded, and they did so without the conveniences afforded by the modern surveillance state. They brutally persecuted

---

36. Benedict Anderson, *Imaginary Communities: Reflections on the Origin and Spread of Nationalism* (New York: Verso, 2016), 11-12.

any dissident ideologies, especially Christianity, forced the peasantry to spy on each other, compelled registration at local Buddhist temples, and locked down the country from any outside trade and influence. Then, to provide a theoretical underpinning for the transformation, the regime synthesized a new Japanese religious tradition from components found within their borders already, and in the process instituted sweeping changes to the family and societal structure in general.

One of these key social shifts under the Tokugawa regime included the de-centering of "the clan" in favor of "the household."[37] This tight policing of the boundaries of the family enabled the authorities to sharply circumscribe the people's filial loyalties, which posed the primary competitor to national loyalty. These twin duties of filial piety and national duty drew primarily on Confucian ideals about how one relates to family and the state. Since the wars of previous eras owed their motivations to clan competition over networks of power and resources, the success of the nationalist project hinged on narrowing down the clan structure in order to replace it with household units and national loyalty. This filing down of the extended family network was also accompanied with rigid social class distinctions and codes about how to relate with those of different classes. Social and economic mobility was severely curtailed, marriages needed to be registered and approved with local magistrates, and strict codes governing diverse aspects of social life were implemented.[38]

To ensure compliance with these shifting social changes, the Tokugawa regime also employed (1) the *danka* system and (2) the *go-*

---

37. Joseph M. Kitagawa, *Religion in Japanese History* (New York: Columbia University Press, 1990), 152.

38. Ibid.

nin-gumi arrangement. The *danka* system required all families to register with their local Buddhist temple, thus defining in legal records the extent of their household and also raising nominal barriers to secret Christians by requiring one to step on the *fumi-e*.[39] The *gonin-gumi* or 'group of five' system extended this surveillance into all of social life by designating groups of five families who were responsible for monitoring and reporting on each other's behavior.[40] These groups ensured that civil and social codes were being honored, and they served to identify early signs that something suspicious might be happening, especially regarding any secret practice of Christianity or certain undesirable Buddhist sects.

Such sweeping changes do not come without a human cost though. While it's counter-intuitive to think, peace is ultimately backed by the threat of an overwhelming violence which overshadows every possible conflict. For instance, the immense power of the Roman military provided the foundation of the famous *Pax Romana*, uniting within the empire's borders many warring tribes and clans who had to learn to live together under Roman law because they did so under the threat of being crushed by the strongest military in the world. The free flowing networks of trade and ideas which flourished in the Mediterranean world had as their background a looming violence which secured the

---

39. Neil McMullin, *Buddhism and the State in Sixteenth-Century Japan*, (Princeton, NJ: Princeton University Press, 1984), 245.

40. Makoto Fujimura, *Silence and Beauty* (Downer's Grove, IL: IVP Books, 2016), 104.

safety of this vulnerable network.[41] Immense violence was necessary to bring about this lasting peace and stability.

History is riddled with violence. Not only is nature red in tooth and claw, but human beings also turn against one another in vengeance, greed, or sport. This violence seems to found the very nature of civilization itself, as Sigmund Freud famously postulated, for the structures of human society aim primarily at repressing and redirecting these vital forces at work within humanity and which constantly threaten to burst their bounds to wreak havoc amongst us. Rene Girard emphasizes that human community cannot move beyond the most elementary levels of subsistence if it cannot contain the violent feedback loop of revenge. If an eye for an eye makes the whole world blind, then the vengeful spirit threatens to turn the world into a massive conflagration of brothers killing brothers if the spread cannot be stemmed by some communal mechanism.

---

41. We have witnessed the same thing in our own time, especially from 1945 to 2001, as the United States' immense wealth and military power allowed it to dictate a "rules-based international order" which relied on the petro-dollar, democratic government, and the free flow of trade to drive conflicts around the world into an underground status for many years. In the shadow cast by the USA's power, the world experienced an unprecedented spread of international goods accompanied by safe ocean travel and porous borders. All of this was backed by violence, or at least, its threat — a threat made all the more credible by the devastated state in which most of Europe and Asia languished in the aftermath of WW2.

Becoming Japanese with the *fumi-e*

This peculiar relationship between violence and peace is intimately related to the problem of sovereignty which we introduced at the beginning of this chapter. The peoples of the Japanese archipelago struggled to unify under a stable government and achieve a long lasting peace because no single group was able to establish an all-encompassing system of violence which could suppress all the other actors constantly contesting the status quo. The glut of tiny kingdoms and the constant jostling of ambitious elites created a situation in which no one could definitively claim any long term consensus about who should rule. However, with the rise of Oda Nobunaga and the triumph of Tokugawa Ieyasu, one group of men did finally manage to find the precise arrangement of violence which could bring all the disparate pieces of Japan into a durable complex which could persist over time.

How does one achieve such an enduring work of national unification through violence? This violence cannot operate simply at the external level where it always appears as an outward negativity intruding into the lives of political subjects. If the regime's violence remains only at this superficial level of coercion, it will inevitably stir up feelings of resistance and various modes of rebellion which will constantly boil just underneath the surface, waiting for an opportunity to erupt into full-blown opposition.

In the long run, pure fear through the application of violence can't forge the lasting peace which a nationalist regime hopes to achieve. The sort of violence which forges nations must be *internalized* to become durable. The person must learn to identify with an image of ideals and wholeness, thereby coming to experience themselves through this invisible membrane of the ideology which shapes their life-world. The mechanisms of control must become internalized in such a way that the person becomes auto-regulating and complicit in their own subjugation. The Tokugawa regime astutely realized that people must be re-molded through social pressure and outward violence until they come to internally desire their own servitude. This labor of engendering in their population a new set of desires demanded that the Tokugawa regime devise updated strategies for the production and circulation of a new identity amongst the social body.

This brings us to the *fumi-e*, that most ingenious psycho-technology which plays such a central role in Endo's novel. The *fumi-e* begins to answer the question of how a fisherman in Goto village on the southern tip of Kyushu may come to experience himself as "Japanese" in the same sense that someone in the heart of Kyoto or Edo might.

In his essay "Fumi-e Culture," Makoto Fujimura argues that the Tokugawa regime re-forged Japanese society through the experience of a collective trauma embodied in the *fumi-e*. Fujimura interprets the *fumi-e* as a symbol which captures the repression, self-denial, and violence upon which Japanese society as a whole rests.[42] "The nail which sticks out will be hammered down," goes the old proverb, and Japanese people have been hammering themselves and others down so long that the

---

42. Fujimura, 103-105.

pain has had to go underground, just like the Japanese-Christians did when the Tokugawa regime banned Christianity.

As everyone steps on the physical *fumi-e* forced upon them by the regime— using a denial to bind them together in community — they nonetheless also possessed a personal *fumi-e* which they step on in their hearts. Echoing Endo's own words, Fujimura laments how the denial of their most precious and personal experiences stands at the heart of what it means to be Japanese today. They must betray anything which might make them different or individual, sacrificing it silently for the sake of the group's outward harmony and the appearance of unity.

Fr. Rodriguez comes to a visceral understanding of the profound toll that this secrecy has taken on the Japanese-Christians — "I have already told you that Mokichi and Ichizo have expressionless faces, much like puppets. Now I understand the reason why. They cannot register on their faces any sorrow — nor even joy. The long years of secrecy have made the faces of these Christians like masks."[43] Part of the brilliance of Endo's work is seeing in this highly specific experience of the Japanese-Christian a universal aspect of the contemporary Japanese experience — that which one worships inwardly must be outwardly denied. Religion, the deepest thing of the heart, becomes a private matter which one is expected to sacrifice at a moment's notice for the sake of a mere formality. Over time, this continual repression causes a hardened exoskeleton to develop over the internal wound, and one's face must become a mask, hiding the suffering underneath.

This newly emergent Japanese identity which is forged through the psychological violence of stepping on the *fumi-e* enables a trans-his-

---

43. *Silence*, 33.

torical experience which binds the Japanese people together across the boundaries of space and time. Through the experience of this collective trauma, "the nation" begins to appear in the heart of each person as a Whole in which they come to participate through the denial of themselves as a subject. The subject has the power step back from the social collective at any moment in order to assert the truth over and against the community, and thus this subjectivity must be renounced to preserve the Whole. The renunciation of the individual's experience of freedom, love, and worship which takes place in stepping on the *fumi-e* is required to create a socially-constructed self and to construct a social in which that self finds its place.

As they are both fictions, the self and the nation are correlative with one another — the person imagines that they are a self, and this self is dramatized in relation to the equally imaginary object "the nation" which serves as a totalizing whole in which the self understands itself as a part of some greater whole. This whole provides the frame for the self's individual meaning, and the person's adjusts their self and their resulting behavior in accordance with this perception of the grander whole. An imaginary loop is formed and enacted, and the world is changed by the modifications wrought in the individual by the continual repetition of this loop. Through their imaginary participation in the ideological object of "the nation," the fisherman in Goto, the samurai in Kyoto, and the courtesan in Edo all come to spontaneously think, act, and change their lives on the basis of their relation to this fictional social totality.

In the foregoing description, we are trying to describe a strange object — an "objective fiction" — which exists in so far as it is continually reproduced by the social collective, but which also only exists through the radically personal relationship which each individual imagines themselves to have with it. The nation does not exist; only a multiplicities of nations which are imagined and spontaneously experienced in each person. Yet, through the collective force of the singular actions of each individual, the nation is conjured into a kind of reality in so far as it can exercise real effects by changing people's behaviors and ideas in the actually existing world. In this way, the nation comes to possess a life of its own.[44]

Exclusion and the new social synthesis

In this social formality of stepping on the *fumi-e,* some*thing* is excluded from the social realm in order that the group might be made whole, for the whole can only come to exist by ejecting the thing which

---

44. The philosopher Nick Land helped to coin the concept of the 'hyperstition' (a play on the word of 'super-stition'), a concept which describes the way in which things can be brought into existence simply through insisting on them with such prolonged intensity that they *become* real. Hyperstition works much like summoning — by the belief that something will hearken to our ritual of summons, we act differently in the world and thereby give efficacy to the power which we summoned. Once people begin to behave *as if* something is real, the enactment of that thing will eventually *make* it real. Something which never existed before can eventually exercise actual agency in the world through the power of hyperstition, much in the way that swarms of anonymous actors on the internet can meme entire jokes, identities, and worlds into reality. This fictional object "the nation" is also a hyperstition created by a swarm of humans who have been reduced from persons to selves.

disturbs its unity and harmony. There is always something or someone which does not *fit*. The *fumi-e* has no place in the Whole.

The one who steps on the *fumi-e* thus testifies to this gap in the social field, even as they cover it over and bury it. The act of stepping reminds us of this dark undercurrent which threatens at every moment to tear the fabric of society apart by introducing a contradiction or antagonism which would render the group's smooth functioning impossible. In order for everyone to know their place, for every question to have an answer, and for every part to be reconciled to the whole, something or someone must be excluded from the social field to found this structure. The fictional object "the nation" can only come about through this exclusion of whatever contradictory element prevents society from fully closing into a complete structure which has a place for everything and everyone without exception.

We have already seen how the ideology of Japan has to repress and exclude its racially and religiously diverse past in order to conjure the image of an ancient people called "the Japanese." As wave after wave of immigrants arrived on the shores of Japan from far flung places along the Pacific Rim during the Yayoi period, they brought their genetic and cultural material with them. This is not ancient history — this was going on even after the death of Christ! However, even more recently, as Japanese scholars traveled to China to study Buddhism, or Korean emissaries arrived in Kyushu with word from the continent, or Chinese merchants docked in Japanese ports to sell exotic wares, a unique ecosystem of human interaction sprang up which could not be strictly defined as purely Japanese. Despite their image today of being a highly idiosyncratic people, the Japanese have cultivated their idiosyncrasies through a continually repressed process of hybridity. They are hybrids who must forget that they are hybrids.[45]

The Tokugawa regime had to lean on this principle of hybridity too, but without acknowledging that is what they were doing. Thus, as with all ideological construction, one element needed to stand in for all the other contradictions which had no place in the system — Christianity thus came to symbolize that contradiction which needed to be excluded to found the new Japanese religious identity. As Inoue's parable of the king and his four wives makes clear to Rodriguez, the Tokugawa regime's strategy relies on constructing Japanese-ness through an exclusion of what is characterized as 'foreign.' This alien element which creeps into society disturbs the group's harmony, divides people's loyalties, and enables the emergence of new subjective stances which may begin to question the status quo.

We encounter the logic of exclusion in the edict of Tokugawa Hidetada in 1614 which marked the official beginning of the Tokugawa

---

45. Even the Japanese language speaks to this bewildering hybridity. The Japanese employ three different writing scripts (Kanji, Hiragana, Katakana) for writing different types of words — Kanji are Chinese characters, whereas Hiragana are syllabic and used for specifically Japanese words or articles. Katakana were developed for writing and pronouncing foreign words. Today, even words for everyday objects are derived from some foreign version of the thing, like 'pan' for bread or 'tabako' for cigarettes. All of these are appropriated, integrated, and their origins erased.

regime's systematic persecution of Christians.[46] The edict reads like a blend of various religious views all sitting uncomfortably alongside each other. The ideas of the gods (*kami*), the Negative and Positive principles, and the Buddha find themselves brought into a chain of equivalences in which each can be interchanged for the other. The three primary religious traditions in Japan — Shinto, Confucianism, Buddhism — appear all woven together in the text of this edict, indicating the intellectual work that the Tokugawa regime was doing to subjugate all of Japan's religious discourses under a single dominating ideology of the state.

The document follows a theoretical progression in which the indigenous gods are first proclaimed as the original fountain of Japanese religion, and these gods are then immediately equated with the general cosmic principles of Negative and Positive. The text then asserts that Japan is a land which reveres the Buddha, and that the great scholars of the past retrieved this ancient teaching for the Japanese people

---

46. You can find the English translated text of this edict in Joseph Jennes' *History of the Catholic Church in Japan, from its beginnings to the early Meiji period (1549-1873) ; a short handbook* on pages 126-128. The text is out-of-print and expensive, but you can access a free digital copy at Archive.org : https://archive.org/details/historyofcatholi0000joze

Note that at this point in time, Tokugawa Ieyasu had stepped back from the role of Shogun, and appointed his son to function in his place, although he still retained the full functional authority of governance (Drummond 87).

from China.[47] Thus, Shinto serves as the mythical origin point of the Japanese people, Confucian law and cosmic principles as the guide for arbiter for good and evil, and the Buddha and his benevolence as the height of spiritual teaching and blessing. All of these supplement each other, working together to create a new ideological synthesis which will justify the regime's actions and lay the groundwork for the citizen's duty of loyalty to the state.

The religious rhetoric in the edict ultimately culminates in a denouncement of the *Bateren* (padres), the Christian missionaries from Europe. The Japanese-Christians are not themselves mentioned or attacked in the document, but are rather portrayed as part of the Japanese people who are in danger of being lead astray by this new religion which perverts the knowledge and piety which the Japanese people have supposedly possessed of old. Already we can detect here the shift in inquisitorial strategy which we see carried out by Inoue in Endo's *Silence* — the padres are attacked as a foreign influence who will lead the poor Japanese people into a perversion of good and evil, and thus the people must be protected from the padres (and, ultimately, from themselves!). This type of paternalistic language typically suffuses authoritarian rhetoric, justifying violence against its citizens in the name of their best interests.

---

47. Of course, to cover over this detail that Buddhism was *received* from elsewhere, the text reminds the reader that the Buddha's teaching's always travels East, which is a frequently cited maxim used by the Japanese to portray themselves as the culmination of Buddhism (seeing as there is nowhere further East to go from Japan) rather than those who received a later and less primordial version of Buddhism.

However, the perversion the padres are accused of is very precise in this document, and the specific denouncement on the part of the Tokugawa regime brings us back to our point we have been hammering all along — Christianity at every moment threatens to upset to the social order. While the edict justifies the persecution of Christian missionaries in Japan by claiming that they "disbelieve in the way of the gods, and blaspheme the true law, violate right doing and injure the good," the example that it immediately provides is oddly specific and illuminating — the edict claims that the Christians "run to a condemned man and begin to worship him."

Now, we can take this a number of ways, so let's unpack what might be going on here — first of all, we can see that the way in which Japanese-Christians would honor and venerate martyrs could easily create the image that Christians worship criminals. Japanese-Christians and European missionaries would show up in force at the execution of Christians in order to sing psalms and pray, creating a public display of solidarity with this figure who has been deemed an enemy of the state. However, it does also get complicated, because Christians were caught in genuine wrongdoing at certain points, such as the Okamoto-Daihachi incident, which preceded the promulgation of this edict, in which a Christian daimyo was exposed as a collaborator in an unlawful conspiracy.[48] Another black mark for Christianity was the execution of a coiner named Jirobioye who was a Christian, who despite the fact that he was an actual criminal, many Christians showed up to witness his execution and kneeled to commend his soul to God.[49] Situations

---

48. The details are not extremely relevant, but to learn more, consult Boxer, 315-317.

49. Boxer, 316.

like this remind us that we cannot decisively avoid moral ambiguity in our analysis, as we have been seeing throughout our exploration of the often sordid history of Christians in Japan.

However, I think we have to see the Christian practice of forgiveness at work here in this pronouncement, for, lest we forget, it was escaped and converted criminals who first led Francis Xavier to the shores of Kyushu in 1549. Those who draw near to despised and rejected people imitate their Lord Jesus in his willingness to get his hands dirty with the ambiguity and contradictions of the lives of others, especially in the practice of grace and forgiveness. As he dined with tax collectors and prostitutes, he drew the ire of the religious elite who prized their own (imaginary) purity about all else. Further, Jesus himself even became a criminal, an enemy of the state, who was sentenced to death and executed in much the same way that many of the Japanese-Christians were themselves.

This charge that Christians "worshiped the condemned" thus contains a greater range of meaning than perhaps the authors of this document intended.[50] The claim undeniably cuts straight to the heart of Christianity — the violence of love and its many practices of resistance, such as hope, forgiveness, and reconciliation. This conceptual ambiguity cannot be fully escaped, for God is drawn precisely

---

50. It's interesting to see how this charge also appears in Christian encounters with Buddhists in China, where Chinese scholars accused Mateo Ricci of worshipping a condemned criminal. See James Baskind, "The Matter of the Zen School: Fukansai Habian's *Myotei Mondo* and his Christian polemic on Buddhism" *Japanese Journal of Religious Studies* 39, no. 2 (2012): 313.

to the site where deviancy and wickedness are found. This notion that Christians worship the condemned indicates the profound threat which the freedom of God represents to all totalizing systems in all their various manifestations — ideological, political, and theological. The Gospel proclamation which each Christian carries will inevitably drive them towards those people and places in society where social violence performs its cruel operations in the name of the community's identity and purity.

We referenced Rene Girard briefly earlier in relation to the problem which vengeance poses to the body politic, but we did not actually do justice to the answer which Girard poses for this dilemma. He does not prescribe more violence to solve the problem of revenge, seeing that such an approach would be futile. Instead, his work elaborates an extended investigation of the function of the *scapegoat*, which is that element of the community which is ejected for the sake of forging a renewed social unity. The scapegoat has the community's problems symbolically laid upon it, and then those conflicts can be removed from the social totality by sending away or killing the scapegoat.

The scapegoat must be sent away because the element of impurity which is disturbing the community is pinned upon it, just as Hidetada's edict portrays Christianity as this alien and perverse force corrupting the community through its insidious penetration. To achieve a new national consciousness, the Tokugawa regime employed the scapegoat mechanism, ultimately slaughtering and suppressing the Japanese-Christians to create an artificial communal whole to found their enduring political stability. In stepping on the *fumi-e*, the Japanese person kills the scapegoat in order to restore order to the community. This ritual of exclusion grants them entrance into the imaginary collective which is being constructed through their act of sacrifice.

Conclusion

In this chapter we have embarked on a grand tour of political theory and its practice, but we have tried to keep it tied to the concrete details of the Japanese situation at every point in our analysis. We are describing a concrete situation in which the Japanese as real people who share physical space found themselves struggling to achieve a more lasting peace and a higher level of flourishing. Japan has been such a fragile and tenuous thing for most of its history, always on the verge of wiping each other out through warfare, and if they didn't manage to kill each other there was always the volcanos, typhoons, and famines to contend with. The story goes that the divine ancestor Ninigi selected the beautiful bride 'Princess-Blossoming- Brilliantly-Like-the-Flowers-of-the-Trees' (*Ko no Hana Sakuya Hime*) instead of her less attractive older sister 'Princess-Long-as-the-Rocks' (*Iwa Naga Hime*), thus condemning his posterity to be "as frail as the flowers of the trees."[51]

As the various fiefdoms which composed the patchwork called Japan emerged from the tumultuous Sengoku period, a cloud of new possibilities emerged for what these communities could be together. The Japanese people were in the process of discovering a grander unity which could facilitate a civilizational step forward in terms of art, politics, and culture. Although the Christian Church from Europe arrived to share the good news of Christ with them, it was ultimately up to the people of the Japanese archipelago to discover for themselves the answer for how to live together. They and they alone must carry that responsibility for themselves. What would it look like for them to live out the community of God's love in the precise place where they found themselves?

---

51. Cobbing, 9.

Endo in his novel seems to be desperately wondering how Christianity and being-Japanese could be reconciled, but the story which he tells indicates for us that there was a time when the opposition between these two was not as set in stone as it seems to us today. There was nothing destined or historically necessary about a Japanese identity which opposes itself to Christianity. As we study the history of the Tokugawa regime, we begin to see all the various social, political, and psychological mechanisms which were needed to create a Japanese-ness which was in opposition to Christianity. This vision of the Japanese identity which excludes Christianity *tout court* is a historical artifact. Since this opposition was constructed by human hands, could it not also be undone by these same hands? Endo's story testifies that under different circumstances a new synthesis could have been achieved in the past, and we must never forget that a new synthesis always lies ahead in the future. What labor will the people of Japan need to undergo to meet the unique set of challenges they face today, and what role can Christianity play in what the Japanese people will become? The answer has not be arrived at yet. More work remains to be done. In that, there is hope.

3

THE POLITICS OF JAPANESE BUDDHISM

Introduction

In 1605, the Christian convert and former Zen Buddhist monk Fukansai Habian penned his *Myōtei mondō* (The Myōtei Dialogue)[1], an extended fictional dialogue between a Buddhist noblewoman and a Japanese-Christian nun. This text by Habian represents the earliest surviving written work from an indigenous Japanese-Christian scholar in which they articulate a a comprehensive critique of the dominant Buddhist religious framework in Japanese society, and also point towards a viewpoint on Christianity which, while influenced by Western sources, remains an immanent attempt to contextualize Christianity within the Japanese consciousness.

Habian's prior training in a Zen Buddhist monastery (likely of the Rinzai sect)[2] uniquely positioned him to navigate Japan's religious and philosophical territory, a world which would have been wholly

---

1. Baskind, 310.

2. Ibid.

unfamiliar for Western missionaries. He puts this mastery of the Buddhist canon to work in the *Myōtei mondō* in which he systematically exposits and critiques the teachings of every official school of Japanese Buddhism, as well as Pure Land Buddhism, all with the aim of asserting the superiority of Christianity and its ethical vision over its religious rivals.

Despite the attention given to particular doctrinal formulations, the question of ethics is paramount for Habian. In *Myōtei Mondō*, Habian aims all his arguments at supporting the claim that Buddhism cannot provide the resources to sustain moral behavior. For Habian, Buddhism represents a sophisticated form of nihilism, both metaphysically and (consequently) morally. The teachings of Buddhism, regardless of what any sect's particular flavor might give it, amount to an insistence on the need to realize the emptiness of all things. Habian argues therefore that enlightenment understood in this way does not provide any of the motivations or notions necessary for one to make judgments about moral behavior or to find the will to act on those judgments.

Habian's critique of Buddhism raises a strikingly similar question to the one which also runs through this book — does the revival of interest in Buddhist thought represent a practice of genuine liberation or does it provide another sophisticated trap in which we might unwittingly entangle ourselves? In this chapter, we explore that question from the angle of asking whether the history of Buddhism to this point in Japan furnishes any evidence that Buddhism can generate the moral or intellectual resources which might motivate an emancipatory framework which could lead to liberating outcomes for the poor and the oppressed.

As we cast our minds back to the Shimabara Rebellion which we discussed in chapter 1, a question might strike us — how come Buddhism never produced a similar uprising in the country's history? Why does it seem to have fostered a passive and submissive populace instead of people and leaders willing to sacrifice themselves to achieve greater levels of freedom and flourishing in solidarity with the most vulnerable of society? This conspicuous absence may indicate a symptom of a deeper malady affecting the historical system of Japanese Buddhism, and perhaps even the broader Buddhist tradition.

For the claims that I'm making in this chapter to be persuasive, we'll need to start by learning a bit about the history of Buddhism in Japan, as I'm trying to make a historical argument, not merely per-petuate needlessly combative religious polemics. That being said, I do believe that the historical evidence supports my interpretation of the abysmal track record which Japanese Buddhism has for articulating and motivating any sort of politics of liberation for the people of Japan. Throughout its history, Buddhism in Japan has served as either a state-funded bureaucracy or an inert private practice of piety, neither of which mustered the resources to resist the ruling regime and its supplementary network of aristocratic families.

This history also provides crucial context for Habian's critique in his *Myōtei mondō*, located as it was in his own time and social location. We might fruitfully read his argument that Buddhism cannot provide the necessarily underlying mechanisms for ethical behavior as deriving not from sophistical disputations about metaphysics, but rather from a consistent drawing out of the social implications of the nihilistic claims of the Buddhist religious establishment in Japan.

By the claim that Buddhism cannot motivate ethical behavior, I do not take Habian to preclude that a Buddhist community could incul-cate pro-social behaviors, for we know from experience that sufficient social pressure can produce desired behaviors in people. As a Japanese person, Habian would have viscerally understood the power of the social collective to extract compliant behaviors. In fact, this is the bet of the Tokugawa regime in their persecution of Christians — that the Buddhist religion is more likely to foster in the populace the pro-social behavior which they believe will be conducive to build a strong and cohesive Japanese nation.

If Habian's account of Buddhist doctrine is correct though, his argument would entail that a Buddhist community would be in contradiction with its own teachings about the nature of reality and the non-existence of the self were it to exercise its social influence to conform its members to a moral code which presumes to judge behavior as right or wrong. There would be nothing distinctively *Buddhist* about such a community, its actions, or its ethics. Such a Buddhist community might find that they have enforced a certain conception of Japanese politeness instead of following the Eightfold path, and they will have entirely missed the Buddha's attempts to help them realize the emptiness of all phenomena.

But let us radicalize this even further — pro-social behavior is not synonymous with morality. I think that Habian is concerned not simply with whether one's religion can support a system of pro-social behaviors, but rather with the trickier question of whether one's religion can motivate them to choose the right thing when it's hard, unpopular, or risky. Can you speak truth in the face of danger, or stand up for the oppressed when you are hit hard with the pressure to back down? Can Buddhism's teachings or practices provide what one needs to engage in *this* type of resistance? A morality which only does what is popular is no morality at all. That would be more like an ethic of self-preservation. Instead, a truly robust ethics must provide the freedom to dissent from evil practices because one commits themselves into the hands of a power which is higher than any particular political community.

The Brazilian-Catholic Archbishop Hélder Câmara famously said "When I give food to the poor, they call me a saint. When I ask why the poor have no food, they call me a communist."[3] These words call to mind other Latin American priests who struggled on behalf of the poor in their countries, especially those priests who were martyred — figures such as Ignacio Martín-Baró and Óscar Romero. What can give us the courage to broach such difficult questions, and perhaps even, as both Martín-Baró and Romero did, to live in such a way that will get us killed?

Habian speaks of how Christianity can motivate moral behavior because it posits a reward or punishment in the afterlife based on our actions in this life. In this way, he reveals the necessity of positing a beyond to life in order to articulate an ethical realm — life must be able to produce a value higher than itself. Without something operating within life which is nonetheless of greater importance, we become slaves to pure utility, shackled to a logic of efficiency which will ultimately reduce human beings to nothing more than error-prone and dysfunctional machines.

The irony to be appreciated here is that we must have something we are willing to die for if we want to truly live. When we eliminate death as a pure negativity opening up the realm of freedom, we also lose the capacity to live as human beings. In what ways does Buddhism attempt to foreclose this negativity, and in what ways does Christianity hold space for that negativity, mobilizing it in concrete experience towards God's purposes?

---

3. https://www.goodreads.com/quotes/20321-when-i-give-food-to-the-poor-they-call-me

This chapter proceeds to investigate these questions in three movements — one historical, one textual, one philosophical. First, we will learn about the historical process whereby Buddhism was introduced to Japan, how it was institutionalized, and what it became over time, especially in relation to the Imperial court and elite structures of power. We will then transition into a reading of Fukansai Habian's *Myo Tei Mondo* in order to survey and consider the sweep of his arguments in the text. Finally, the chapter closes by bringing the reader into an encounter with some contemporary critiques which echo's Habian's arguments, especially in the philosophy of Slavoj Žižek.

The introduction and growth of Buddhism in Japan

Buddhism as early political technology

While Buddhism likely arrived in Japan earlier than the official accounts indicate, these interactions would have simply been due to the general circulation of people and goods across the China Sea, and they seem to have left scant historical evidence, as well as lacked any wider societal impact.[4] Thus, scholars consider the effective beginning of Buddhism to Japan to originate from an official envoy from King Sŏngmyŏng of the Paekche kingdom, a small country located on the Korean peninsula at that time.

The *Nihon Shoki* (an official historical account compiled by 720 AD) records that in 552 AD King Sŏngmyŏng dispatched emissaries

---

4. William E. Deal and Brian Ruppert, *A Cultural History of Japanese Buddhism* (West Sussex, UK: Wiley Blackwell, 2015), 25.

and retainers to the Japanese imperial court, carrying "a gold and copper statue of Śākyamuni Buddha, ritual banners and canopies, and several volumes of sūtras and commentaries."[5] In his accompanying message to the royal court, King Sŏngmyŏng highlights three things about Buddhism — First, that the doctrine of Buddhism is high and difficult to obtain. Second, he praises the Buddha's teachings for how it has granted his kingdom's every wish, providing them everything they could have asked for. Finally, he closes by noting in passing that every nation from India to Korea has accepted this new doctrine.[6]

Initially, the Japanese elite did not fully unite around the idea of importing this new religion to their country. A number of prominent aristocratic families exercised their influence primarily by stewarding the rituals, stories, and worship of native Japanese deities, and thus they naturally pushed back against the introduction of this new religion Buddhism by expressing worries about the potential consequences of abandoning the service of their ancestors' gods.[7] Other elites saw this an opportunity though, and the Soga family which championed the cause of Buddhism in Japan eventually settled the matter of aristocratic opposition by way of a military conflict which concluded decisively in 587.[8] The supremacy of Buddhism as the new state-instituted religion proved a step forward in uniting the people, the elite, and the state around a shared conception of "Japan."

---

5. Ibid., 21.

6. Ibid.

7. Kasahara, 53.

8. Deal, 29-30

Taking a step back though, we can characterize Buddhism's introduction to Japan primarily as a top-down project of the elites attempting to import an entirely new civilizational structure from the continent. We already see intimations of this in King Sŏngmyŏng's original message to the Japanese court in which he highlights both Buddhism's power to materially bless the nation and its widespread adoption across the Asian continent.

King Sŏngmyŏng's comment about Buddhism's widespread adoption signals that Buddhism functions as a medium of trans-national culture for the international elite of southern and Eastern Asia. Thus, to import Buddhism was not to simply adopt a new religion, but rather to gain entrance into a prosperous and advanced inter-national political network with the Chinese civilization at the center of this complex.[9] This was something the Japanese elite desperately wanted, especially as they found themselves relegated to a remote Western corner of the Asian region, and were generally considered such a backward and reclusive nation as to be hardly even worth mentioning in the historical records of other nations.[10] They primarily had diplomatic relations with the kingdoms on the Korean Peninsula, such as Paekche, who were themselves primarily importing Chinese thought-forms and ways of life.

At this time in east Asia, Buddhism played an important religious and cultural role in what we might call the larger "Confucian civilizational complex." This Confucian complex was an interlocking

---

9. Ibid., 23-24.

10. Chinese records have only sparse and sketchy mentions of Japan — called "Wa." Learn more: https://factsanddetails.com/japan /cat16/sub105/entry-5289.html

system of cultural and political achievements which were developed in China, and later conceptually re-packaged and exported to the Korean peninsula. When King Sŏngmyŏng sent his Buddhist emissary to the Japanese court, he was offering them the opportunity to avail themselves of the achievements of Chinese civilization — a rich history of art and poetry, sophisticated native philosophical traditions in Taoism and Confucianism, innovative new religious forms like Buddhism, advanced scientific technology, and a structured and scalable political system of bureaucratic governance.

Buddhism represented more than a new religion to the Japanese elite — it was the key component in a larger complex of arts, religion, technology, and statecraft which formed the foundation of their Chinese and Korean neighbors' civilizations. From the very beginning of its history in Japan then, Buddhism was primarily a tool prized and employed by the elites to achieve civilizational advancement in tandem with increased political control. Its truth or its ethical vision was not a consideration at all. The question was — what can it *do* for *us*?

The growth of the Temple system

The Japanese imperial court in Nara established Buddhism in Japan primarily by funding and constructing a system of temples which served as cloisters for monks and nuns who were responsible for performing rituals on behalf of the kingdom, as well as reading auspicious sutras (Buddhist texts) intended to accrue karmic blessing for the nation. [11]

---

11. Kasahara, 66.

This temple system effectively made the monks, the nuns, and the entire Japanese-Buddhist leadership into government employees from the outset. The monks and nuns who occupied the state's monasteries received a salary from the government, tax exemptions, and even immunity from state police entering temple grounds. Further, all the clergies' physical needs were provided for by the land which the state granted to the temples, even including serfs who would live on the land to work it to produce food for themselves and the clergy in the temple.[12]

In exchange for these benefits, the clergy were assigned a strictly delineated set of duties, which included a demanding set of rules regarding their conduct and a regular schedule of rites to be performed in order to secure blessing and prosperity for the nation. With state-funding, legal immunity, arable land, and even subservient labor, the temples could become a world unto themselves, totally disconnected from the realities of everyday life.

Initially, the imperial court recognized and established six official schools of Buddhism — Kusha, Jojitsu, Sanron, Hossō, Kegon, Ritsu[13] — and these all controlled a number of larger and smaller temple networks concentrated in and around the palace located at Nara. The practice of any schools of Buddhism other than the state sanctioned ones were strictly forbidden, and the monks and nuns of the state-sanctioned schools were required to remain shut up in their cloisters, unable to travel amongst the people spreading the Buddha's teachings.[14]

---

13. Ibid., 68.

14. Ibid., 63.

This prohibition on itinerant teaching seems to betray that the elite did not conceive of Buddhism as a person's path to individual salvation, but as a complex metaphysical framework for accommodating, venerating, and obtaining blessing from an increasingly complex pantheon of celestial beings, both inherited from Chinese Buddhism, but also through syncretic absorption of indigenous deities pre-existing Buddhism's arrival. In light of these circumstances, the Buddhism which was practiced in monasteries and nunneries had little to no relevance to the lives of normal people, both because of the strict cloistering of the clergy, but also because the temples derived their income both directly from the Imperial court's coffers and from the usufruct which they enjoyed from the land and servants provided to them by the government. While local shrines dedicated to indigenous deities were often operated by local families and relied on the donations and visitations of the locals for support, Buddhist complexes had no such need, and could afford to ignore the spiritual needs and concerns of the general populace. They weren't paid to concern themselves with the people since the mandate they had received from their employer, the Imperial court, did not include anything about actually proselytizing the populace.

Despite the irrelevance of Buddhist practice to the daily lives of Japanese peasants, the role of clergy still held a powerful allure for commoners as it offered the only path available for gaining social standing without having to have been born to a family of upper rank. In this new role of Buddhist clergy, the government had created a high-status political role which was theoretically open to anyone who was willing to dedicate themselves to studying Buddhist texts and to practicing the strict lifestyle code of the monastery. While, in practice, the upper ranks of the Buddhist leadership at the most prestigious temples began to become bloated with the second and third sons of noble families,[15] the pathway of the monk or nun became so popular that the government had to institute quotas for how many new clergy could take monastic orders each year.[16]

As the aristocratic families became more deeply intertwined with the leadership of the most powerful temples, and government money's constant flow into the temples had increased their numbers, power, and influence, the six schools became inextricably caught up in the constant political maneuvering of the nobles. With all the temples concentrated in the region of the city of Nara where the imperial court was also located, the Yamato regime began to develop a sense of claustrophobia. Consequently, in 794, they moved their capitol a little over 30 kilometers northeast to the location of present-day Kyoto, and strictly forbade any of the Buddhist schools to follow them there.[17] The government and the religious establishment had become too close in both physical and political proximity, and thus the Imperial court took drastic measures to get some breathing room from the constant in-fighting of the nobles.

While at first blush this would seem to have increased the Imperial court's power relative to the Buddhist establishment, history shows that it actually had the opposite effect in the long run, especially when we couple this development with a few other important factors. With their government salaries, private land, and legal immunity, the Buddhist temples were rapidly becoming private micro-fiefdoms which were carving out a space for themselves inside the nation, almost like

---

15. Ibid., 50.

16. Ibid., 63.

17. Ibid.,

a parasite within a host. Further, the largest temples had begun to establish satellite temples in other regions — called "temple branch systems" — which means that the Buddhist leadership were effectively acquiring land, funds, and people for themselves, all while maintaining a system of government-backed hierarchy. When one adds in the emergence of a class of "warrior-priests" (*sohei*) living on temple grounds to defend it (and even attack other temples!)[18], you have a situation in which the Imperial court of the Yamato regime woke up one day to find themselves with functionally sovereign kingdoms hiding in plain sight inside their borders, all while *subsisting on the state's tax revenue.*

If we think back to the governance challenges we enumerated in the second chapter of this book, especially the problems that ambitious elites can create for the ruling regime, the establishment of the Buddhist temple system created an invaluable vector for aristocratic families to accrue influence, wealth, and functional sovereignty to themselves, as well as maneuver themselves in relation to the Imperial court in order to sap their resources and take a larger slice of the pie. Effective governments have to remember that the other elites are always waiting in the wing to replace their regime, and in the meantime these elites will take any opportunity to enrich their own position within the kingdom.

Popular Buddhism in the Kamakura period

The Buddhism which was practiced in the government-sponsored temple system largely followed the doctrine and rote practices which

---

18. Ibid., 90.

they received from the continent. However, two figures changed this by pioneering new forms of Buddhism which were home-grown in Japan. The work of Kūkai and Saichō catalyzed religious innovation within Japanese Buddhism,[19] particularly by trying to understand Buddhism as relevant to the question of the individual and salvation, rather than simply as a complex system of ritual. Did Buddhism present a path for the individual's salvation, and if so, what were the ideas, teachings, and practices should be emphasized as leading to salvation?

Kūkai, the founder of the Shingon sect, and Saichō, the founder of the Tendai sect, each traveled to China at different times to drink from the ancient wells of Buddhism on the continent, although they both had begun to read texts and synthesize their idiosyncratic interpretations before they made their pilgrimages to receive their official dharma transmissions in China.[20] These men received the imperial charters to start their own schools of Buddhism, thus becoming the forerunners to introduce some level of religious competition to the existing 6 schools which had previously been established by the government.[21] The Tendai complex *Enryaku-ji* at Mt. Hiei would become a particularly powerful temple, so powerful in fact that Oda Nobunaga would raze it to the ground in 1571 to stem its influence.[22]

---

19. Richard Bowring, *The Religious Traditions of Japan 500-1600* (Cambridge: Cambridge University Press, 2005), 113-114.

20. Ibid., 116-119 (Saichō) and 135-137 (Kūkai).

21. Kasahara, 76 and 104. Also see Bowring, 153.

22. George Sansom. *A History of Japan: 1334-1615* (Tokyo: Charles E. Tuttle Company, 1963), 284.

I've had to forego quite a bit of interesting history about these two figures, as well as the details of their doctrinal distinctives, simply because it would likely be more distracting than illuminating for the reader, but we need to include Kūkai and Saichō in our narrative because their work in forging new schools of Buddhism in Japan paved the way for an explosion of popular or lay Buddhisms which would appear in the Kamakura era (1185-1333) about 400 years after they founded their schools. While the Shingon and Tendai schools still fell within "Old Buddhism" (*Kyū Bukkyō*), many of the figures who founded new and significant schools of "New Buddhism" (*Shin Bukkyō*) during the Kamakura period studied at Mt. Hiei in the Tendai school at some point, and thus the tradition established by Saichō eventually came to serve as a catalyst for widespread changes in the religious landscape of Japan.[23]

The Kamakura area saw an unprecedented growth of new schools of Buddhism, but not all of them were welcomed by the Buddhist establishment or whichever regime happened to be in power at the time. The significance of these new schools resided primarily in how they went against the national, ritualistic, and formalistic attributes of established Buddhism which was practiced in the government-sponsored temples. These new schools took their message of salvation to the masses, sharing the teachings of the Buddha with individuals, exhorting people to seek personal salvation, and emphasizing simple practices such as meditating or chanting. These simple practices could be performed anywhere at any time, no ritual implements or dharma transmission required, and thus figures such as Shinran (1173-1263) and Dōgen (1200-1253) transformed Japanese Buddhism in their

---

23. Kasahara, 157.

process of democratizing it. No longer did people need to take vows or submit to a strict code of monastic living to practice Buddhism.

Personal salvation becomes a theme which will appear again and again in the new schools of Buddhism. This taps into a concern which also animated Saichō's Tendai tradition, a passion we see most clearly when he came into an intense rivalry with a Hosso priest named Tokuitsu concerning the question of whether all beings possess Buddha-nature or whether only some do.[24] Tokuitsu taught that there "five natures" or types of beings, each endowed with differing spiritual capacities based on their nature, whereas Saichō argued that every creature can realize the emptiness of all things and thereby attain release from suffering through enlightenment. He found Tokuitsu's view abhorrent because it implied the existence of a whole class of people who were consigned to never achieve enlightenment, condemned to wander in illusion with no hope.[25]

If Buddhism was only practiced by monks and nuns who are cloistered away in a temple complex and subjected to rigid lifestyle codes, how could anyone attain the state of bliss taught by the Buddha? If the people cannot hear or practice the faith, how can they be saved? This concern for personal salvation thus becomes a radicalizing idea which motivated significant religious innovation during this period, and which also put pressure on established Buddhist schools to reform their own teaching and practices. These movements and their values left an indelible mark on the religious consciousness of the Japanese people, and in many ways, they tilled the soil which would eventually become receptive to this foreign religion, Christianity.

---

24. Kasahara, 77-78.

25. Ibid., 78.

Nobunaga's unification and Tokugawa's policies

Our account here will pass over the Muromachi period (1336-1573), which was nearly three centuries marked by constant warfare and political instability. We're not delving into this period in detail because it did not significantly alter the trends which we've already outlined in the previous section about the Kamakura period — how the practices and teachings of personal salvation introduced a dividing line between the democratized lay Buddhisms and the established schools of the temple system.

Even as lay Buddhist movements proliferated throughout the Kamakura and Muromachi periods, the Buddhist temple-system continued to ascend in importance on the political landscape of Japan. This was still true when Oda Nobunaga undertook the task of returning peace to the country by unifying the clans which had been engaged in nearly constant armed conflict since the Ōnin War (1467). The many new schools and lay movements had not mustered anything like political organization to this point, but rather intermingled with and co-existed alongside the official operation of the temples which continued to exercise their political influence.

Oda Nobunaga would, more than any figure until that point in Japanese history, manage to forge something like a unified Japanese state. While he wasn't able to complete the job in his lifetime — that was left to his successors, Hideyoshi and Tokugawa — through his military campaigns and political policies he successfully broke the power of the landed nobles, the Imperial court, and the Buddhist temple system, ultimately laying the foundation for the subjugation of the elites at the hands of a military government under his successors.

Historical records portray Oda Nobunaga as a violent and irreligious man who mocked those that would criticize his lack of piety. It's said that he held no reverence for religion, deities, or the supernatural, and seems to have held beliefs more akin to a Norse warrior — today we are here, tomorrow we are gone, so let us be brave and glorious in our actions, not even fearing death.[26] Perhaps because of this total lack of reverence for religion, he possessed an unusually clear-eyed vision of the entrenched political power which the Buddhist temples possessed. His actions indicate that he understood how desperately he needed to break the military and economic power of the Temple system if he had any hope of successfully unifying the nation. If he didn't address the problem of the temples head on, these micro-kingdoms nested inside the nation would bitterly oppose him at every turn, undermining even his victories.

He implemented two particular policies which served to choke the Buddhist Temple system. First, his "land policy" in which he seized and re-organized land, and (2) his "urban policy" in which he took control of markets and commerce.[27] By seizing land, he cut off the Temple's legal immunity, their base of operations, and their source of self-sufficiency derived from agriculture and slave labor. By taking control of the urban markets, Nobunaga began to draw down the Temple's outside funding sources and revenue, forcing them into operating with tighter budgets and fewer resources. This was also a way for Nobunaga to control the private wealth of the elite in general, because it choked their commercial and tax revenue while making them more dependent on his vassals and central government.

---

26. McMullin, 88.

27. Ibid., 162.

While he certainly wasn't against allying himself with temples who demonstrated their desire to forge a beneficial relationship, mostly notably the Shingon school concentrated in and around Kyoto, he would often play both sides of the table by having these same temples fight the temples which opposed him. Thus, he would conduct campaigns in which he had temples fight other temples ,rather than putting himself in a bad light by using secular warriors to kill religious clergy.[28] This tactic had the additional benefit of causing both temples to wear themselves down through fighting, thus weakening even those temples which allied themselves with him, and reducing both parties' power in the process.

Hideyoshi Toyotomi, Oda Nobunaga's successor, continued this work of forcing the Buddhist temples to submit to the military authority of the shogunate. He divested many of the largest and most powerful temples of their land holdings by returning them to their original owners . In some cases, he confiscated as much as 90% of the temple's holdings.[29] Hideyoshi broke the military power of the two largest remaining temples, Mt. Koya and Negoro-ji. The temple Negoro-ji he destroyed, burning its over 2,700 buildings and killing its 2,000 warrior-monks,[30] while the other temple was forced to submit after witnessing this violent display. When Mt. Koya submitted, they signed a document pledging to return their land to its original owners, to restrict their activities purely to scholarly pursuits, and also to no

---

28. Ibid., 160.

29. Ibid., 238.

30. Ibid., 237-238.

longer harbor criminals or fugitives.[31] These three actions formed the three prongs of Hideyoshi's strategy to break the temples — divest their land, take away their military power, and revoke their legal immunity.

Tokugawa Ieyasu also continued the policies of his predecessors which divested power from the Buddhist temples, monks, and scholars, although he differed in choosing to ally himself with an emerging synthesis of Neo-Confucian social ethics and Japanese folk religion. As approached from the perspective of this emergent framework, Buddhism needed to be tightly circumscribed and controlled so that it could be effectively assimilated into the religious mosaic the Tokugawa regime was cobbling together. The Tokugawa regime approached this problem not so much by destroying Buddhism, but rather entangling it with the government and making the temple system more dependent on the Shogunate.

The implementation of the *danka* system perfectly encapsulates of this strategy. We referenced the *danka* system in the last chapter when we turned our attention to the social violence which the Tokugawa regime committed against its people in pursuit of a unified national consciousness. The *danka* system was in full force by 1640, at which point every Japanese household was required to be registered with a local Buddhist temple.[32] While this certainly increased the revenue and patronage to the Buddhist temples, in reality, the Buddhist temples were now thoroughly ensnared with the Shogunate's social policies and legal enforcement. So, while Buddhism was ostensibly

---

31. Ibid., 238.

32. Ibid., 245.

promoted by the regime, temple participation was reduced to the level of perfunctory government registration.

To summarize the story thus far — the introduction of Buddhism to Japan was an astro-turfed elite project to gain Japan access to the cultural, technological, and political resources of the Confucian civilizational complex which had developed on the continent. This state establishment of Buddhism mutated over time into a vector for elites to accrue political influence, legal immunity, and even military power. At the same time, many popularizers brought new variations of Buddhism to the masses, ones which emphasized personal salvation and the ability to practice outside of the state-sponsored temple system. In order to bring about a unified Japanese state, Oda Nobunaga and his predecessors had to implement a series of decisive policies to break the power of the Buddhist establishment and control these lay Buddhist sects which were spreading amongst the people.

Setting the stage for Habian's *Myotei Mondo*

Th preceding historical narrative takes us all the way up the 17th century, dropping us into the fraught moment in Japanese history in which Endo sets his novel *Silence*. Regime-sponsored Buddhism plays an under-stated role in Endo's novel *Silence*, appearing only in so far as it plays the role of the assumed religious background of the Japanese people. Just like with the Shimabara Rebellion, this crucial political and ideological context is left unspoken by Endo, but once we understand it we start to see its fingerprints all over the text. However, I think that we cannot fully appreciate the import of Rodriguez's decisions without understanding this history, because it is with this Buddhist establishment that Rodriguez ultimately chooses to comply.

He assimilates himself into this historical institution and tradition of practice.

In *Silence*, right after Rodriguez is captured, we meet a Buddhist priest who plays the role of Fr. Rodriguez's handler and a go-between for Inoue.[33] This priest represents the political and religious establishment which contrasts itself with the dangerous foreign religion of Christianity. He pursues a number of differing strategies to undermine Rodriguez and begin sowing seeds of doubt, but the binding thread of his rhetoric in their first conversation amounts to — "If you force on people things that they don't want, they are inclined to say: 'Thanks for nothing!' And Christian doctrine is something like that here."[34] He says that he has studied Christianity in the seminary, but that he does not think it should be introduced to the country.[35] In this way, he postures himself as both open-minded but also resolute to protect his people from ideas he has deemed deleterious to their flourishing.

Inoue and the Buddhist priest presents themselves to Rodriguez in such a way that Buddhism appears to have an unassailable and natural place within the Japanese identity. However, in Kyushu at least, this had certainly not been the case even a few decades prior, as Fr. Rodriguez is quick to point out in his exchanges with the Inquisitor. Christianity had spread throughout Kyushu, and even had outposts in the capital city itself. There were Christian daimyos who presided over Christian realms. Even the Buddhism which predominated in

---

33. *Silence*, 92-97.

34. Ibid., 94.

35. Ibid.

the countryside was often highly syncretic and superstitious, with the official forms being performed only in a perfunctory manner because of the requirement to register with a local temple. Since the official forms of Buddhism could not really be practiced by the lay people who were not under monastic vows, many de-institutionalized and lay forms of Buddhist piety were practiced by the people outside of the bounds of the official schools' teachings.

We've already seen how the 16th and 17th centuries marked the largest drawdown in Japanese Buddhism's influence which it had ever experienced. At the hands of three successive military leaders, the Buddhist temples and various schools had been brought to heel, and thus were no longer enjoying the privilege which they had grown accustomed for the past thousand years. Shadows of their former selves, the Buddhist temples had become places for tranquility and scholarship, no longer powerful fiefdoms with warrior-priests or politically influential clergy. The drastic measures taken by Tokugawa Ieyasu and his predecessors to break up and re-organize the Buddhist temple systems had been successful at eliminating their political power and converting them into a governance tool for enforcing social uniformity. By the time that Fukansai Habian would have begun his training as a monk, the Buddhist temples had been functionally reduced to places for rites, texts, administrative records, and housing clergy. While the monks continued to maintain set apart lives of ritual purity and strict behavioral protocol, their social role was largely confined to rituals of cleansing, funerals, and state record-keeping functions, as well as studying and preserving important religious or artistic texts. This is why we find ex-Fr. Ferreira living in a Buddhist temple copying out European science texts which the regime was desperate to get its hands on.

This speaks to the ultimate interests of the operation of the Buddhist system in Japan at the time — it was largely an extension of the state's governing apparatus, and the religious teachings served either to reinforce or at least not impede the effective governance strategies of the nascent Tokugawa regime's unification and homogenization efforts. While there were no doubt many zealous practitioners of the faith who closely studied texts, propounded profound teachings, and pushed themselves in the rigor of their practices, the entire institutional structure functioned in a deeply complicity with the state, relying on a brokered truce which codified co-dependence. From this perspective, the proliferation of personal piety was not necessarily desirable, but at least not seen as a threat to the system's true aims. As long as the people continued to officially register with the temples and denied their Christian faith by stepping on the *fumi-e*, the regime had secured what they desired most — a compliant populace.

So little influence did the official schools have on your average Japanese person that Habian sees these forms of personal Buddhist piety and practice which preached salvation for all beings functioning as Christianity's primary religious competitors for the hearts and minds of the Japanese people. Personal forms of Buddhism supplemented the emptiness of the ritual compliance which institutional Buddhism demanded. They served as the private meaning-ful supplement to outward conformity to social strictures and ritual requirements. One could still register at the local temple but study and carry out their daily practice in another tradition entirely, all with the hopes of attaining to the bliss of enlightenment as taught by the Buddha.

This explains why in the *Myotei Mondo* Habian makes the Christian nun Yutei's interlocutor an adherent of Pure Land Buddhism, an un-official and itinerant Buddhist school which enjoyed wide popularity amongst the people. Founded by Hōnen and popularized by

Shinran, Pure Land Buddhism preached a universal salvation irre-spective of one's spiritual lineage or mastery of Buddhist teachings — one simply had to chant the name of the Amida Buddha, calling upon him to save you. Habian culminates his discussion of the eight official schools with a final refutation of Pure Land, which seems to signal a particular anxiety to address the threat which Pure Land represents to Christianity's adoption in Japan. Pure Land preached a 'Western Paradise' to which one goes when they die, offering a blissful place in which the Amida Buddha helps all people easily attain enlightenment. Since this was probably the closest approximation to the Christian notion of heaven that one could find in any contemporary Buddhist school, it receives special treatment and refutation in Habian's text.

Habian's *Myotei Mondo* demands closer scrutiny, both because it positions itself as a polemical and apologetic text within Kyushu's complicated religious terrain, but also because it presents an indige-nous Christian's critique of the established religious framework of its day. While institutional Buddhism structured public and political life, many private forms of Buddhism were also on offer for lay people to take up and to practice. With Buddhism providing one the key ideological underpinnings of the Tokugawa regime's grander political architecture, the stakes couldn't be higher in Habian's undertaking to critique the Buddhist ethical vision, and to recommend the Christian one in its place.

Buddhism as a species of nihilism

To state Habian's thesis in *Myotei Mondo* very succinctly — he claims that Buddhism cannot motivate ethical behavior because it denies both (1) the existence of a self which could be ethical and (2) the experience of an after-life in which that self could be rewarded or punished for its actions in this life.

In making this argument, Habian relies on three specific premises:

1. Buddhism teaches that all things are nothingness and that, consequently, selfhood too is an illusion. This means that the belief in a self which could act ethically is an illusion which must be surpassed in order to attain enlightenment.

2. Christianity motivates an ethical life by positing an eternal soul which will persist into an after-life where God will judge our actions, offering reward or punishment on that basis.

3. Buddhism only *appears* to offer an after-life which could motivate ethical motivation, namely, karma and the cycle of samsara, but Habian refutes this by demonstrating how the use of "skillful means" renders this language purely allegorical and ultimately only provisional.

This section will focus on unpacking premises 1 and 3 in particular, as they compose the substance of his critique of Buddhism, but a few preliminary remarks are in order —

First, in making this overarching argument, Habian focuses primarily on the existential dimension of the religious schools, rather than their ritualistic or collective benefits for which the Japanese elite originally prized Buddhism. As the cohesion of social groups were breaking down and people were developing an increased consciousness of the individual *qua* individual, the newer schools of Buddhism thrived on this personal dimension of religious practice and piety. Displaying a consciousness of this shift, Habian leaves out any extended discussion of the social consequences of Christianity, instead choosing to focus on the beliefs and affects which make up the believer's personal relationship with God, the state of their soul, their moral decisions, and the Final Judgment.

However, I want to note that we can certainly recognize that his emphasis on moral decision-making nonetheless heavily implies a concern with the good of the community. The actions of the individual always affect, and even directly constitute, the collective. Although Habian's discourse furnishes evidence that the individual was emerging more prominently as a locus of ethical questioning, a Japanese thinker would still not have separated the self and the group in ethical reflection as sharply as a Westerner would in a similar theoretical context. Thus, I take it that while he restricts himself to discussing the individual alone, Habian does not exclude the individual and their decisions from any reflection on the question of communal flourishing, but rather leaves this extra step of reasoning up to the reader. While it falls outside of the purview of his apologetic goals in the text, the social implications of his arguments about moral decision-making are inescapable, as we will see.

Second, I have chosen in this chapter not to focus on Habian's positive arguments for Christianity as successfully motivating moral behavior by way of reward and punishment. I will argue elsewhere in this book how Christianity motivates a solidarity with the oppressed and seeking the good of others,[36] but Habian's critique of Buddhism and his defense of Christianity technically constitute distinct arguments, and thus we can choose to remain agnostic at this time about

---

36. Chapter 5 – 'A Theology of Freedom' puts forward an account of how freedom forms the core of the Gospel message, but how this freedom is also *for* the other. It pushes us outwards and towards the contradictions in our world.

whether reward and punishment in the after-life are the best framework for motivating ethical behavior. We are more interested in this chapter about the accuracy of Habian's argument against Buddhism in which he portrays it as a species of nihilism, and what type of effects he believes this nihilism would cause in the individual.

Third and last, premise 1 functions as the core of Habian's argument against Buddhism, and I think that point 3 constitutes his rebuttal to the primary objection against his argument. He needs to establish both of these premises for his argument to work, but if his response to the rebuttal in premise 3 does not hold, then premise 1 will fail as well. With all that said, let's dive in.

The emptiness of all phenomena

In first section of the *Myotei Mondo*, Habian displays through the mouth of the Christian nun Yutei an encyclopedic knowledge of the most crucial texts in Buddhism, and he uses these to elaborate the teachings of the eight schools of state-sponsored Buddhism. Ultimately, through his exegesis he demonstrates that all the schools converge on a core shared teaching — that enlightenment is the pure realization of absolute nothingness.[37]

This characterization of enlightenment instructs one to realize the essential emptiness of all things, thereby abandoning all desire which might attach one to the various illusions that we experience in consciousness. At the center of Buddhist teaching stands the denial of

---

37. Fukansai Habian, *The Myotei Dialogues: A Japanese Christian critique of native traditions*, translated by James Baskind and Richard Bowring (Leiden: Brill, 2016), 66-67.

both the reality of the self and the reality of the external world, all aimed at the elimination of the suffering which arises due to our becoming attached to the constantly changing phenomena in experience.

Despite its characterization today as a "world religion" complete with texts, rituals, deities, and various schools or lineages, Buddhism originally arose as a therapeutic response to the problem of suffering, a response which the Buddha grounded in a reflection on the operation of consciousness. In consciousness we experience ourselves as subjects to whom objects appear, or are given, and the Buddha finds in this experience of consciousness itself the roots of our suffering as humans. The appearance of objects with distinct essences to a subject which is also separate from these objects is, in the Buddha's analysis, nothing more than an illusion. Buddhism reasons that if what is ultimately real is that which is permanent and does not change, then we are forced to admit that nothing at all is real. All things which appear to be objects are actually the flux of infinite change in which all phenomena are so inextricably interdependent that they cannot be said to be anything in and of themselves.

Buddhist *dharma* (teaching) extends this critical move even to the self — there is no thing (no-self, *anatman*) for objects to appear to, for in taking ourselves to be an object to which other objects are presented, we make the exact same error as before. Enlightenment consists therefore in realizing the illusory nature of all things, and that one *already is* Buddha-nature, which is absolute nothingness. Enlightenment must surpass consciousness' illusion in order to penetrate to the original groundlessness of all things, including our-selves.

The nun Yutei explains the Buddhist critique of consciousness to the lady Myoshu by using the analogy of mistaking a rope for a snake. In mistaking a rope for a snake, one's belief that the rope is a snake has no reality at all, because the belief is simply wrong. This taking a rope to be a snake is what we do when we take objects which appear to consciousness to have reality or substance. However, as Yutei explains, the rope has a *provisional* reality for us in that its appearance has arisen as the result of having been acted upon. A "rope" is simply the name we give to the form of straw arranged in this way and used for this purpose. Ultimately, the rope's ultimately reality (if such a word can even be used) is simply straw, and so too are objects simply nothingness, that is, lacking in any independent or unchangeable substance.[38]

Consciousness takes the unchanging object to be a bounded and definite thing, possessing a form and a nature which persists across time, but in so doing simply objectifies the continual process of change which underlies our conscious perception of reality. In truth, only absolute nothingness lies behind this appearance of this subsistent thing, and the experience of other objects as chronological persistent and separate cannot be established rationally.

In light of this critique of both phenomena generally and the self in particular, Yutei contends that Buddhist enlightenment cannot sustain any coherent notion of the after-life, but actually repudiates the idea of any*thing* which *could* experience life after death. Without a subject who can experience things, there could neither be torment in hell nor reward in paradise. Indeed, death can be neither an end nor a continuation, for all things simply are emptiness itself. This confession of the emptiness of all phenomena also precludes any notion of a deity or divine being which could reward or punish individuals in the after-life. In short, the corrosive acid of this Buddhist nihilism does not leave any ethical notion untouched.

---

38. Ibid., 72.

The doctrine of skillful means

In response to Yutei's systematic exposition of the nature of Buddhist enlightenment, Myoshu raises the question of why Buddhist literature seems to speak about an after-life. Yutei concedes to Myoshu that on the surface the various Buddhist sects *appear* to teach an after-life, but she says that this is not an after-life but rather a "redefinition."[39] She demonstrates this with another exposition of the teachings of the ten schools (including Pure Land) in which she draws out the difference between teachings which are "provisional" and which are "true." This language of "provisional" vs. "true" refers to the Buddhist doctrine of "skillful means," a teaching principle which functions at the heart of Mahayana Buddhist practice.

Myoshu provides the reader with an example of how the doctrine of skillful operates when she claims that "he [the Buddha] temporally manifested his *samsara* and *nirvana* aspects."[40] She professes to Yutei that, despite appearing to us in the shape of change and passing away, in reality, the Buddha's true nature is boundless in age, and that he attained enlightenment in a primordially unattainable past. He only manifested himself in this age under the guise of *samsara* (the cycle of death and rebirth) and *nirvana* (enlightenment) due to his desire to promulgate to all sentient beings the wisdom which leads to enlightenment. In this particular instance, the doctrine of skillful means would have us realize that the practitioner Buddhist must look beyond the earthly manifestation of the Buddha in order to see the

39. Ibid., 105.

40. Ibid., 66.

true Buddha-nature which reveals the state of absolute nothingness in which every conception of the Buddha is surpassed. In order for true enlightenment to take place, the Buddhist practitioner must be able to look beyond the appearances, the rituals, the ideas, and even the Buddha himself — one must kick the ladder away once they have climbed up, so to speak.

Yutei argues that the language of an after-life in the official schools and the language of a "Western Paradise" in Pure Land both serve to conceal the precise nature of Buddhist enlightenment from the ordinary lay person.[41] The practitioner must realize the unreality of all things to attain enlightenment, which includes even conceptions of death or the after-life. Yutei contends that Pure Land Buddhism simply shrouds a thoroughly orthodox understanding of Buddhist enlightenment with its metaphorical language of a Western Paradise where one is re-born and experiences blessing after death.

Based on Habian's comments, we can also extrapolate that the notions of of karma and re-incarnation also play this preparatory role in Buddhist thought — the accrual of karma to re-incarnate as a higher being is all in service of being born as a creature with a greater capacity to attain enlightenment. But the attainment of this enlightenment consists precisely in realizing that one already *is* enlightened in themselves, and that no further no knowledge, ritual, or deed is required. This means that the notion of ascending the levels of samsara by way of the good karma may initially serve to draw one to into the faith and motivate a consistent practice, but in the long run, clinging to this understanding will itself become a hindrance to enlightenment. Through a consistent practice — whether it be reciting the mantras,

---

41. Ibid., 120-127.

sitting *zazen*, or reciting the name of Amida Buddha — one comes to realize the emptiness even of the methods which lead one to enlightenment's threshold. This is the true practice of the Buddha's teachings.

Contemporary echoes of Habian's critique

Buddhism and Phenomenology

Habian's location in time and space meant that he only had so much data to work with from his own experience. However, history has been extremely kind to Habian's argument, and the actions of the prominent Buddhist groups both during the subsequent Christian persecutions and also during WWII corroborate Habian's centuries old criticism concerning Buddhism's inability to muster substantive resistance to the political establishment. In many ways, his claims have continued to be vindicated long after he originally penned his critique.

The philosopher Slavoj Žižek cites this sordid history of Japanese Buddhism repeatedly in his philosophical work,[42] frequently pointing to Brian Victoria's book *Zen at War* which presents a comprehensive historical picture of the failure of Japanese Buddhist groups to resist the imperial and nationalist ideology which motivated Japanese military expansion in the early 20th century. The established Buddhist organizations even took an active role in the ideological formation of citizens and soldiers psychologically to cope more effectively with the

---

42. Slavoj Žižek, *Sex and the Failed Absolute* (London: Bloomsbury Academic, 2020), 90-91.

conflict. He quotes D. T. Suzuki in particular who argues that "it is really not he but the sword itself that does the killing. He had no desire to do harm to anybody, but the enemy appears and makes himself a victim."[43]

However, just as with Habian's own arguments, the historical argument is also rooted in an ideological critique. While a Buddhist may attempt to object that these nationalist collaborators fell short of the ideals of Buddhism's teaching, Žižek provides us with an updated version of Habian's argument when he demonstrates that the philosophical positions espoused by Buddhist popularizers such as D. T. Suzuki flowed from their Buddhist approach to life.[44] Their political complicity embodies a strong tendency already organically within Buddhism to marginalize the question of subjectivity and emancipation. We would be more accurate in saying that the political capitulations of Japanese-Buddhist groups finds itself in consonance with their philosophical commitments and attendant practice, not in contradiction with them.

Because Buddhism aims precisely at the annihilation of the experience of being a subject, it strives to eliminate the very standpoint from which one *could* resist ideology. Without the experience of freedom found through being a subject who can abstract themselves from the totalizing Whole of an ideological superstructure, the human being cannot achieve any sort of perspective from which they could critique the system in which they find themselves enmeshed. The subject only appears in that minimal distance from our context which allows us to

---

43. Quoted by Žižek at the bottom of page 91.

44. Ibid., 90.

notice new and different possibilities. Only the subject can recognize "what could be otherwise" in our world.

Žižek takes recourse to Edmund Husserl's phenomenology to provide a contemporary foil in relation which he can elaborate his critical account of Buddhism.[45] In developing his phenomenological method in the late 19th century, Husserl wanted to ground the study of consciousness in an objective science of experience. To do this, he proposed the "transcendental reduction," which he described as a stance one can take in their mind where they simply observe their stream of experience without judgment about the reality or un-reality of the objects presented to them. Rather than the mundane attitude we typically take towards experience in which we concern ourselves with whether what we observe is true or false, the phenomenologist temporarily adopts the standpoint of one watching and noting the flow of experience as it passes us by, all with the goal of trying to discern the patterns and structures which might emerge. These recurring patterns point us towards ineliminable aspects of experience or structures of consciousness which indicate for Husserl where we might start to discern the essence of things.

Žižek points out the resemblance between Husserl's method of "bracketing" reality and the Buddhist method of enlightenment as the ego-less realization of the emptiness of phenomena.[46] Both methods rely on something akin to a meditative state to achieve this way of seeing. The practice of meditation which serves as the core of Buddhist practice adopts this standpoint of the transcendental reduction whereby the judging activity of the ego recedes and consciousness is

---

45. Ibid., 89.

46. Ibid., 93.

allowed to simply flow in pure observation. The infinitely receded standpoint from which one peers, whether they be the phenomenologist or the Buddhist, finds themselves in the strange position of being an observer of their own bodily experience, buffered from the happenings of the world, and perfectly caught up in the continual flow of other phenomena.

This un-attached standpoint generated by the phenomenologist and the Buddhist creates the conditions for rationalizing our own complicity in the cruelty, absurdity, and injustice which make up our experience. Through meditative practice, there arises within us the sense that these things do not *really* involve *us*. Whatever we are is something infinitely receded, perhaps even non-existent. Our experience of being involved in the world is reduced ultimately to an illusion which must be surpassed in order to attain a higher level of peace and felicity. These philosophies of withdrawal encourage the practitioner to take a non-active stance towards consciousness, and in so doing they purport to ease suffering and dissolve philosophical conundrums.

But, what happens when we ask about the politics which flow from such varieties of subjective stances? What type of a political subject would a bracketed or enlightened individual become? Habian's sophisticated critique of Buddhism from within the experience of living in a Buddhist society allows him to ask this question of how Buddhist ideology shapes the ethical vision of the Japanese people.

The Ideological Self and the Free Subject

Near the end of his exposition of the Buddhist schools, Habian relates an anecdote about Pure Land Buddhism's devotees, and the vignette he paints for the reader obliquely but effectively raises this problem of the relationship between individual subjectivity and communal practice within a Buddhist context—

> "So Pure Land adherents ring their bells, shake their heads, and chant '*namu amidabutsu, namu amidabutsu*' without a thought for anyone else in the neighborhood, and when they really get going to an outsider it sounds just like the heave-ho you hear as men pull up their boats from the sea.

> It would seem that to make people chant the *nenbutsu* like that is designed to bring them to a state of no-mind. This is what [Ippen] was referring to in his verse "When chanting there is no buddha, no self, only the sound of *namu Amidabutsu*."

> The character for mind is a combination of 'sound' and 'mind.' So when they completely lose themselves shouting out '*namu admidabutsu, namu amidabutsu*' they have no thoughts of the Buddha or others around them; all that remains is sound. The voice is wind; the wind is Amidha.

> In which case, it is obvious that, in light of the above, 'Amidha' is the name of the dharma realm as Void. The underlying meaning is that when we die, sentient beings return to the Void; they become nothing.

So the Pure Land school also believes there is no aft
erlife."[47]

This passage presents, on one level, a mocking complaint which
bemoans how the Pure Land practitioners insensitively disturb all
their neighbors with their incessant chanting, but Habian also hints
at a more pernicious claim — the chanting doesn't necessarily serve
the function which the practitioners believe that it does.

Habian's comments here contain for us a key lesson about how
ideology functions. As the chanter works on themselves through their
religious practice, they are being changed, but not in the way that
they assume they are. The Pure Land practitioner may be taught that
through chanting *namu Amidabutsu* they will be ushered into the
Amidha Buddha's Western Paradise when they die, but actually the
chanting serves to annihilate the self, and induces a state of mind
in which one 'returns to the void.' Such a result is more accurately
oriented towards the teachings of Buddhism than the devotee realizes!
In this way, what they *do* speaks the truth which the mind cannot.

In Habian's vignette of the thought-less chanters who achieve
no-mind with their oblivious heave-ho, we find a wonderfully illuminating and satirical dramatization of the role which the self plays in
a larger ideological structure. This self has a fantasy of what it is, and
the particular way that the self imagines itself provides an explanation
for what they are doing, much like the one who imagines themselves
acting their part in the grand fictional whole of "the nation." Their
actions thus have an internal meaning, speaking the truth about who
this person is, but their overall effect is to obscure what is going on at
a structural, social, political level.

We see here a self-conscious avoidance of the truth which exists
at a material level — self-conscious because it cannot rid itself of the

nagging feeling that there is something it's missing, that it has been tricked into a bad deal so to speak, but it also presents a genuine avoidance because the self has veiled itself from this truth which it so desperately avoids. Not quite "they know not what they do" — rather, they know what they are doing but, having blinded themselves to this, they have nonetheless come to believe their own self-deception.

However, as Habian points out in his explanation, *the truth is always revealed unconsciously through speech*, even in absence of our conscious intentions. He refers to the characters which make up the sign for 'mind' in Japanese, being composed of two components, 'sound' and 'heart' (or 'spirit'), which Habian places in the context of Buddhist doctrine to reveal the true operation of chanting — the repetition of sound leads to an obliteration of mind, which leads to the attainment of absolute nothingness, which is enlightenment.

In speech, the subject is at work disrupting the fantasies and images which the self envisions to situate itself in its world. Words operate in a different way than images do, because they require the act of alienation which takes place in representation, whereas images seduce us into an identification with them. Further, images live in the mind and possess an ideal quality, whereas word and signs possess a materiality to them which resists our manipulation and which can take on a life of their own in absence of our using them or intending them. The subject who appears in the materiality of speech is a gap or a lack in the smooth order of the self's imagined world, an irrupting of the inconvenient truth and all its disastrous consequences for our walled-garden existence.

Admittedly, we have to acknowledge that the self which appears within the realm of images plays an important role in understanding the different ways that human beings can be free. For while the self is formed in early childhood in response to the need to unify and master the overwhelming intensity and impotence the infant experiences in their body, the child becomes a subject later when they step into the world of language in which they can symbolize themselves through speech. The formation and acquisition of the self brings a sort of freedom in that the child can, through their attachment to this image of themselves as a unified whole, achieve a new level of control over their body. This allows them to separate from mother and cultivate a new and creative relationship with their environment. However, in the long run, this ego which the child has identified themselves with becomes an anchor which weighs them down. This image of the self lives primarily in the imagination, and thus keeps the human being locked up in a narcissistic fixation, not admitting any outside intrusions or augmentations. The sanctity of the image is threatened, and thus it becomes a source of anxiety and aggression for the human being who must constantly contend with the intrusions of the Real in order to protect and maintain this self.

In contradistinction to the narcissism of the imagination inhabited by the self, the world of language is inherently social. In fact, the sociality of language precedes the child's existence and their acquisition of its powers, for this system of signs and their uses pre-exists the child in time. The child must adopt them, negotiate with them, and find a place for themselves within this already existing structure. The 'I' which operates in language allows me to get outside myself by becoming-other into a sign which I can then share with others. In turn, they can share signs with me, and in so doing, we are connected and can share an experience of our world together.

Where is the freedom in this objective structure of language though? Isn't language more like a cage in which we are trapped and unable to say what we want? If we are finding our place in language, doesn't this seem a more apt description of what happens when we step into an ideology? Language enables a higher attainment of freedom for the human being than the imaginary realm of the self because language cannot full close in on itself like fantasy does. It cannot become a complete loop or totality, for every system of language is inherently incomplete or "non-All" in Lacanian terms. While linguistic systems can aspire to completeness in their ambitions to enable the speaker to express and re-make their whole world, there can be no language which contains every other language (in Lacanian terms, this means that there is no "metalanguage.") — each language takes a standpoint upon the world, one which is inherently partially and interested, and thus cannot be ultimately universal.

We see this in two particular features of language, ones which psychoanalysis in particular focuses on — (1) the Master Signifier and (2) the Subject. The Mastery Signifier is the sign in any linguistic system which stands in for the gap which causes the system to be incomplete within itself. The Master Signifier thus represents a void or a total lack of understanding — the Platonic notion of God as 'One' provides a good example of this. This concept has no positive content, but rather serves to cinch together the system by putting a sign in place of a void. Just like the concept of God, this Master Signifier becomes a point where lack and excess coincide, for precisely at the point where the system breaks down do we also experience the void as an infinite excess — the "luminous darkness" of St. Gregory of Nyssa, for instance.

The Mastery Signifier points us to the first instance in which a linguistic system is incomplete, but the Subject points us to the other — the position of the speaker cannot be fully represented within speech, that is, a sign must stand in for the one who is speaking, but this sign will always be inadequate or ambiguous. You already inherently understand that this is the case. You've likely asked yourself before why someone is telling something to you. In a situation like this ("I am a very honest person" the stranger says to you), you realize that there is a gap between what is said and the one who is speaking it, and you sense that this position from which the words are spoken involves the desire of another person. This gap between the words and the place from which they are spoken determines so much of what language means, just as the same words spoken by one person in a particular context would be perfectly normal but in another context would seem ominous or inappropriate. However, the signs themselves can never fully represent the subjective standpoint from which they are spoken, which creates a constantly disruptive experience of the subject which "twists" or "taints" speech.

To the self who craves infinite actualization in the world of the imaginary, language with its failures and gaps feels like an insufferable limitation, but it's precisely this incompleteness which language possesses that it opens up the space for humans to engage in free actions. Language as a non-All system which cannot fully foreclose itself thereby opens the human being out onto an encounter with the Other and our shared world through the social exchange of signs. This confrontation holds the power to cut across our fantasies, both individual and collective, and to introduce a tear in the fabric of our imagined world, thus allowing us to see a new possibility for being-together in a world which exceeds our own private conception of existence. The subject appears as a void in language, acting as a disruptor which puts us in touch with an Outside.

In ideology, there is no Outside. Every outside must be simply another extension of the inside, always putting itself at our disposal for a full integration into our fundamental fantasy about our identity. To reference the conceptual framework from the last chapter, Kyushu served as the contact barrier where the Yamato inside could encounter and contend with the Outside, the rest of the world in all its difference. However, by closing down the country in complete isolation, the

Tokugawa regime plunged the entire Japanese people into a collective psychosis. A psychotic state is one in which a person does not make that full transition into language, thus becoming trapped within the every shifting realm of images, unable to be able to gain a firm grounding in the hardness of language. They adopt the standpoint of feeling watched, feeling that they are being controlled, believing that words are secret messages from a spiritual entity, and insisting that an outside party is operating their body from somewhere else. The world of images creates this profound unfreedom because, ironically, it does not include a true alienation in which the person can be excised from a self-enclosing totality.

The nationalistic person which the Tokugawa regime aims to produce then is, in the final accounting, the enslavement of a self which inhabits a firm ideological structure in which everything has its proper place — it can foreclose on itself, leaving no room for doubt, questions, or resistance. This psychotic self experiences the constant flux of images without any firm footing to introduce a cut into the seamless fabric of the fictitious world constructed by the nationalist living which the Tokugawa regime ruthlessly implemented. Therefore, Buddhism in Japan became complicit with the regime in so far as it failed to deliver a *subject* rather than a *self*. The teachings and practice of Buddhism allows the self to retreat into a private immediacy which amounts to nothing more than the individual experience of a collective fantasy, and thus the self which Buddhism wishes to abandon leads the individual back into an invisible ideological structure in which they are bereft of any resources to resist the way of things. The practitioner has re-imagined themselves, but without becoming any more free in the process. Such a self has only managed to construct for itself an elaborate system of excuses for refusing the responsibility of being a free subject, thereby accepting the cage which they have collaborated with others in building for themselves.

Conclusion

The fate of Fukansai Habian

We have paid close attention in this chapter to Fukansai Habian's polemical arguments, but we would be remiss to pass over a great historical irony — Fukansai Habian himself also became an infamous apostate, just as the zealous Fr. Rodriguz falls into apostasy in Endo's *Silence*. Habian became a Christian in 1583, wrote *Myotei Mondo* in 1605, but has clearly apostatized by the time he writes a Buddhist refutation of Christianity titled *Ha Daiusu* (Deus destroyed) in 1620. Hailed as a consummate debater who converted his opponents and put rival religions to shame, this once celebrated figure Fukansai Habian brings together many of the political, social, and religious conflicts which we have been investigating so far in this book. A double apostate — leaving Buddhism for Christianity, and then returning to Buddhism once more. In *Ha Daiusu*, he marshals almost the same arguments and texts against Christianity as he quoted in *Myotei Mondo*, as though he is debating himself.[48] There is something of an immense sophistry in all of this... but why?

I suspect that the apostate Buddhist priest who stands by Rodriguez's side throughout his inquisition in *Silence*, tempting and

---

48. George Elison, *Deus Destroyed* (Cambridge, MA: Harvard University Press, 1973), 142-143.

taunting him at every turn, represents a figure of Fukansai Habian. This Buddhist priest in *Silence* indicates that he has studied Christianity in seminary, but has since turned away from it now. In Rodriguez's first encounter with him, Fr. Cabral is mentioned, and this serves as a hint about why this priest (and perhaps Fukansai Habian) later turned against Christianity, despite their initial enthusiasm. We briefly mentioned Cabral in the first chapter, noting that he led the Japanese mission but seemed to harbor a disdain for the Japanese people, even describing them as "conceited, covetous, inconstant, and insincere."[49] and the Buddhist priest's comments in *Silence* obliquely indicate that Cabral's treatment of Japanese-Christians as inferior contributed to a lasting resentment which some converts held against the Christian Church in Japan. After all, we know that Cabral actively prevented Japanese brothers from being admitted to the priesthood.[50] Could Fabian have been slighted for a promotion or ordination?

However, we also have a letter from a Jesuit priest in 1621 who reports a different perspective, saying, "It will be thirteen years ago that Fabian, who was at the time our Irmão, fled the Comp with one of the several devout women who lived a common life in a House adjoining ours in Miyaco, and soon thereafter he abandoned the faith of Christ."[51] While we don't know much beyond this anecdote, this snapshot brings color to the character of Habian, painting him like a zealous young man with a knack for debate but with little control over

---

49. Baskind, 309, quoting George Elison, *Deus Destroyed* (Cambridge, MA: Harvard University Press, 1973), 16.

50. Baskind, 309.

51. Quoted by Elison, 155.

his passions — an intellectual gun for hire who moves on when he loses interest, and turns with bitterness against his past attachments. He's a relatable figure in our own age in which the fiery zeal of converts seems plastered across the internet, from the Protestant convert to Eastern Orthodoxy ("orthobros") to the evangelical youth group kid turned bitter atheist. What happens when the zeal fades, the doubts set it, and faithfulness gets painful?

What then can we take away from Fukansai Habian's works? We could probably go a few different ways, depending on our inclinations. From one angle, we might read his apostasy as a vindication of his work — the nihilism of the Buddhist subjective stance enabled him to switch his loyalties like switching lovers, ultimately coming back into the fold of the Buddhist establishment to live out the rest of his days on the public dole in exchange for some polemical literature. This interpretation is, of course, highly biased towards the truth of Christianity and its claims about uniqueness. But I personally think that the way Habian could vacillate between the two positions speaks to the way that his faith was ultimately undergirded by something other than intellectual conviction, that is, he was cast about desire. In this way, perhaps, he was no more faithful to Buddhism than he was to Christianity. Though he had a glimpse of the emptiness of Buddhism, and paid lip service to the value of right and wrong which Christianity seemed to teach, he remained nonetheless within the realm in which one needs punishment and reward to act ethically. It would seem that he never managed to discover that next stage of the ethical life in which the Law becomes internalized through the spontaneous practice of love. Let us listen to Habian's warnings along the path even as we learn how to tread where he himself never managed to go.

4

—·—

Compassion, the inquisitor's weapon

Introduction

To this point, this book has taken a look at the historical circumstances in which Fr. Rodriguez's story unfolds, all with the
aim of forming a holistic opinion about his decision to step on the
fumi-e. Now, we must delve into the pain and contradiction of Rodriguez's existential experience as a Christian under persecution. We
must interrogate how Fr. Rodriguez arrives at his decision to step on
the *fumi-e* in apostasy. This our exploration aims primarily at forming
a judgment about *the fidelity of Rodriguez's decision to the teachings of
Jesus.*

In taking this approach, we take Fr. Rodriguez's quandary seriously
as one who understands his own act of apostasy *through* the lens of his
Christian faith, and even as an *expression* of his faith in Jesus Christ.
Silence is a text written by a Christian about the experience of *being*
a Christian, particularly a Christian who struggles with a weak faith.
To honor Endo's theme of spiritual struggle, we must grapple with
how he portrays Rodriguez's decision to step on the *fumi-e* as an act
of placing himself into the Lord's care *even in his apostasy.*

We are interested above all in the question of whether Rodriguez's actions can be said to accurately reflect the life of one who is becoming more like God as they walk with Christ in discipleship, because Endo's book, in tortuous and oblique ways, asks this same question about Rodriguez (and by extension, the author himself). Is Rodriguez's decision compatible with the practice of Christian discipleship as expressed within the exceptionally unique circumstances in which God placed him, or does he betray the core of the Gospel message in his decision to step on the *fumi-e*?

To be clear — "exceptionally unique circumstances" do not function here as a way to *excuse* Fr. Rodriguez for his actions. That would be too easy of an approach. No, the question here is more difficult. Rather, this investigation concerns whether the constellation of circumstance in which one enacts their obedience to Christ's teachings can produce actions which appear radically different from how one might act under a different set of factors, all while remaining faithful to Christ's work nonetheless.

Christ himself seems to hint in this direction, such as when he commands that "he who is not with me is against me," [Matthew 12:30] and yet at another time claims that "whoever is not against you is for you."[Luke 9:50] The book of Proverbs too seems to speak to the circumstantial nature of wisdom — saying at once "answer a fool according to his folly," and then immediately "do not answer a fool according to his folly." In these seemingly opposed injunctions, we begin to glimpse the contextual nature of human action, not thereby succumbing to a radical pessimism about judgment generally, but becoming more circumspect in our approach to thinking about human decision-making and actions.

This book tries to avoid the pitfall of claiming no judgment is possible, while also not advocating a reflexive legalism which slavishly follows the Law's text alone. The existence and length of the Talmud in the Jewish legal tradition reveals that such a close adherence to the words and procedure of law inevitably lead us into a proliferation of ethical contradictions requiring an ever-expanding literature to attempt to contain their spread. We will thus refuse to reduce ethics to the rote interpretation and application of legal formulas. In so doing, we also follow the example of our Lord, who swept aside the legal quibbling of the Pharisees in order to assert the essence of the Law's demand in each moment in which he found himself.

Instead, this book understands ethics as a practice of a discipleship which entails a dynamic relationship with the living Jesus Christ whose whole body of commands, teachings, parables, and examples we seek to enact in our lives as God works in us in the time and place where we find ourselves. The disciple acts under a cloud of obscurity, not knowing the future, not knowing all the facts, and not seeing all the possibilities, and as such they must play their role with humility, open-handedness, and even creativity, rather than simply being an actor who rehearses a routine which has already been laid out.

Two primary dimensions compose the narrative of events by which Fr. Rodriguez arrives at his decision to apostatize — one structural and one existential.

First, the structural dimension encompasses the work of the Inquisitor Inoue to devise and deploy a comprehensive strategy calculated to exploit the Christian priests' compassion for victims in order to induce them to apostatize.

Second, the existential dimension includes Fr. Rodriguez' own internal experiences of this external process whereby he is lead to arrive at the point where he becomes able to choose apostasy in a way which sufficiently aligns with his self structure.

Strictly speaking, these two dimensions are inextricably related. The physical and psychological environment which the inquisitor Inoue carefully curates for Fr. Rodriguez has as its goal the production of a certain subjective experience within the priest, and all of Inoue's actions inevitably produce a corresponding perception within Fr. Rodriguez's internal life. This makes it fraught to parse out what should be treated under the heading of structural versus psychological.

However, I take it that every situation possesses some terrain of interacting power relations, and while these are rarely so simple as one agent purely oppressing another, I think we have good grounds to assert that Inoue exercises more power over Fr. Rodriguez in nearly every way that matters. As the one with the agency to shape the state of affairs in accordance with his designs, I assign to Inoue those structural dimensions of the situation, whereas Rodriguez must undergo the situation into which Inoue thrusts him against his will.

On these grounds, I treat Rodriguez's psychological navigation of this terrain in which he finds himself distinctly from Inoue's stratagems. I proceed under the assumption that the structural belongs to the realm of Inoue's exercise of power over Fr. Rodriguez and his environment, whereas the existential dimension of the narrative belongs to Fr. Rodriguez's experience of his own self, beliefs, motivations, and general interiority in the midst of this world which Inoue constructs for him.

To hearken back to the methodological note in the introduction about this text presenting a structural-political reading of *Silence* more so than an ethical-existential reading [note], in this chapter, we begin to understand why that is the case. As the one with the power to mold the shape of Rodriguez's reality, Inoue's perspective on the state of affairs is closer to the truth of the matter than Rodriguez's existential experience of his religious captivity in Japan. Rodriguez's ethical and existential experiences are *included* in the state of affairs, and are accounted for in Inoue's designs (although, not *all* of them), but as products of Inoue's manipulation they diverge from the collective reality of the Japanese people, and thus serve the interests of Inoue, the one who aims to produce those very experiences.

This is not to claim that Rodriguez is an automaton who exercises no power of choice, or that his experience is straightforwardly an illusion. Rather, we are raising a philosophical question which demands further elaboration, although it will not receive the full treatment it deserves here — what is human experience? How does perception function? And how does the will operate? In what ways is the truth of understanding also founded on the operation of an illusion?

In our account of Rodriguez's experience, we will see the two dimensions of structure and subjectivity interacting constantly, and although the structural receives a priority in its proximity to the truth of the matter, the existential register also always speaks the truth — it simply does so with a different voice, often through misdirection or in a displaced manner.

What does Inoue do, and what do Rodriguez undergo? These are the defining questions.

This chapter's structure

This chapter proceeds in two primary parts, with a single connecting section in between.

The first section of this chapter explores Friedrich Nietzsche's critique of pity which provides the underlying theoretical account for the second section in which we analyze how Inoue leverages victims and compassion in his strategy to lead Fr. Rodriguez into apostasy.

These two sections are connected by a brief section in which I highlight the notion of "the helping relationship" in which the priest Fr. Rodriguez finds himself, and especially the unique psychological hazards which the priest experiences in discharging their particular configuration of the "helping relationship." I claim that the exercise of care and the activity of helping provide one of the defining themes which mark the role of the priest, and that the peculiar nature of this helping relationship shapes the priest's subjectivity in certain ways, making them more susceptible to certain types of experiences. The context provided by Nietzsche's critique of pity will help us understand why this is the case and what these hazards are.

The final section of the chapter analyzes in detail the primary strategy and core tactical components of Inoue's overall comprehensive plan for producing apostasy in the priests. We will first consider Inoue's strategy under the general heading of "gaslighting," before then proceeding to elaborate what I take to be the four tactics which make up the core components of his method for producing apostasy — (1) staging cordial dialogues, (2) permitting the formation of a prison parish, (3) depriving Rodriguez of violence, and (4) providing Fr. Ferreira as a model.

Nietzsche's critique of pity

Friedrich Nietzsche clearly intuited the centrality of compassion to the Christian religion, and consequently made his critical account of pity a pillar of his critique of Christianity. Strictly speaking, Nietzsche does not critique the notion of compassion *per se*, but rather uses the German word *mitleid* (*mit* - with, *leid* - feel), often translated 'pity.' In light of this nuance, I contend that Nietzsche is really developing an alternative account of *empathy*.

While the concept of empathy has a recent provenance in our moral vocabulary, empathy and compassion do seem to be two closely intertwined notions, almost as though empathy has come to function as the secular organizing concept for all the "sympathetic" acts which involve some form of pro-social feeling of solidarity or connection with others.

Nietzsche's alternative account of *mitleid* illuminates what people are doing when they perform an act of empathy, and his account does this by cutting against our beliefs about what we *think* we are doing in the empathic act. The way then that Nietzsche de-constructs empathy's self-delusions possesses important ramifications for our investigation of Fr. Rodriguez's experiences and motivations which lead him to apostatize.

I once encountered a meme which I return to whenever I think about Nietzsche's critique of pity. The unknown creator of the meme masterfully (and with requisite mockery) captured the critique that Nietzsche is trying to launch against empathy. I present the meme below:

Top text: I'm an empath. Bottom text:
Sometimes I can tell how people are feeling
simply by deciding how I think they feel in
my own mind and instantly believing it.

This meme nutshells what Nietzsche thinks is going on when we perform an act of empathy — we imaginatively project the other person's mental state, immediately believe our own projection, and then adjust our actions based on our own projection.

Typically, this is not what we think we are doing when we are exercising empathy. While this meme primarily aims its mockery at woo types who trumpet the efficacy of their empathic powers for divining the inner world of others (we all know these people), the critique really hits us all. We all operate as though in our empathy we are inhabiting the other person's experience, and Nietzsche points out that this just isn't the case.

In fact, he goes on in his work to contend that our mundane intuitions about our own empathic acts fail on a number of grounds —

First, since each human being is radically unique, we strictly cannot "put ourselves in another person's shoes," so to speak. This doesn't mean that humans can't share sufficient commonality to achieve some minimal level of understanding, but it should serve to chasten our confidence about our ability to project into another's subjectivity. At the very least, we should be honest about what we are doing when we attempt to do so - we are imaginatively projecting. Each person is a singularity, so to speak, constituted through a distinct chain of historical events, personal experiences, and biological realities. We therefore display an immense hubris when we glibly claim that we can step into another's person's world.

Second, we have no way of verifying whether our projection was correct or not. Because we cannot directly inhabit the other person's experience, and we only have their own self-reporting about the matter to go from, we can only ever make extrapolations about another person's inner states. Ultimately, we cannot know if we were right *even if the person behaved as expected,* for there are a myriad of alternative subjective structures which can produce the same external response but for many different reasons. Thus, we can think we were right when we were really just lucky.

Third, our projection often says more about ourselves than it does about the other person, primarily because the only resources we have for constructing the projection stems from our own reservoir of experiences and reactions. Thus, our empathic act consists primarily of a *narcissistic* projection. We can only see what we have already put there to see, which is to say, ourselves. Not only do we not have the same experiences as the other person, but we also know for a fact that we only have our experiences (which are not their experiences). The empathic act is therefore poisoned with our subjectivity from the very start.

Notice that Nietzsche is *not* making this argument from any claims about human beings as having a nature which makes them *inherently* self-interested or narcissistic. Although Nietzsche believes that human beings *are* self-interested by nature, the veracity of that claim is irrelevant to the critique which he makes of empathy. Instead, he's making an argument about what is and is not possible in the realm of mutual understanding. He's simply arguing from the structural limitations of the experience of relationality itself, that is, the inherent boundaries of what it means to be an embodied creature encountering other embodied creatures.

Nietzsche's critique presses us by insisting that, due to the limitations of human consciousness, our most common reflexive and unexamined intuitions about what we're doing when we think we are empathizing are, strictly speaking, impossible. We aren't actually doing what we purport to be doing — we are *not* entering the other person's experience. We are imagining a projection of their experience based on our own set of experiences. We use our imagination to consider what it would be like to undergo those experiences, how we would react to them, what we think that pain might feel like, and what type of view we might have of the world from that position.

If then, for a moment, we accept Nietzsche's account of what is actually happening when we empathize, then what does he think that *compassion* is?

For Nietzsche, the exercise of compassion is a self-serving act which seeks to extinguish the internal pain which has become inflamed by witnessing another's suffering. When we see another human being suffering, we experience both physical distress (our body tenses up, our heart races, our palms get sweaty, etc...) and mental distress (pain, anxiety, fear, guilt, etc...), and this internal pain is only intensified by the empathic act which we inflict on ourselves in which we use our imagination to project ourselves into their suffering.

Let us put it this way — the act of compassion is aimed at accomplishing what we believe will relieve the other person's pain *so that we might assuage our own pain.*

Nietzsche notes how compassion drives us *towards* the other, which might superficially appear altruistic, but the compassionate act resembles any attempt to relieve pain in that it motivates us to locate and draw near to the wounded region which is the source of the pain. In the situation of compassion, while the pain exists within our hearts, the drive to extinguish this pain causes us to make ourselves more proximate to the source of that pain — the suffering person before our eyes.

The human is committing something of a mistake here though, although it's certainly a convenient mistake for the sake of the group's health. By witnessing another's pain, our own internal pain becomes inflamed, and yet this pain drives us towards the other under the pretension that the pain we are feeling *is* the other's pain, not our own! While we believe that our aim is to relieve the other person's pain, underlying this belief is the deeper operative desire to relieve our own pain.

Nietzsche does not claim that the desire to relieve the other person's pain is entirely fabricated, but rather that it's not the only operative desire, and further, that it's certainly not the *primary* drive in the scenario. Rather, the pain we imagine in the other provides a plausible but ultimately incorrect rationalization for one's altruistic behavior, and thus it serves to obscure the situation more than it does to illuminate it. The belief that we act primarily to relieve the other's person's pain is not inherently fake or hypocritical, but it becomes so when we insist on it as the primary explanation which we offer to ourselves or others.

While some might pan this claim as cynical, we can simply point out that even cursory experience of human behaviors provides an abundance of evidence that humans are most satisfied when they *feel* they have helped someone, regardless of whether they have actually helped them or not. Many folks are happy to stop short of the actual helping if only they can achieve a sufficiently plausible experience of feeling as though they have helped the other person. When we give the homeless person a dollar, have we helped them? We do not know, but the pain has subsided, and so we are no longer curious about what happened.

The Christian Scriptures also explicitly warn against the self-satisfaction which would cause one to stop short of true aid — St. James asks the readers of his epistle, seemingly to their shame, "If one of you says to them, "Go in peace; keep warm and well fed," but does nothing about their physical needs, what good is it?" (James 2:16) Good intentions are not enough to truly love our neighbor, but often good intentions *feel* like enough.

While we might know deep down that what we are doing is not good enough, we easily fall into the impression that it is, even deriving satisfaction from our own paltry deeds which offer only a hollow amelioration. When we see the sad puppies on the commercial and donate money to the organization in response, that might make the pain go away for a time, but the pain did not disappear because the puppy's suffering was actually extinguished. This clues is in to the original source of the pain — it was not the puppy's, but rather our own.

Here's the surprising cash out of Nietzsche's analysis — his work helps us ask "how can we *actually* help people, rather than be controlled by a compassion which seeks to relieve our own pain?" Now we can start to see how, in this account, compassion is both the thing which drives us towards the person to help them but *also* serves as the single most difficult obstacle to surmount in the quest to actually help them.

Nietzsche thinks that people are way *way* too confident about their ability to help other people. We take for granted that we can see a person's situation, diagnose the problem, and provide the solution. But part of what he wants us to see from his analysis of empathy's shortcomings is how compassion distorts our ability to properly diagnose issues and provide effective help. It does this by first distorting the incentives in the situation — shifting them from helping the other person to helping ourselves — and then covering over that the distortion has taken place. Ironically, compassion is what helps us get close to the problem, but once we have gotten close, we have to have our compassion mastered such that we can force ourselves to sit with it while we truly focus on the unique person right in front of us. Compassion must be overcome in the service of the person whom we wish to love.

Compassion is especially bad in situations in which a solution is either not possible or very ambiguous, and Nietzsche contends that more situations are like this than we generally think. Compassion creates a mental pressure that pushes early and fast for a diagnosis so that it can quickly implement a fix to make the pain go away. The desire to help becomes a mechanism that causes us to rush through our analysis and propose a shoddy solution, because while we think our goal is to help, it's more accurate to say that we are seeking to relieve our own internal pain.

This is how we find ourselves in our contemporary situation where a vast network of non-profits, program managers, NGOs, development officers, social workers, and volunteers can fundraise, circulate, and divert immense sums of money from around the world into poorer countries for all manner of programs, but with middling results at best. We send an incredible amount of funds overseas to implement very limited and fragile stopgaps to structural issues, and this makes us feel good enough about ourselves to carry on from day to day, all while we ignore the pressing needs in our own backyard. We have done our part by "doing something."

But, Nietzsche wants us to ask, has the doing something done something?

Slavoj Žižek often jokes that Starbuck's has created the epitome of ideology by embedding the symbolic notions of justice and charity *within the products themselves*. The large corporation says "We donate 1% of the proceeds of this water bottle to help children in Africa," or "We only use fair-trade beans so you know the hard working farmers are getting a livable wage." Then the products' prices are marked up accordingly. They have, Žižek points out, built the cost of assuaging your guilt of consumption right into the product, so you can enjoy the consumption of their product without shame. Buy, drink, go in peace.

In our haste to make a diagnosis, Nietzsche also wants us to see how we are tempted to assign blame to a guilty party. In general, the assigning of blame and the meting out of punishment comes much more readily to humans than careful analysis and problem solving, and this doubly so when operating under circumstances of pain, anxiety, or duress. Nietzsche devotes large portions of his work to revealing the operation in humans of a vengeful spirit (*ressentiment*), and while we don't have space to get into that analysis here, this tendency to want to exact suffering from a guilty party as a "solution" to the suffering of an other plays an uncomfortably important role in the way that compassion operates in our hearts and minds.

Nietzsche's work thus challenges the predominant modes of contemporary ethical discourse which emphasize concepts such as care, harm, safety, empathy. Of special interest to us in this book, the foregoing account of Nietzsche's analysis indicates how the inquisitor Inoue can weaponize victims against Fr. Rodriguez. Inoue understands the dynamics of compassion, how the sight of the victim produces a corresponding pain in the heart of the witness which arouses our powers of compassion, and ultimately compels us *to act*. Someway. Somehow. We *must* do *something*. Anything at all. This is the power (and terror) of *care*.

The hazards of the helping relationship

We inhabit many "helping relationships" in our lives, from that of mutuality with our neighbors to the encounter with the beggar in the street, and even the professional roles of counselor, educator, or advisor. We take these relationships of mutual aid and support to be mundane parts of living in a society, but they harbor hidden levels of complexity we are liable to overlook. Even as they make up the basic texture of our lives, they also present a minefield of hazards.

Nietzsche's critique of empathy makes a vital contribution to the question of the nature of the helping relationship. His work asks, for instance, about the ways that helping can be motivated by selfishness, or how our feelings about helping and its underlying relation can distort true aid. He also raises the question of iatrogenesis — harms which are introduced by the act of helping — in exploring how such harms originate or might be avoided.

I use the phrase "the helping relationship" here to refer to the activity of entering into a relation in which one attempts to improve the state of affairs of another entity, object, or person, guiding them towards greater flourishing or actualization, sometimes including doing for them what they are not fully able to do for themselves.

Despite its centrality to human life the helping relationship remains one of the most under-theorized phenomena in our daily activities. While it provides a source of great joy and immense frustration to us all, we tend to take our ability, technique, and capacity to help for granted. We see someone in need and we act. They thank us (or perhaps not), and we move on with our day. But how effective was our help? And how did we know that we solved the real problem? It's easy to fall into an auto-pilot mode where we don't stop to check or reflect on our practice of helping.

As a relation between two different persons, the helping relationship entails navigating the thorny ethical dilemmas inherent to working with an other person while nonetheless respecting them *as an other*. Rather than subsuming them into our own being and destroying their distinctness which confronts us in their own uniqueness, the helper must navigate a relationship in which they believe that they have better insight into the other's situation than the other has themselves, while also not doing violence to the other's agency to choose or not vitiating their responsibility for their own actions.

The terror and frustration of the helping relationship is ultimately that you can lead a horse to water, but you can't make it drink. Only the horse can be responsible for whether it drinks or not. In this way, the helping relationship entails a profound help-lessness on the part of the helper, and thus demands a radical humility which pushes back against the false confidence which compassion instills in the wounded mind seeking to silence the alarms going off.

A horse will only drink, in this example, if at least four conditions are met — (1) intuits its lack, (2) sees the solution for its lack, (3) exercises the will to act on that solution, and (4) has available the means to obtain the solution for its lack. The helping relationship can target conditions 1, 2, and 4 by helping someone to see their lack, helping them to discover a solution, or providing them the resources they need to take hold of that solution. While those three conditions can founder under certain circumstances, the fundamental dilemma of the helping relationship is that one cannot change condition 3, that is, to impart to the other person the will to take hold of the situation — the drive to *live*, or rather, to kill what is killing them. To respect the other as other demands that we leave to them the realm of willing and acting. In the context of compassion, that includes giving up the means of assuaging our own pain, and placing ourselves at the mercy of another who we cannot control.

This terror of helping in which we put ourselves at the mercy of another explains why so much of what passes for helping actually amounts to a ritual for protecting ourselves from the anxiety and pain of the helping relationship. We give money in order to avoid a direct encounter with the other, paying someone else to have that encounter on our behalf. When we are confronted by the other, we try to find the quick solution rather than walking with them to find the right solution. Sometimes we must walk with them without even knowing for certain if a solution can be found! Our lives are scaffolded by complex practices which serve to buffer us from the trauma which others have the capacity to inflict on us simply by confronting us in their un-controllable other-ness.

We are accustomed to speaking about occupational hazards, but we typically conceptualize these dangers as potential physical accidents, or perhaps the social stigma attached to certain lines of work. However, we cannot overlook the psychological hazards posed to individuals when they repeatedly enter into specific social roles, especially the helping relationship.

What happens to the mind and heart of one whose job is to help people day in and day out, especially if these people in need of help are desperate, dissatisfied, or ungrateful? We can think of servers at restaurants, but we can also consider doctors, nurses, or teachers. How does entering into such a role on a daily basis re-shape an individual's sense of self, perhaps even in deleterious ways, and what long term effects will this have on how they see themselves in relation to others?

The helping relationship poses a minefield in this regard, and while Nietzsche's critique of pity effectively raises these questions for us, his account also illuminates the actions of the Inquisitor Inoue as he exploits the dynamics of the helping relationship in which Fr. Rodriguez stands towards the Japanese-Christians, thus mobilizing the minefield of compassion as the core of his strategy for securing Fr. Rodriguez's apostasy. To extract formal apostasy from Fr. Rodriguez, Inoue simply exposes the priest to the psychological hazards which are unique to his particular kind of helping relationship.

As a priest, the helping relationship in which Fr. Rodriguez found himself was like none other in his society— a direct mediator of God's forgiveness through confession and His presence through the sacraments. We might even speak of this particular variety of helping relationship more abstractly as the "Shamanic relation" —a helping relation where the shaman becomes the material link between the worshipper and the divine, providing a conduit of exclusive access to the spiritual realm.

Roman Catholic theology in particular, more so than Protestantism, cultivates this dependence of the worshiper on the priest through the theology and function of its priesthood. For example, unlike in Protestantism where the worshipper confesses their sin directly to God to receive forgiveness, we see in the story of *Silence* how the Roman Catholic practice of confession stipulates that the worshiper must confess to and seek absolution from a priest in order to receive God's forgiveness. Fr. Rodriguez's internal monologues show that he is clearly aware of the gravity of his calling and the function he serves to the Japanese-Christians, and their reverence for his sacred objects and rituals seems to bear this understanding out. This burden weighs heavily upon him, especially as he is called upon again and again to hear Kichijirou's confession and provide him absolution.

The *Jii-sama* (the elder) in the village where Rodriguez and Garrpe reside when they first arrive in Japan explains that he has performed baptisms on some of the infants in the village — note that this practice would not be prohibited as church teaching has historically admitted some latitude for lay people to perform baptisms under extreme circumstances. However, the Eucharist is treated differently in church teaching. Lacking a priest, the Japanese-Christians in the village have not tasted the Eucharist in years. Since Roman Catholic theology teaches that the bread and wine become in their essence (if not in their outward qualities) the very body and blood of the God-man Jesus Christ, such an activity was reserved solely for priests who had been trained and ordained by the Church. This only serves to heighten the uniqueness of Fr. Rodriguez's role as priest, and especially the responsibility which he bears for connecting God's people to their God through the Eucharist.

Inoue preys upon the exclusivity of this connection to God which Rodriguez provides the people in order to produce in the priest the feeling that the Japanese-Christians are suffering *for him*. His unique presence in Japan is criminal and unwanted in the eyes of the nation's leaders, and thus the *kurishitan* are condemned to suffer, whether it be in his presence or in his absence. There is no good choice however, because he either remains and the persecution continues or he leaves and deprives them of the vital connection to God which he provides them with through confession and the sacraments. By framing the dilemma in this way, Inoue forces Fr. Rodriguez to choose between his own soul and the souls of the Christians over whom God has given him charge.

While we as the readers have enough distance to discern that the Japanese-Christians are suffering on account of Inoue's capricious exercise of politically sanctioned violence against a religious minority group, Rodriguez has a harder time of anchoring himself in that reality, and this is one such hazard of the shamanic variety of helping relationship which plays such a central role for his personal identity and self-understanding. The way that Inoue gets inside the psyche of the Christian priest to turn Rodriguez's motivations and intentions against himself displays a keen understanding of the inner experience of being a Christian. You can't break Christians if you operate from the perspective of an unbeliever — you have to get inside the experience of being a Christian in order to destabilize their world internally.

Inoue's strategy for producing apostasy

On gaslighting

The concept of "gaslighting" enjoys some provenance in contemporary ethical discourse, especially in the realm of medicalized self-help speech. Mental health theorists warn people, particularly women, to pick up on signs of gaslighting, which is deemed a favorite technique of narcissists (a group people are constantly warned to be on guard for). Wikipedia notes that the concept of gaslighting did not gain much currency until the mid-2010's, which also closely coincides with the explosion of Very-Online discourse about identity, self-care, and mental health. The term derives from the movie *Gas Light* (1944), which was itself based on a play of the same name, in which the main character Bella becomes the victim of her scheming husband's secrecy and psychological torment, leading her to doubt her own sanity.

Unfortunately, proponents of the term gaslighting undermine its usefulness sometimes by taking the concept to the extreme of labeling even the act of asking questions or theorizing about alternative explanations as gaslighting. A hysterical version of this paranoia about gaslighting posits total unassailable authority to first-personal impressions and spontaneous speech about one's subjectivity, violently resisting any attempt whatsoever to provide an alternative explanation for an experience or to expand one's range of possible interpretations. Within this framework, even dialogue itself becomes a traumatic psychological harm and a form of attempted manipulation.

However, let's be clear — gaslighting *is* real. In fact, a central claim in this chapter is that the inquisitor Inoue gaslights Fr. Rodriguez into inhabiting a world where he, and not Inoue, is responsible for the torture of the Japanese-Christians. By inaugurating this psychological landscape for Fr. Rodriguez, Inoue shifts the responsibility for action from himself to the priest Fr. Rodriguez. Knowing that Fr. Rodriguez experiences himself through the lens of his priestly calling, Inoue ruthlessly exploits this vulnerability through a strategy of systematically gaslighting Rodriguez about how the world works.

Gaslighting includes a range of tactics designed to achieve two primary objectives — first, to comprehensively undermine the victim's sense of their own ability to perceive reality or trust their perceptions, and second, to progressively build dependence on the perpetrator to provide the certainty and interpretive framework which the victim becomes less able to generate for themselves. Inoue cultivates both of these elements through a masterfully crafted kabuki theater of experiences which he feeds Rodriguez, all with the ultimate aim of leading Rodriguez to the belief that apostasy is the only way out — the only way to fulfill his duty of love as a priest. Only through apostasy can the priest end the torture of the Christians who God has put him in charge of.

Inoue relentlessly employs standard gaslighting tactics, including shifting blame for the state of affairs onto the victim. The victim must be made to feel that they are the cause or the source of the issues — they're crazy, they're ignorant, they've evil, they're wrong, whatever. The perpetrator simply has to continuously shift the blame for the events to the victim until they become bereft of the necessary psychological resources to resist the perpetrator's designs.

In a gaslighting situation, the perpetrator will cultivate their place within the state of affairs so as to always appear to be the pure one, the helpful one, the consummately well behaved one, the one who can do no wrong, whereas somehow, in every scenario, the blame for all the problems will find its way back to the victim's account. In fact, we will examine how the first component in Inoue's strategy is precisely these formal dialogues through which he positions himself as hospitable, eminently reasonable, and rationally detached. For the gaslighting to be successful, Rodriguez must both believe that he is the problem *and* that Inoue's interpretation of the state of affairs offers the only solution.

In an overwhelming situation where the perpetrator's ability to press the victim is practically unlimited, such as in the case of the Inquisitor Inoue's mandate from the regime to deploy any means necessary to control Christianity in Kyushu, the victim ultimately has to decide between adjusting themselves to the psychological world which the perpetrator has created for them or going completely insane. Fr. Rodriguez, by navigating his own idiosyncrasies as well as the pathologies of his shamanic role as priest, manages to find a path to come to terms with the world that Inoue inaugurates for him, and does so in a way which somehow aligns with his re-constituted self-structure. This adaptive mechanism of re-orientation and resignation leads him finally to his decision to exit through apostasy, giving Inoue what he desired all along.

The components of Inoue's strategy

We have described Inoue's strategy as that of gaslighting Rodriguez, but speaking even more concretely, what does Inoue *do* to undermine Rodriguez's perception of reality?

In this next section, I outline the four core tactics which compose Inoue's strategy, and we will see how each tactic reinforces Inoue's central aim, which relies on some key concepts inherent to Nietzsche's critique of pity — weaponizing victims in order to generate a sense of compassion which makes Rodriguez manipulable in ways his role as priest makes him especially liable to.

When Rodriguez first meets Inoue[1] , he does not even realize that he has met the Inquisitor Inoue. Rodriguez is blinded by the grand narrative of martyrdom into which he has cast himself within his mind and heart, and this makes him unable to see the short old man in front of him for who he truly is — a brutal and calculating opponent who understands the psyche of the priest better than Rodriguez does. In fact, their first encounter contains the seeds of everything which will follow. In a way, Inoue intentionally reveals his hand, knowing that Rodriguez will completely miss the meaning.

As Rodriguez sits on the ground in the jungles of Kyushu, hands tied behind his back, a short Japanese man sits down on a chair in front

---

1. *Silence*, 89.

of him, all the while swatting flies and complaining about the heat. This self-evidently important person casually addresses Rodriguez with some pleasantries, before finally turning to the crux of the matter — "It all depends on you whether or not they are to be set free."

The first opening in the conflict. The gaslighting begins. Although Rodriguez and the Japanese-Christians were forcibly captured and detained by Inoue and his retainers, it becomes Rodriguez's fault that the Japanese-Christians remain in captivity. He is the only one who can free them, and he can do that by giving Inoue what he wants.

Inoue reveals his intention to exploit the psychological hazards of the priestly role through weaponizing victims — "Now, if you are really a father at heart, you ought to feel pity for the Christians. Isn't that so?" "Punish me alone," Rodriguez shoots back. He seeks the martyrdom which he craves. But Inoue denies it from him, instead shifting the blame for violence to Rodriguez, making him the guilty party who will become responsible for the suffering of the Japanese-Christians. "It is because of you that they must suffer," he says before abruptly leaving.

In this short exchange, Inoue reveals everything about his plan, except for the final blow — the revelation of Fr. Ferreira — which he holds back, keeping an arrow in his quiver. However, even though he reveals his plan to exploit Rodriguez's sense of compassion born from his duty as a priest, and that this compassion and duty will deepen his sense of responsibility for their suffering, it remains to be seen what particular tactics which produce in Rodriguez this particular subjective stance and outlook on the world.

To accomplish his aims, Inoue employs four primary tactics, all structured by a cyclical arc which progressively intensifies the situation with each repetition. Inoue structures time and events into a cyclical movement of peace, confrontation, and violence in order to cultivate a certain sense of reality in Rodriguez. The cycle exhibits something of the following structure — A long period of inactivity persists, which is unexpectedly interrupted by an invitation to cordial dialogue between Inoue and Rodriguez. Within a few days of the dialogue, Inoue's retainers administer a *fumi-e* test for the Japanese-Christian prisoners. Then, depending on whether the Japanese-Christians defy the *fumi-e* or not, sudden and seemingly random bouts of violence will follow. After the shocking episode of violence, a long period of inactivity sets in, starting the cycle over again.

This cycle of peace, confrontation, and violence includes three main tactics which are aimed at producing in Rodriguez the subjective conditions necessary for apostasy to occur, and Inoue retains a final tactic to push him over the edge once these conditions are met — (1) staged dialogues, (2) the formation of a parish in prison, (3) depriving Rodriguez of martyrdom, and finally, (4) providing Fr. Ferreira as a model for apostasy. We will explore each in turn, connecting each back to the primary subjective structure of the priest in his helping relationship and its attendant psychological hazards.

1. Staged dialogues

The novel *Silence* is punctuated by a number of dialogues between Rodriguez and his captor. More so than anything which Inoue says in these dialogues, the psychological function these dialogues are paramount. Inoue stages them for the effect which they are intended to produce in Rodriguez. Setting aside any analysis of the ideological framework which operates in Inoue's side of the dialogue, the reality is that it's actually irrelevant whether Inoue believes a word of what he's saying. For him, words are merely tools for psychological manipulation. He is a rhetorician who openly questions the existence of any universal truth. In fact, he claims that he doesn't even care whether Rodriguez accepts his claims or not; he aims only for Rodriguez to comply. Intellectual assent is unnecessary as long as outward submission can be secured. The threat of Christianity must be effectively neutralized, and achieving this objective does not necessarily require that he change Rodriguez's mind about any intellectual matters.

However, looming behind every one of these seemingly free and cordial dialogues stands an unspoken threat of violence, and Inoue's barely concealed fangs serve to indicate the true nature of the situation in which Rodriguez finds himself. We can pick up on this implicit threat more nakedly in the less adept conversational maneuvers of Inoue's assistant, the lapsed priest who comes to speak with Rodriguez sometimes in Inoue's place. When Rodriguez argues Inoue's assistant to a stalemate in a religious debate, he quickly resorts to veiled threats of violence before abruptly ending the confrontation. This pivot on the part of the assistant suggests, in my mind, that he still harbors too much hatred for the priests and resentment against Christianity to be a truly great inquisitor like Inoue. Inoue maintains a clinical approach to his work — a torture master with cold and calculating mien slowly extracting a confession from his victim, exploiting the very emotion of compassion which he has inoculated himself against.

Inoue constantly cultivates this clinical distance from Rodriguez, positioning himself as eminently well-mannered, magnanimous, and treating the prisoner Rodriguez with a generosity only afforded to a foreign dignitary. Rodriguez only ever sees Inoue when they are sitting together having an intellectual discussion, often after Rodriguez has been cleaned up or been permitted to wear nice clothes. In these encounters, Inoue wears traditional Japanese attire, sometimes sitting drinking tea, always peaceful and speaking in an even voice. He never flies off the handle at Rodriguez, and he always permits Rodriguez to oppose him and speak his mind freely. As we mentioned earlier on, this constitutes one of the core strategies of gaslighting — the perpetrator constantly postures as the long-suffering and steadfast one who graciously bears with the victim's delusions which are creating the difficult state of affairs at hand.

Further, this is also why Inoue is never present when actual violence occurs. When violence does take place, it's always carried out by some nameless retainer who is acting on orders which have filtered down from above, lacking a clear origin or responsible party. The blood never appears to be on Inoue's hands. In fact, Inoue is not even physically present when Rodriguez apostatizes. Whenever there is violence against the Japanese-Christians, an apostate always stands by Rodriguez's side, tempting him — either Inoue's assistant or Fr. Ferreira. Inoue does not tempt, he does not physically abuse, he does not even appear to be the source of violence. He at all times maintains the facade of the consummate gentleman who calmly insists on the course of action which Rodriguez must take to resolve the current problematic state of affairs.

We've seen how these dialogues shape Rodriguez's experience of his imprisonment through positioning him vis-a-vis Inoue in a certain way, but we can also observe how they act at a purely structural level to mark time in a world without clocks or calendars. Through the cadence of long periods of inactivity punctuated by dialogue and subsequent violence, Inoue begins to control the rhythms of Rodriguez's own ability to introspect and hold together his self-structure. In a way, Rodriguez starts to lose hold of the tempo as Inoue becomes increasingly able to get inside his head. Rodriguez's confinement does not stop at the physical — it extends even to the chronological, and by extension, the psychological.

However, Inoue doesn't want to control Rodriguez simply for the sake of control — he's not a megalomaniac. He's an observant student of human behavior and an astute practitioner of psychological manipulation, so he works only to obtain this control in order to ensure he has at his disposal the necessary tools for producing his desired outcomes. Inoue uses these dialogues to plant doubts in Rodriguez's mind, and once these doubts are planted, they must be fed and given time to grow. By controlling Rodriguez's outer sense of time, Inoue begins to influence Rodriguez's internal sense of self, which means that he can begin to guide Rodriguez towards an apostasy which aligns with his re-shaped self-structure and self-narrative.

In the components of Inoue's strategy which we will investigate subsequently, we'll see how each tactic engenders a tension or a pain in Rodriguez which Inoue weaponizes through his control of the entire cadence of Rodriguez's inner and outer experiences.

2. The priest's prison parish

Rodriguez notes how the first tranquility which he experienced in Japan, was, ironically, found in captivity. As he is confined to a small wooden prison cell in a military compound, he finally experiences the freedom of not having to conceal himself. He can now openly discharge his calling as a priest without fear of capture precisely because he has already been captured. His greatest fear behind him, he has only now to inhabit the tenuous space between life and death where he and the Japanese-Christians live their daily lives.

Life in prison is bare, but continues unabated. An almost preternatural calm settles over Rodriguez as the days roll on. The time becomes defined by long periods of uneventful days in which Rodriguez establishes for the Japanese-Christians their own rhythm of singing, chanting, prayer, and confession, something which they would not have even been able to experience in their home villages. In a strange twist, the Japanese-Christians in prison too are more free to engage in the practice of their faith than those on the outside who remain hidden in the villages of Kyushu.

We can view Rodriguez's actions as that of organizing a parish within the prison As Rodriguez ministers to this needy people, and these Christians experience, perhaps for the first time, the regular life of being a member of an open body of believers, both parties experience a profound enjoyment which would have been inaccessible to them outside the walls of the prison. The body of believers residing within the prison compound constitute a Christian people who worship and live as followers of Jesus, all under the leadership of the priest Fr. Rodriguez.

Lest we forget, Rodriguez has only freshly emerged from his seminary training, and thus, for the first time he too is experiencing what it's like to openly act in his role within a parish. Although he first ministered to the hidden Christians of the village of Goto, this experience of a prison parish would likely be exhilarating for the young man who had taken vows and trained extensively for years in order to one day assume this priestly role amongst God's people. In allowing the formation of this prison parish, Inoue provides Fr. Rodriguez and the Japanese-Christians with a special form of enjoyment around which their self-experience can coalesce.

Inoue permits this prison parish to form, even fostering it by allowing Rodriguez to not remain confined to his cell, precisely because he knows that establishing and deepening the bond between priest and parish will work against Rodriguez in the long run. Inoue allows Rodriguez to derive this satisfaction from his "playing priest" for the imprisoned Christians. As the cycles of waking, serving, and sleeping continue on seemingly without end, Inoue lulls Rodriguez into a sense of comfortable complacency in his role as prison priest for his prison parish. Thus, Rodriguez becomes bound to the fate of the Japanese-Christians, and through solidarity he finds that his compassion for them has greatly expanded.

As he develops this priest-parish relationship, he assumes a greater sense of responsibility for each of the Christians under his care. Ultimately, this makes their death and torture all that much more painful for Rodriguez. The more he begins to identify with his parishioners, the greater his compassion will be when they become the victims of violence, and the heavier will be the burden which he carries for them in his heart. Their suffering becomes his own pain and travail. With this, Inoue is betting that the temptation to apostatize will only grow more intense the more that Rodriguez assumes responsibility for the prison parish.

3. Deprived of victimhood

Inoue never orders violence against Rodriguez. The violence against the victims — the Japanese-Christians — never includes Rodriguez himself, and thus Rodriguez never becomes the victim which he always imagined he would become.

While simultaneously inflicting pain upon Rodriguez by forcing him to view the violence perpetrated against his parishioners, we can also see that Inoue *deprives* Rodriguez of the violence which Rodriguez wishes to undergo for himself. In this deprivation of violence lies a number of the core psychological components of Inoue's strategy for producing apostasy, as well as some insights about Rodriguez's own pathologies.

As was discussed previously, Rodriguez must be made to feel that the Japanese-Christians are suffering on his account. The violence they experience makes Rodriguez feel that they are receiving what *he* deserves, deepening his sense of responsibility for them and his feelings of guilt about being treated well in prison while the other padres (including his companion!) suffered fates worse than death. His flock is under attack, and this causes him an intense emotional pain, not only as one human witnessing another in pain, but as one watching a wolf devour the helpless sheep which Rodriguez has a responsibility before God to shepherd even unto death.

Throughout the novel the reader encounters an interesting line which recurs frequently during scenes in which the *kurishitan* are tortured — Inoue's assistant will add an aside in his explanation to Rodriguez that "these Christians have already apostatized." The message is clear — "They are suffering on your account. Even their own apostasy cannot save them from this scourge." Only Rodriguez can set them free from this torture through his own apostasy, and thus this simple aside embodies the stakes which are at play in any violence against the Japanese-Christians.

While I think it's likely that the claim that the Christians have already apostatized is a lie, it ultimately doesn't matter, because the psychological effect on Rodriguez is all that is desired, and this seems to be achieved if we judge by Rodriguez's response. Everything in the situation continuous compels Rodriguez towards the inescapable belief that he can be their only salvation — he alone is responsible for their torture, and the only way to set them free is to sacrifice himself. And what priest, modeling himself after Jesus Christ, would not sacrifice himself just as his Lord did? This is Inoue's masterful bet.

Beyond his sense of guilt though, we can't help but notice that Rodriguez also *desires* to be punished. Rodriguez requests again and again that he should be punished, but he never is. So while he's certainly in travail and guilt at watching the *kurishitan* be killed and tortured while Inoue never lays a hand on him, there is another element operating here — enjoyment. Despite his physical and psychological torment, Rodriguez derives an immense amount of *enjoyment* from his identification with the sufferings of Christ. Throughout the story Rodriguez conceives of himself through the lens of persecution, heavily identifying his own experiences with the narrative of Christ's persecution, betrayal and crucifixion. As he casts Kichijiro in the role of Judas Iscariot, and himself as Jesus the betrayed and persecuted, he seems to derive a perverse enjoyment from this way of seeing himself and his predicament. This way of seeing his trials through the lens of the life of Christ has served to keep him together mentally and emotionally throughout this difficult journey in Japan.

Inoue knows the symbols through which Rodriguez conceptualizes himself — his identity he clings to for meaning — and consequently deprives Rodriguez of the martyrdom which he desires most of all. One wonders if Rodriguez unconsciously came to Japan seeking this very experience, both out of a sense of thrill of adventure and a zealous inclination to test his faith. The ideal of the martyr animates Rodriguez's deepest conceptions of himself, and thus the way that Inoue withholds violence from him makes him unable to fully unite himself to that archetype which he holds out for himself.

Rodriguez's pain must have been multiplied when he witnessed the brave and holy death of his comrade Fr. Garrpe, at once his beloved and trusted companion, but also someone he must now secretly envy because he received the blessing of martyrdom which God through Inoue withholds from Rodriguez, prolonging his suffering and softening his resolve through a comfortable existence in prison. By never letting him become an object of violence, Inoue prevents Rodriguez from enjoying the martyrdom which his priestly psychology and quasi-messianic self narrative naturally fosters in his subjectivity.

Instead, Inoue gives Rodriguez the opposite of what he desires — peaceful and quiet days in a seemingly never-ending captivity. How will Rodriguez persist in his own self-understanding without the support of the narratives which previously provided him with such meaning and enjoyment? Now that Rodriguez has become bereft of the resources he has relied on to this point in his life, Inoue's bet is that he can provide Rodriguez with an alternative self-structure, one which allow him to carry on in a way which aligns with Inoue's interests as well.

Inoue has stoked the flame of Fr. Rodriguez's pious passion for martyrdom, and yet he has given him no opportunity to satisfy this desire to come under any sort of holy suffering. Instead, in time, Inoue will open up a path for Rodriguez to enjoy the sweet travails of martyrdom. Inoue simply has to show him the way forward by providing him with a convenient model.

4. A model for apostasy

Thus far we've seen how Inoue leverages a cycle of peace, confrontation, and violence to break Rodriguez. Inoue also cultivates a clinical distance from Rodriguez by using cordial dialogues and his conspicuous absence at events of violence, while also tacitly promoting the formation of a prison parish which deepens Rodriguez's sense of compassion, duty, and solidarity with the Japanese-Christians in prison. By then depriving Rodriguez of the martyrdom which he craves, Inoue leaves Rodriguez bereft of the psychological tools which would enable him to derive enjoyment his situation, and to thereby make sense of it.

As Inoue disavows his responsibility by continuing to insist that Rodriguez is the only one who can save the Japanese-Christians, Rodriguez increasingly experiences himself as the one responsible for the ongoing suffering, torture, and death of the *kurishitan*. All of these structural and psychological mechanisms combine to put Rodriguez in the ideal psychological conditions to apostatize. He simply needs one final element — a model.

Inoue has used the formal dialogues to introduce doubts into Rodriguez's mind about the possibility of a positive relationship between Christianity and the Japanese people. Even if Rodriguez has not been swayed intellectually, the seeds of doubt have nonetheless been planted simply by virtue of him being exposed to an alternative perspective which runs uncompromisingly at variance with his own. Inoue makes his view more plausibly simply by his unswerving insistence on the same key talking points. Rodriguez cannot make sense of his own predicament through the usual narrative mechanisms and archetypes by which he has conceptualized himself to this point in his life — the priest, the martyr, the faithful Christian — they have all become unsettled and undermined by the experience of his imprisonment, and by his confrontation with Inoue's alien worldview.

Inoue knows that Rodriguez is ready to fall, but he needs a push. More precisely, he needs someone who can devastate the last shreds of his identity while simultaneously providing him an alternative model of selfhood for him to step into. Rodriguez doesn't realize it, but he has become sufficiently malleable as to be open to another model of self-understanding. He simply needs to meet this model.

Inoue has this model waiting obediently in the wings to meet Rodriguez at the most opportune moment. The (ex-)Fr. Ferreira who the young priests so zealously sought has already forged this new path of apostasy which Rodriguez now walks down. He developed and pioneered this new model of the apostate priest living in Japan under the thumb of the Tokugawa regime, and thus Inoue finally brings Rodriguez to Ferreira only once he knows that Rodriguez's mind has been rendered open to adopting Ferreira as his model of escape.

The meeting between Rodriguez and his old teacher — this apostate priest Ferreira — casts down every last illusion Rodriguez had about why he was even in Japan. Seeing the melancholy and obedient Ferreira before him brings his mission to an anti-climatic end, and ultimately renders it a failure as he discovers that his worst nightmare has come true. Since Ferreira had provided a formative model for Rodriguez as he pursued his priestly calling in the Jesuit Order, the appearance of the apostate Ferreira before Rodriguez's eyes embodies every intellectual doubt and every spiritual failure to which Rodriguez viscerally fears he may succumb for himself. He fears his own weakness of faith and the softness of his will. Then the very paragon in his mind of a Jesuit full of knowledge, burning with love for God, and skilled in service, sits cross-legged before him, head bowed like the Tokugawa's dog. This scene devastates him, leaving him emotionally unmoored as he sees the teacher and leader he had revered reduced to a downcast shell of his former self, not to mention a regime collaborator who produces flimsy propaganda for a rival religion.

When they first re-unite, Rodriguez hears Ferreira — now named Sawano Chuan — repeat back to him all the talking points which Inoue has rehearsed in their dialogues. Rodriguez was, of course, hoping to hear a brilliant rebuttal from his former teacher, and was relying on him to provide the counter-arguments which would bolster his own spirit. Instead, he finds a man writing a defense of Buddhism and its critiques of Christianity, as well as handing over to the Japanese regime the details of Western science and technology all while he actively disparages the religious and philosophical underpinnings of the very

European culture which developed those insights. Rodriguez cannot believe his ears when he hears his once-teacher openly agree with Inoue that Christianity can find no purchase in Japan. Everything about Ferreira's situation — from becoming a Buddhist monk to taking a Japanese wife to producing anti-Christian propaganda — signals a total resignation to the regime's ideological line. We see no evidence of even a hint of Ferreira's attempt to resist total subservience to the political establishment's demands.

Rather than Inoue being present for his apostasy, Ferreira becomes the one who accompanies Rodriguez as he faces the *fumi-e*. Ferreira says, "You are about to undertake the most painful act of love which has ever been performed," before leading him out of the cell into the yard where the *fumi-e* waits in the dust. This is, in fact, the first and only time Rodriguez personally faces the *fumi-e* in the novel's entire narrative. When he stands before the fumi-e, surrounded by the groans of tortured Christians, Rodriguez finds that the voice speaking in his ear is none other than a fellow apostate who stepped on the *fumi-e* before him. Ferreira stands by his side, offering a perverse companionship as they both peer over the edge into a black, unknown abyss of unbelief. Ferreira's presence offers the possibility of a solidarity in this overwhelming suffering, a new figure of the martyr which Rodriguez can step into, quite literally, by trampling on the face of Christ.

Conclusion

In the end of *Silence*, Inoue wins. He gets what he wants. Ferreria and Rodriguez sit and inspect merchandise all day to ensure that no Christian objects are smuggled into Japan. They quietly live out their lives, faithfully apostatizing every year as a continued show of their subservience. The *kurishitan* are abandoned, like sheep whose shepherds have left them to wander on the crags and cliffs. In all this, we must not lose sight of the fact that the Japanese-Christians are betrayed at every turn. Even by the very Church which shared the good news of Jesus with them, their leaders and teachers have fled before the sword of the enemy, fearing for their own safety and consoling themselves with the secret faith they may (or may not) harbor in their hearts.

In this chapter we have looked at how the inquisitor Inoue weaponized victims against Fr. Rodriguez to lead him to his fall. I think the question of the hazards of compassion and care has a wide ranging relevance to our current context. How do the tactics which Inoue employed mirror the strategies of our own leaders and elite institutions today? What can we understand about our own experience by seeing it through the lens of cyclical violence which serves to disorient us and prepare us to accept alternative identities and lifestyles? In what ways does the demand to resolve trauma or "to do something" feed into the regime's overall strategy of control and social transformation? Nietzsche's critique of empathy is more relevant than ever in our age of governance which justifies itself in terms of the rhetoric and principles of care.

These questions also lead us into our next chapter, which explores the question of liberation within Christian theology. This book and its author place *freedom* at the heart of God's life and the message which He sends in His Son. God's work in us and through us orients itself to this lodestar of freedom which is lived through the power of the Spirit. What does the Gospel look like if we center liberation as its primary theme, and what does this freedom entail? It at least drives us to investigate the manifold and clever cruelties which are perpetrated by those who oppose themselves to God's freedom, and who instead seek their own self-aggrandizement at the expense of others. Men like Inoue exercise a pitiless power which could not be further from the heart of God. These powers and principalities are the very ones which St. Paul tells us that Jesus broke and openly shamed on his cross. This is the message of freedom which we live in and live out as we walk in faith with God. I am convinced that Rodriguez lost sight of this in the pitch black hole in which he found himself at Inoue's hands. We need to understand how we can not be like him. We need to think hard about how we can *resist*.

5

—.—

A Theology of Freedom

Introduction

The title of this book is *Ideology and Christian Freedom* — but if we have spent four chapters addressing the history and experience of ideology, when do we get to talking about freedom? And further, what makes this freedom distinctly Christian? We cannot put off any longer the theological question of *liberation*. Instead, we must grapple with this theme of freedom which runs through Endo's book, and use the story of Rodriguez and the Japanese-Christians to reframe and renew a liberation theology for our times.

This chapter could have been written any number of ways. Freedom is a broad topic, but also an intensely personal one. At the outset though, let me highlight that the freedom which we will be exploring cannot be restricted merely to the realm of the personal. We cannot escape the personal experience of freedom, for it finds us wherever we are, but it's a crucial part of Rodriguez's mistake that he believes he can achieve the freedom of salvation in isolation from his Japanese brothers and sisters in Christ. This is why I prefer the terms liberation or emancipation, although I will use the word freedom throughout, because these words evoke an image of a free *people*, not simply a crowd of free persons. Indeed, freedom cannot be fully understood without a direct engagement with the question of living in a community with others.

We have to re-center the notion of freedom as the heart of Jesus' message, rather than continuing to go along with the way that evangelical Christians have disproportionately emphasized personal forgiveness in salvation. Such a method of evangelism seeks to save persons, not a people. The evangelical overemphasis on personal salvation also directly mirrors the secular mistake that Jesus is simply another spiritual teacher of the likes of the Buddha or Gandhi who came to spread a message of peace and point to a higher human potential. Both groups have to wrestle with how Jesus actually spoke and acted when he was alive — his burden was to proclaim the apocalypse (unveiling) of the Kingdom of God, to point to the new type of social relations which would define God's kingdom, and to prepare people to enter into this kingdom through faith and repentance.

Repentance seems an archaic concept to us today, but it's one eminently worth reviving. It cuts to the heart of the human condition in which we are inescapably *free* — the one who repents turns away from how things are (Greek: μετάνοια, *metanoia*, changing one's mind), and instead turns with their whole person towards a new way of living. Repentance speaks to this power to choose something radically new. The animal caught in the mechanical function of its instincts does not exhibit the capacity for this rejection of the status quo which can intervene in its circumstances to bring about a fundamentally changed course of life. This is our great blessing but also our terrible burden as human beings.

This book also carries the burden of Jesus' message of freedom. Wherever he went, Jesus preached the practice of discipleship which walks with God through His Son in the power of His Spirit. This collective liberation will include things like the practice of forgiveness, reconciliation, and love, but the binding thread is that through the Spirit-filled community God is creating a free people made up of free persons. The first free community was the Trinity — the infinite love shared by the Father, Son, and Holy Spirit — who chose to call creation out of nothing (to make an Other!), and then to graft that creation into that community of freedom, thereby expanding the fellowship of freedom to fill the whole heavens and earth. The good news of Jesus Christ is not that we get to enjoy a blissful castle in the sky when we die, but rather that we are invited into God's life now and forever. This is an utterly staggering message.

However, if we confess that this emancipation which God works in His creation must be lived and experience communally, we have found ourselves firmly in the realm of the *political*. The proclamation of Jesus' life, death, and resurrection cannot be filed down to a personal myth or an individual spiritual experience, for it explicitly inaugurates a new sort of political community. This polis has a different type of king and is marked by the strange ways in which its people acts and organizes — "You know that the rulers of the Gentiles lord it over them, and their high officials exercise authority over them. Not so with you. Instead, whoever wants to become great among you must be your servant, and whoever wants to be first must be your slave." (Matthew 20:25-27)

Why else would Jesus spend so much time confronting the leaders of the Jewish community if he did not have the questions of leadership and community as one of his primary thematics? We do Jesus a disservice when we move too quickly to abstract him from his Jewish context. Jesus was a Jew who preached his message on the basis of what the Torah taught, and he explicitly says that he primarily came to the

Jewish people. But his work also radicalizes Judaism from the inside by drawing together and emphasizing the universal and emancipatory threads which run through the Torah. From God's promise to make Abraham a blessing to *all* nations to Isaiah's visions of a new heavens and a new earth, Jesus works his way outward from the Jewish tradition to expand God's community of freedom to all people.

If what Jesus teaches about God is true, then the Gospel is as much for the Japanese as it is for the Anglo-Saxons. Wherever this message goes and to whomever it comes, a repentance can take place in which the old is negated and transformed by the appearance of a new possibility for living together. This negative labor of repentance in which the old dies and the new is born constitutes the essence of human freedom which is also a participation in God's freedom. The Japanese-Christians which Endo paints so vividly for us in his novel have taken up this work of trying to follow God in a land and amongst a people where the message of God's liberation is entirely new. In this encounter, they are allowing themselves to be changed as they explore what it could look like for them who are situated in their time, location, and social milieu to find their place in what God is doing in the earth as He reconciles all things to Himself.

As I've been trying to indicate throughout the more historical sections in this book, I think that these theological considerations indicate that Japanese-Christians were not a fifth-column for the European powers, but rather saw themselves as loyal to a different kingdom — God's kingdom — breaking into the world in Jesus Christ, making them fearless to oppose the oppressors they were once so afraid of. The Japanese-Christians offered no ultimate allegiance to the kingdoms of this world, whether European or Japanese. In this way, they mirror the first Christians who lived and moved within the Roman Empire, living counter-culturally and eschewing the dominant ideologies of the empire.

Wherever Christians go, we are a threat. Not because of any attachment or loyalty we might have to whatever hollowed out empire we happen to be living in at the time, but precisely in our *lack of attachment* to the things of empire. We are suspiciously *un*-attached to the things which the nation would have us elevate, worship, and sacrifice ourselves for. Our mode of living and of valuing life is not grounded first and foremost in our people group, language, or cultural rituals — all the stratagems which power uses to ensnare our bodies and minds. All these things are expendable, if the situation calls for it. Certainly if they are not repugnant to God we will not go out of our way oppose them, but if they are evil, we will simply refuse to comply, and we'll carry on doing our own thing until they either join us or kill us. That's how these things tend to go.

This stance I have just outlined has become unpopular in contemporary Christian discourse, for reasons which we will discuss in greater detail in the conclusion to this book, but suffice to say that many would accuse me of defending or supporting an enlightenment liberalism which continually works to undermine any forms of attachment to people, place, or culture. We will address that charge in a future chapter, but I want to be clear that this book is an exercise in refusing to throw the baby out with the bathwater. In our haste to question the Enlightenment project of a secular rationality from no-one and no-where (which absolutely needs to be critiqued), we should not risk losing the profound achievement which is the subject who can act outside of the political and structural flows in order to intervene in their world, thereby changing it.

While the Enlightenment failed to recognize that our particular location with a people and place provides the basic form of our freedom, we must remain alert to the ways that our social, political, and cultural location also presents profound dangers to our freedom. For instance, the revolution which American conservatives so loudly applaud came about only because of the profound insights of the Enlightenment which opened a radical horizon for the colonists to abstract themselves from the ideological structures of divine kingship and national colonialism, and to instead enact a universalizing gesture which granted inalienable rights and divine dignity to the individual. In order to fight for their freedom to determine their own goals and laws, they first needed to experience themselves as free, and this requires a specific level of abstraction from one's context. If we oppose the cultivation of this sort of freedom, would we not squelch the very sort of subjects who could have risen up in revolution in the first place? We must be careful not to kick away the ladder, thinking that we have arrived at a higher place, for the practice of freedom must be renewed daily, and more importantly, with each generation.

Ultimately, as we learn to cultivate this freedom, we will find ourselves siding again and again with the contradictions in society, over and against the wholistic claims of the social totality which spins a fictional web to ensnare the subject by making of them a self. The self remains trapped in a narcissistic fixation on their identity, a mental object composed of images and scenes all coalesced around a core of the void at the heart of each human being. In this sense, the self and one's supposed identity belong to the realm of imagination and the primary narcissism of the infant, shutting us up in a funhouse of mirrors all reflecting back on themselves.

Liberation from the specular world of fantasy comes only through the *alienation* of becoming a social creature through participating in language. When we enter into language, we find that we must substitute a sign (a word) for ourselves and our thoughts in order to then circulate those signs socially, and thereby to achieve mutual understanding and connection. Only by entering into this alienating realm of signs can we begin to develop solidarity with others outside of the narcissistic realm of fantasy in which the self and identity keep us trapped. Ironically then, the pain and suffering of alienation becomes the ground of our freedom, and this explains why the process of aligning ourselves with freedom demands that we side with the rejected, the oppressed, and the excluded. The site of the excluded is where the labor of God's freedom unfolds.

A Theology of Liberation

The freedom of God in the Spirit community of Jesus Christ

Many people have focused on different aspects of Christianity, but we cannot deny that from the very beginning the life of Jesus nakedly confronts us with the terrifying practice of freedom. In this sense, a "theology of liberation" is a redundancy, for the whole aim of God's life, and the substance of the life He holds out to His creation, is that of freedom. Everything about the Christian life and story impels towards a participation in the immense freedom which defines the life of the Triune God.

In Luke 4, Jesus stands up in the synagogue and reads from the scroll of Isaiah, saying "The Spirit of the Lord is on me, because he has anointed me to proclaim good news to the poor. He has sent me to proclaim freedom for the prisoners and recovery of sight for the blind, to set the oppressed free, to proclaim the year of the Lord's favor." As he sat back down, Jesus said that these words had been fulfilled in their hearing, and in this way he clearly broadcasted what the beating heart of his ministry entailed.

However, it was not at this saying that the Galilean Jews became furious with Jesus. Luke's account continues on to inform us that they all spoke well of him and admired his "gracious words" after he read this passage, and that they began to wonder amongst themselves about his claim, because they knew that he was Joseph's son. It was Jesus who became irritated at this response — the Jewish reaction to his words was akin to a bourgeois white liberal cooing about how "nice" the idea of social justice is. They had missed the point entirely, and they were treating him like some local kid instead of the Messiah who came in judgment.

Jesus began to rebuke them, and he did so in terms that really bite. He spat back that a prophet is never accepted in his hometown, and he proceeded to remind them that this was why God sent the prophet Elijah to be cared for by a Gentile woman in Sidon, even though Israel had many widows Elijah could have stayed with. Only at this mention of the role of Gentiles in God's plan did the people in the synagogue become enraged!

Naturally, these Galilean Jews think Jesus' words of liberation are "gracious," until they are brutally confronted with one of the many difficulties which liberation entails — being reconciled with their enemies and relinquishing their feelings of ethnic superiority. They are not ready for the practice of freedom, which presents a profound danger to their egos and their stable identity which they secretly prize more than God's plan of promised redemption for the world.

Jesus clearly hearkens back to the Old Testament tradition of the Prophets, both in his choice of the Isaiah passage and in his characterizing himself as a prophet who is rejected in his hometown. In doing this, he taps into the theme of freedom which also runs deeply through the corpus of Israel's Prophetic literature, animating not only their savage critiques of Israel and her people, but also their unshakeable hope which proclaims a future work in which God will inaugurate a freedom which human ability cannot achieve in its own power.

Jesus says that he has come to proclaim the "year of the Lord's favor" — this is an eternal jubilee in which one is released from their debts, allowed to return to their home, and set free from the burdens of kings, oppressors, and creditors. This is the Kingdom of God which is coming into the world, and the political community for which Christ exhorts us to prepare ourselves. St. Mark distills Jesus' message in just the first few lines of his Gospel account — "repent, for the Kingdom of Heaven is near." This Kingdom of Heaven fulfills the promises of blessing and freedom which Yahweh made to his people over and over again, and to which the Prophets testified with their poetic visions and vivid metaphors. These visions were not simply spiritual, but proclaimed peace between the lion and the lamb and foretold such a great abundance that the purchase of food and drink would no longer be necessary. They promised that the poor would be judged with equity, and the wicked would be utterly destroyed. These blessings which Yahweh holds forth in His kingdom are social first and foremost. They point to a human community animated by the love of God.

This encounter between Jesus and the Jewish community provides us with some clues about God's plan for freedom. Chiefly, this freedom involves being *for the other*. The freedom which God possesses, and which in the Gospel we come to experience and share in, is the freedom to be so full of life that we can give ourselves to another rather than remaining shut up within ourselves. This freedom is, ironically, an experience of compulsion, where our life springs from an abound-

ing well of generosity — the fountain which never runs dry, which is
Jesus Christ himself.

Consider Paul's words in 2 Corinthians 3:17 — "Now the Spirit is
the Lord, and where the Spirit of the Lord is, there is freedom." Christ
tells his disciples that he has to leave so the Spirit can come [John 16:7],
and thus in the outpouring of the Spirit at Pentecost we get the most
vivid picture this side of the eschaton of the Kingdom of God marked
as it is by freedom. The Spirit's outpouring on God's people as they
prayed and worshiped together in Acts 2 indicates for us that freedom
finds its culmination in *community*, that is, in a collective experience
of a life which exceeds each of us individually. Thus, not only is this
freedom *for* the other, but it must also be practiced *with* others.

This new experience of freedom immediately compels the New
Testament community to share the good news of Christ with all peoples, to worship God, to learn the words of Christ and his Apostles'
teachings, to partake in the sacraments, and to draw together into
a community of love and mutual aid. In this account, the Spirit is
showing us what the life of the liberated creature looks like — loving
community and thankful worship.

The freedom which Christ calls us into as he emancipates us from
the powers of the world, the Devil, and Death, are inescapably social,
as the early Church clearly realized. Having received the Spirit, they
had become bound together into a new type of communal life, one
which was defined both by the personal practice of devotion and the
concerted labor of social love. They sold their possessions to share with
anyone who had need, they met together regularly, and they shared the
meal which Christ commanded them, thus becoming bound together
as the family of God who shares in the life of God Himself through
His body and blood.

The New Testament church enacted what Paul describes in Galatians 5:1 — "It is for freedom that Christ has set us free." Paul's claim here seems like a tautology at first glance — we are set free to be free? — but Paul is saying that freedom is a way of living in the world. The freedom which Christ won for us was a release into a certain mode of existence, and this freedom for which we have been set free must be *lived* to be understood. This is why Paul immediately warns the Galatians against falling back into the burdensome yoke of the Law, which is the way of being in the world from which the one in Christ has been freed — the vicious circle of striving to be loved.

The way of the individual who lives under the demands and guilt of the law represents for us the chief temptation when we consider freedom, and is the dominant picture of freedom which our contemporary society espouses in its ever-expanding discourse on freedom and liberation. This freedom of the sovereign individual who stands underneath the command to endlessly enjoy, to acquire objects, and to assert their identity is no freedom at all, Paul wants the Galatians to see. The freedom which Christ inaugurates, and which the Spirit community of the New Testament embodies and proclaims, differs radically from the freedom trumpeted in our capitalist societies today. Our culture bows to the capitalist imperative to liberate every desire, all in the service of commodifying and financializing every desire of the human heart.

However, this supposed freedom to pursue one's desires without inhibition transforms imperceptibly into a slavery to one's pathologies, and puts one at the mercy of the constant manipulation perpetrated by those masters of persuasion at work in our society today. This unquenchable demand to liberate desire also feeds into the mission of the biopolitical nation-state which seeks to quantify every human need in order to bureaucratize care, and ultimately, to eliminate suffering itself through the proper application of public policy and scientific technique. These two work together — the market generates the libidinal demand for products by producing the objects and experiences which will exacerbate this demand, and the bio-political state responds to the cry of this vulnerable populace demanding ever more care to protect them from the dysfunction of society and the violence of the system.

Against the bacchanalian demand of capitalism to liberate every desire and against the all-consuming biopolitical project to master suffering through scientific technique, Jesus Christ and his church instantiate the practice of freedom as *love*, not desire. While our culture worships desire above all, the Christian understands that desire is highly variable, easily manipulable, and regularly deceived and deceiving, whereas love operates through a violent insistence on what is good and true, staking even its own life to oppose anything which would bring its beloved to ruin. This love is not the greedy and consuming void of desire which cannot be satisfied, but becomes instead a fountain of excess which satisfies itself only with its own overflowing.

In one sense then, love is a radical negativity, one which runs contrary to the infinite positivity of the feedback loops of desire we are constantly encouraged to ensnare ourselves in. This positivity of desire accelerates the more we indulge it, trapping us in a loop of dissatisfaction with no brakes. Love can short circuit this cycle by introducing a radical break where one thing in the world becomes elevated above all the others. By singling this object out from the general economy of things, everything else starts to pale in comparison with the beloved, and the beloved becomes a point of radical freedom through our dogged insistence on its supremacy, even against all other claims to the contrary.

However, in another sense, this love is also the purest positivity, for it requires no reference point outside of itself. Love creates its object through its loving, for love is also the infinite affirmation of its beloved. Love sings a song over its object, making a declaration about its object, and thereby transforming it in the process. Love even unites itself to its beloved through an extended process of entanglement and mediation in which its own life becomes inextricably bound up its beloved. In this way, love as an insistent lack and existent excess are paradoxically united.

Love is the foundation of any resistance to the powers of this world, and consequently for any effectual practice of freedom, for this love's being from God makes it the one thing which this world cannot control or calculate. God's love is power because it is "useless." This useless love does not optimize, instead it forgives the accuser, it reconciles enemies to each other, it generously gives things away knowing that God will provide, practicing a patience which resists the demand to "do something" or to "have the answer." This useless love stands against everything in this world, and God in Christ leads us out from the desert where the cold logic of the machine reigns into the promised land where we can live in the freedom of this wasteful love which overflows like milk and honey.

Where the Spirit of the Lord is, there is freedom — the freedom to love our God, our neighbor, and ourselves. This is the promised and terrible liberation which God in Christ inaugurates on the earth and is now working out with and through us.

Christ's identification with the lowest

A return to liberation theology

This emphasis on liberation undeniably beats at the heart of Scripture, but we can't overlook how susceptible today the concept of freedom renders itself to capture by dominant ideologies. For instance, what many academics call "liberation theology" today exhibits a tendency to get caught up in a particular interpretation of liberation, one which unwittingly falls into the frameworks of the bio-political state which seeks to turn flourishing into an operational process oriented towards the reduction and elimination of suffering. As capitalism and the biopolitical state collaborate to liberate all desires, this insistence on liberation feeds into the project of re-structuring, re-schematizing, and re-directing these desires to flow into newly constructed channels.

Through an insistence on justice as the satisfaction of demand, the liberation theologian ends up carrying water for the continual expansion of the state's bureaucratic systems of care and its sanctioned modes of knowledge production which govern the development and application of these interventions, a monstrous system which threatens to swallow us whole. The activist crying in the street clears the way for the lawyer, the psychiatrist, and the bureaucrat to devise and implement a new solution for these social maladies in which people are traumatized by all manner of repression. The psychoanalyst Jacques Lacan famously said concerning France's 1968 student protests that "As revolutionaries, what you long for is a master," adding ominously, "— you'll get one."

Liberation theology today risks serving as a vehicle of bitter resentment and the vengeful cry of the wounded, believing themselves to be free in casting off their chains while becoming more deeply compromised than ever, ultimately ensnaring themselves and its advocates every deeper in the machine of capital which will grind them to dust without hesitation. Instead of embodying the great freedom which Christ secures for the family of God by ushering in a kingdom defined above all by generosity and reconciliation, liberation theology has allowed itself to become indistinguishable from the secular discourse of identity and justice which is perpetuated by academics, scientists, and activists.

The Latin-American thinkers who developed the first theological discourses which we now recognize as a "theology of liberation" were animated by the same Spirit of Jesus who drove the moneychangers from the Temple or by the fiery passion of John the Baptist who rebuked the Pharisees for coming out to assuage their guilty consciences with baptism. In his attack on the Temple's moneychangers, Jesus accuses the Jewish leadership of laying intolerable spiritual *and* economic burdens on God's people, showing how these two are intimately woven together in the labyrinthine economy of sacrifice and money exchange unfolding at the Temple.

By operating in this same vein of prophetic critique, Latin-American liberation theologians paid with their lives when they spoke out in the same register as their Lord Jesus did. Many were martyred for preaching and organizing against brutal regimes which oppressed the poor and the vulnerable, the very ones who God through His prophets identifies as especially precious to Him. Theological discourses of liberation must appear at precisely this point where economic oppression begins to speak in a religious key, thus tempting the Church to remain silent.

We will not take the time to recount their stories here, although I am convinced that in their martyrdom God vindicated these liberation theologians as His faithful servants. Their blood commends their words to us, just as the cross and travails of the Japanese-Christians killed by the Tokugawa regime testify to the labor of the Spirit of God in their midst. They would not have been killed if they were not dangerous, and what could be more dangerous than the subversive work of God's death on the cross patiently unfolding its power through real historical moments?

However, I theorize that as these subversive liberation theologies from Latin America were imported and taken up in a new American context, they were mobilized in a different political context, eventually becoming enmeshed in various leftist discourses, such as human rights, democratic socialism, and intersectionality. This new constellation of ideological and institutional commitments fundamentally changes the sorts of projects which liberation theology could be enlisted to underwrite. A core set of ideas and their corresponding symbols could be transplanted from their original context in order to become the theoretical underpinning for the activist work of the managerial class in the US, all while allowing them to simulate an emotional experience of solidarity with the South American poor. Through a reflexive and uncritical capitulation to the latest fashions of leftist discourse, liberation theology has sold its birth right for a pot of soup — exchanging the radical material and spiritual change which God in Christ works amongst His people through the violence of love for an ideology which excludes critical voices, segregates peoples based on identity, and celebrates vengeance for past wrongs.

I would contend then that the opposition which has arisen from many conservative Christians today towards liberation theology concerns primarily the way in which it has been mobilized within our particular ideological and political context, and not necessarily the theological ideas which are inherent to the discourse itself. As liberation theology has begun to simply baptize capitalism's never-ending quest to liberate every desire which spontaneously springs from the human heart, it has lost the authentic practice of a Spirit-filled freedom which made it so threatening to the powers of this world in the contexts in which it originally arose.

At its heart, any liberation theology must take the words of Scripture seriously when it talks about God's special care that He has for the poor, the humble, and the oppressed. What liberation theologians call the "preferential option for the poor" leaps off the pages of Scripture if only we are able to read whilst resisting the temptation to hastily explain what certain passages must *really* mean, as opposed to allowing ourselves to encounter what they really do *say*. The vision of justice which we find in a plain reading of the Old Testament's histories, psalms, or prophecies is uncomfortable to us a moderns, wedded as we are to democracy and liberalism — Yahweh's justice *takes sides*, identifying with the one who's cause is being brought against the powers that be, and advocating most especially for those who are most vulnerable. This is no blind lady justice who listens impartially to the renter and the landlord alike.

Yahweh is deaf to the oppressor, but he hears the cries of the oppressed. He draws near to those who are humble or lowly of spirit, whereas Scripture says that he regards the haughty from a long way off. He does not regard the sacrifice of the wicked at all, instead challenging them to reform their way of life, especially in how they treat the poor, the widow, and the orphan. God's spokesmen in the Old Testament, the Prophets, act like attorneys bringing God's case not only against all of Israel, but often specifically against Israel's leadership. While even the poor are complicit in the wickedness and idolatry which ultimately brings judgment upon the nation, Yahweh reserves his harshest words for those who enjoy positions of leadership amongst the people. Their failure is the most grievous of all, and serves only to magnify the suffering of those who dependent upon them for protection and provision.

Since it's their job to lead the people in the statutes of Yahweh, it's a much greater evil when they err, for they lead the whole people astray.

We could heap up examples here, but the central story of the entire Old Testament speaks volumes about the theme of liberation — the Exodus, the origin story of the Israelites, encapsulates both for Jews and for Christians the heart of God as liberator of the oppressed. Yahweh hears the cries of His people who groan under the immense burden of their futile labor and the genocidal violence perpetrated against them. In the book of Exodus, the reader learns how Yahweh sets the Israelites free from the Egyptians who treated them like a slave population to be used up building monuments to the king's ego, to be killed and harmed without consequence, and to be controlled through the brutal practice of infanticide. Yahweh is moved by the tears of His people suffering under these conditions, and He involved Himself in the messy affairs of history to bring about a new way of life founded in the law code which He then promulgated from Sinai.

The life of Jesus taps into the same themes of the Exodus as well — when Jesus ascends the mountain to deliver a new law (his famous Sermon on the Mount), surrounded by his twelve disciples (twelve tribes of Israel), he begins to speak with an authority which shocks his listeners — "you have heard it said, but I say to you..." Law and liberation are intimately connected in Scripture, because freedom is not the throwing off of the Law, but rather a radicalization of the Law whereby its precepts become internalized through the spontaneous practice of love. St. Matthew's image of Jesus promulgating a new law from the mountain hearkens back to this image of Yahweh who, having set the Israelites free from slavery, gives them a new law which will set them apart from the other nations by orienting their community towards justice, mercy, and righteousness.

As the new lawgiver who leads his people into a new exodus, Jesus also clearly identifies in a special way with the poor and the oppressed, just as Yahweh does in the Old Testament. From a plain reading of the Gospels, we can see that Christ relates to the rich and powerful, such as Zacchaeus, in a different way than he does to the lepers and to the blind. He is no less loving, but there is a nuance we can detect in how he chooses to operate in relation to them. He forces himself upon Zacchaeus, inviting himself over to Zacchaeus' house, he seeks signs of repentance from Zacchaeus, The repentance which Zacchaeus offers to Jesus is a costly one — giving half of all his possessions to the poor — which provides authentic evidence of a genuine change of heart.

We observe this same pattern in Jesus' response to the rich young man who approaches him asking how he can attain eternal life (Mark 10:17-27). The young man claims to have kept the whole of the law, but Jesus immediately cuts to the heart of the matter — he commands this rich young man to give away everything he has and to follow him. The text says that the young man went away sorrowful "for he owned much wealth." Jesus then takes this opportunity to decry to his disciples just how difficult an obstacle wealth poses to those who would enter into heaven or follow after God. "It is easier for a camel to go through the eye of a needle than for a rich person to enter the kingdom of God," warns Jesus (Do we really take these words seriously enough today, we who live in such lavish abundance?).

However, in contrast to Zacchaeus and the rich young man, Christ asks for nothing in return from the poor, the sick, and the needy whom he encounters in his travels — sometimes he seeks a confession of faith, and sometimes not even that much! In the case of the lame man who is lowered through the ceiling, Christ heals him on account of *his friends' faith*, raising up the man without any evidence of his possessing faith of his own. In the story of the ten lepers who were healed, although only one leper returned to thank him, Jesus did not for that reason withhold his act of mercy to all ten. Jesus heals the woman with an issue of blood simply by her touching his robe in a crowd, indicating that Jesus heals the needy so instinctively that he at times is not even aware of what he is doing. The contrast should not be lost on us, and it should lead us to consider why Christ welcomes the downtrodden with open arms whereas he acts aloof with the rich. He uses sharp words to provoke the powerful, but he mercifully binds up the needy and the weak.

This is how much Christ identifies with those who are suffering under the yoke of the powers of this world — his heart moves almost on its own. The wretched of the earth are his reward, the ones he purchased with his own life. He shepherds these ones instinctually, whereas the rich he confronts, calling them to follow him while simultaneously provoking them by demanding a costly sacrifice and pointing out the immense barriers they face in following him. Since their complicity with the dark spiritual powers at work in the world are of a higher degree and different sort, he necessarily relates to them differently than he does those who groan under their oppression. The poor are Jesus' people, for he also lived an itinerant life dependent upon the kindness of others, he was reviled and hated by the elites, and he died naked on a cross — the shameful death of a criminal who was despised by all.

Christ becomes the lowest in the *fumi-e*

Shusaku Endo desperately wants us to glimpse this shocking truth about the heart of Christ in *Silence*. As Rodriguez stands before the *fumi-e*, torn apart about whether to step or not, staring at the visage of Christ cast in worn bronze, he hears a voice — "It's okay." The

Japanese phrasing here — *ii yo* — is tender and permissive, almost feminine.[1] "Go ahead." The voice *invites* Rodriguez to step.

The identity of this voice is one of the great ambiguities of the novel, the wheel around which so much of the novel's interpretation must turn. What is this voice, and where does it come from? Is it the voice of resignation and self-justification or is it the tender voice of Christ finally breaking through to his thrashing child Rodriguez? Endo does not seem to know with any certainty, for living with the ambiguity is itself a pivotal part of the Christian life, but in this voice I believe that Endo hears an echo of the beating heart of Jesus who came into this world to become the lowest of the low. In His incarnation, God became so low that no one could be lower than Him, thereby depriving even the lowest sinner of the excuse not to come to Him, for when we stare into the abyss to find our rock-bottom, Christ is already waiting there at our lowest point.

The image of the *fumi-e* is so poignant and fertile in this sense, for Christ was born among us precisely in order to serve as a *fumi-e*, the image of God to be trampled upon for our salvation. He knew this was his mission. As he insisted to his disciples on many occasions, it was *necessary* for him to be killed in order to accomplish the task which his Father had given him. He needed to unite himself with us — the lowest of the low — so that he might raise us up to God. God came to earth seeking the wicked, the wretched, even the apostate, so that He might love them and call them His treasure.

Can we definitively say whether or not having faith in God is a stepping on the *fumi-e*? Every time we sin, do we not step on the

---

1. I attribute this insight to my Japanese literature teacher, Dr. Miho Nonaka at Wheaton College (IL).

fumi-e? In our acts of evil, we dishonor the very image of God, be it in the face of the other or even in our own bodies. And every time we ask for forgiveness, are we not also stepping on the face of the crucified Christ who paid the price for our forgiveness? When we bring our sin to the foot of the broken Christ on the cross, are we not adding another intolerable weight to the already infinite burden of the world's sin which he shouldered on that dark day? Daily we are stepping on Christ, and daily he accepts our foot, just as Rodriguez describes how the *fumi-e* feels so worn, almost as if inviting his foot as he presses into it. In this pressing, Rodriguez also feels the groove of the countless feet of other sinners who have stepped, connecting him to every other desperate and needy recipient of grace who has preceded him in this act of betrayal.

Siding with the contradiction

Rodriguez recounts in his letters how he continually returns in his mind to the face of Jesus Christ, bleeding and suffering with the crown of thorns pressed into his temples. — "I am always fascinated by the face of Christ, as a man is fascinated by the face of his beloved."[2] Just as Rodriguez too was dumbfounded by who God is in Jesus Christ, so too we are also confronted by this brutal contradiction — the God who chose to die. The crown which the King of universe wears is a crown of thorns. What are we to make of this complete reversal which upends all our prior conceptions of... well, everything?

That God is the highest by becoming the lowest cannot be incidental to the message which Jesus proclaimed. St. Paul's theological

---

2. *Silence*, 21.

speculations take the en-flesh-ment of God as the starting point for understanding God, not as something incidental to the God which can be arrived at already through abstract metaphysical speculation. There dwells in God a movement of desire to be *with* us which we never could have expected or foreseen, much less could we have believed the lengths to which He would be driven to go for our sake. This descent of God entails a corresponding loss or an emptying — God is not *unaffected* by this downward transit. His humiliation on the cross is not a sorry tale to be rushed through so we can get to the good part, for we see even in St. John's visions in Revelation that this conquering King, the Lamb of God, even bears the wounds of the cross in His *resurrected* body. Just as St. Thomas experienced by putting his finger into the wounds of the resurrected Son of God, we too may come to see that all the contradictions we experience as finite beings have been enfolded into God's person as well.

If God's humiliation has become his glory, with what other glory shall we also be clothed? Is a servant greater than their master? I am persuaded then that the call of the disciple leads them deeper into the contradictions of existence. In walking this path, the disciple follows in the footsteps of their Lord. Rather than cravenly pursuing a relaxation that comes with the release of life tension's or longing for the almighty thud of some final answer to arrive, the disciple follows the stations of God and His cross as He travels into those wounds and conflicts which structure the nature of our selves, our communities, and our world.

By making Himself the lowest for our sake, Christ rejected both the self-assured identity of the Jews on the one hand and the imperialistic ideology of the Romans on the other, thus decisively demonstrating a gesture whereby one can refuse the options given to them, and to instead choose the third, hidden option — to expose the contradiction which founds the entire state of affairs within which one finds themselves. Having exposed that which is repressed and reviled, we press into it to see what may emerge on the other side. In this way, we become like God.

Christ as the contingent third term

One way to categorize philosophies is whether they admit the existence of true contradictions or not. Is a contradiction only something apparent or can true contradictions exist? Can a contradiction be *true?* I take the incarnation to be just one such true contradiction. God becomes man, the crucified God, the resurrected human, the community of love... at every moment in the story of Scripture we are confronted by a powerful contradiction which pushes the narrative forward. Those who hear the news are at first stupefied and in awe, but at once they come to understand that if this contradiction is *true,* then there is no way that they can stay the *same.* The women who discover the empty tomb run to the apostles, and Peter and John race each other to the tomb to witness it with their own eyes. They need to see the true contradiction for themselves, for everything hinges on the power of the contradiction of the highest God who made Himself low in Jesus Christ.

When we ask whether or how contradictions might be true, we must be clear that we are not talking about a paradox. Contradiction and paradox are subtly but importantly different. A paradox posits that something which does not appear to make sense nonetheless possesses a resolution at a conceptual or metaphysical level higher than our current understanding, whereas a dialectics which works with contradiction maintains that no reconciliation between the two terms of the contradiction is possible — the only path forward is the introduction of a new or third element into the field such that the prior contradiction is overcome through an intensification of the contradiction. This new and higher division re-founds and re-orders the totality in which the contradiction appears, thus fundamentally changing the nature of a state of affairs.

A highly productive exploration of this conceptual conflict confronts the reader in *The Monstrosity of Christ*, a book in which Slavoj Žižek and John Milbank debate the path forward after the much-heralded collapse of secular reason in light of the failures and anomalies which defined the 20th century. As they try to mark out a post-secular way, the difference between contradiction and paradox comes to the fore as a key dividing line in their thinking. Žižek advances Hegel's dialectic of contradiction as the true path through Christianity, to fully realize the revolutionary core of Christianity which we have been exploring here in this chapter's exposition of a theology of freedom. Despite remaining an atheist and a Marxist, Žižek staunchly advocates for the West's fundamentally Christian project of fighting for universal human emancipation. He presents Judaism as a monotheism still haunted by other gods (pure particularity), and Islam as a monotheism of pure universal abstraction (the universal without any particular embodiment), and presents Christianity as the dialectical synthesis which surpasses the two through the event of the incarnation of the universal God as the particular man Jesus Christ.[3]

Milbank follows in the footsteps of St. Augustine and St. Thomas, opposing himself to Zizek's dialectic by advancing an interpretation of paradox which he believes functions at the core of the Christian logic. He emphasizes that Christianity commits itself to a logic of partici-

---

3. Slavoj Žižek and John Milbank, *The Monstrosity of Christ* (Cambridge, MA: The MIT Press, 2009), 87.

pation which relies on 'mediation.' The creature can participate in the life of God through God's mediatory self-giving in the elements of the Sacrament, with Christ as the pinnacle and source of this sacramental participation. For Milbank, the Christian doesn't need to believe that God simply is the man Jesus Christ, rather God became the man Jesus Christ without becoming any less God. In the logic of mediation then, the vast difference between God and His creatures does not prevent real communion and participation from taking place, even if the *what* of this participation remains ineffable.

Milbank contends that Christianity lost this logic of mediation by accepting the nominalist and voluntarist philosophy of Scotus and Occam, ultimately giving us every type of Protestantism (except Anglicanism, apparently?). Scotus' nominalism and Occam's voluntarism renders the cosmos closed off from God and "disenchanted," which makes the paradoxical mediation of God in the creaturely elements utterly implausible. We can't ignore though that Zizek also embraces the logic of mediation, but simply puts forward a different theory of its operation. He introduces a third term into the process of mediation, speaking of a 'vanishing mediator' which instantiates the gap that separates the two terms in the equation. The existence of this void requires that a monstrous particular third term appear in order to function as the true universal. The difference between the two terms constitutes the essence of the two terms. This third term simply is the embodiment of the void that lies at the heart of the universal itself. Only the particular which is expelled from the totality sustained by the paradoxical opposition of the two terms can function as the essence of the whole.

Hence the way the title of the book highlights the *Monstrosity* of Christ, for Zizek contends that Christ plays the role of this monstrous exception who represents the void that separates the two terms God and man. This means that Christ in himself is exactly nothing at all. He is pure contingency, pure void, pure doubt, pure loss, and thus represents the void at the heart of even God Himself. There is no higher synthesis of God and man, but rather a revelation of the mutual coincidence of these two contradictory terms at the site of a visceral nothingness.

Milbank differs from Žižek in that he sees no need for this third term in the Christian notion of participation; the mediation simply is the relationship between the two terms whereby each participates in the other. The Christian simply eats and drinks the Eucharist which *is* the body and blood of Christ directly, no mediation necessary. How this is possible remains unexplained, but an explanation is assumed to exist in the mind of God. However, Žižek's method radically opposes the theoretical approach of participaation on the grounds of the effect which it has on thinking and emancipation. He points out how this paradoxical thinking operates similar to ideology in that it tells the thinker to disbelieve the reality of the contradiction, believe an authority figure's claim, and trust that a higher synthesis exists. In this way, paradox covers over the work of synthesis which is already underway. The assumption of an ineffable higher reconciliation of the two terms cedes that synthetic labor to the powerful who prescribe which terms get to exist in a paradoxical relation to each other. However, it's precisely by taking the contradiction at its face and pushing it to its limit that one finds a powerful engine for new, productive, and liberating thinking.

Paradox asphyxiates this generative power of thinking which can engage contradiction to forge a new synthesis which intervenes in the current state of affairs. In opposing it, Žižek isn't advancing a childish objection to authority as such, but rather a precise psychoanalytic insight about the relationship between thinking, action, and metaphysics. This unseen reconciliation in the mind of God which the paradox supposedly testifies to does not exist in the case of contradiction, but the void which crystalizes this lack of understanding catalyzes a dialectical labor which will, once it has run its course, produce the higher synthesis which was believed to have existed in the first place. Basically, our belief that the synthesis exists is precisely what tricks us into doing the synthetic work which will retroactively make it true that there was a synthesis.[4] Žižek wants us not to lose this movement by falling into the facile formulations of Milbank which posit this reconciliation as pre-given and pre-existent, albeit inaccessible. Being inaccessible, these syntheses cannot be verified, and thus the powerful can say about them whatever they will. The one who believes in paradox needs simply to obey and trust, whereas the one who practices dialectics cultivates a relationship to inconsistencies, gaps, and contradictions which open them to new questions, problems, and concepts.

With Žižek, we confess that the cross of Christ, the death of the crucified God, confronts us with the most excessive contradiction which could be imagined. If we posit a higher reconciliation of this contradiction though, one which somehow rationalizes how God didn't *actually* die or that God didn't *actually* doubt ("it was only in his human nature!") we divest ourselves of the incredible potency of God's incarnational act in His becoming-human. To play on a famous line from St. Athanasius, if we don't go all the way with God's becoming-human then we will inadvertently short circuit the full potential

---

4. For a clearer and more succinct explanation of this concept ("retroactivity"), see my piece "How to change the past" https://www.samsara.clinic/how-to-change-the-past/

of humanity's becoming-God.[5] For Žižek, Christ's death on the cross is what sets humanity free in the sense that not only does Jesus die, but also the transcendent God of the Beyond also dies with him. Thus, we are cast out into existence without a metaphysical guarantor for our actions, forcing us instead to risk ourselves in attempting to achieve a freer society without having the psychological fallback that God will do it for us. Only dialectics can enable us to think in this way, whereas paradox would smother this generative movement by telling us that we don't need to understand how God can become man, and that we should just accept that there is an answer which we are simply unable to think. Instead, we should trust authorities and obey power.

The scapegoat

In his usual provocative way, Žižek calls this third rejected element the "excremental remainder," for this despised object is what remains after the teeth of the universal-particular dyad has worked over the Real, spitting out the leftover which could not be properly metabolized into the conceptual schema. Much like a stool test to analyze gut health, this excremental remainder contains within it the marks of the dialectical labor and the traces of the system's internal dysfunction. In this way, it serves as an invaluable diagnostic artifact.

To engage with the excremental remainder which embodies the antagonism grounding the relationship between the universal and particular in thought puts one into direct confrontation with all parties

---

5. St. Athanasius' dictum that "God became man in order that man might become God" provides an early and radical articulation of the salvation held out in the Gospel message.

involved in society, for one must oppose both those who arrogate to themselves the semblance of universality ("objective truth") and those who reject universality altogether in order to immerse themselves in some particular (Inoue's rejection of Rodriguez's claims to truth). If one rejects both sides, where should they turn? The refusal of both terms in the universal-particular dyad is to side with the scapegoat, that material and conceptual element which through its ejection enables the two terms in the universal-particular dyad to mutually constitute one another.

We spoke of Rene Girard earlier, in chapter two, but we return again here to his concept of the scapegoat. The scapegoat provides us with a visceral image of this metaphysical movement whereby a false universal appears through the rejection of a disturbing element which can find no place in the new schema. This false universal appears universal because it is a particular which has attempted to become an all-encompassing concept through an ejection of its contradictions. The only way then that this particular can become universal is through relating itself to another particular and rejecting the contradictions which arise in relation to this other particular. Thus, Žižek's metaphysical schema posits two opposed elements — a universal-particular dyad on one side and the contradiction which constitutes the dyad on the other, or, in Girardian terms, the particular community and its universal myth over and against the scapegoat. The choice which freedom offers is the ability to choose the contradiction, the scapegoat, instead of a retreat into the fantasy world of the universal-particular dyad which exists only through a denial of the scapegoat's sacrifice.

Girard connects the scapegoat with Christ as well, and builds an entire theory of atonement from his literary and anthropological analysis of the function of the scapegoat. Jesus Christ exposes the powers of the world by becoming the perfect scapegoat — perfect in at least two senses, namely, that he embodies everything which is a threat to the powers of this world, but also that he is perfect in his conduct and lifestyle. This last element ultimately serves to unveil the machinations of power. The hypocrisy of ideology is revealed in the fact that no crime can be pinned on Jesus Christ, for even Pontius Pilate who sentences him publicly proclaims that he can "find no fault in this man." Thus, Jesus willingly becomes the rejected element in order to unmask the scapegoating mechanism which produces false totalities, enslaving human communities in ideologies which foreclose the practice of God's freedom.

In this way, Christianity more than any other religion chooses to side with the contradiction, for this contradiction functions as the very heart of its historical message and spiritual power. God is a criminal, a scapegoat, and because of this his people themselves are drawn to the site of the contradiction which society turns its eyes away from. This is why the Tokugawa Shogunate could say that Christians worship the condemned. Jürgen Moltmann speaks of this as an "internal homelessness,"[6] although we should radicalize this statement to say that the internal homelessness witnesses to a concrete homelessness — the Kingdom of God is always arriving. This is the logic of "the last days" or "the end times" in which every time is the end times, for the

---

6. Jürgen Moltmann, *The Crucified God* (Minneapolis, MN: Fortress Press, 1993), 10. Moltmann identifies this inner homelessness as a characteristic which the Christian faith shares with the political Left. This book's thesis entails that this inner homelessness of the Leftist emancipatory project possesses deep roots in the work of Christ and early Christianity, and that this ought not to be lost or forfeited.

kingdom of Man is always coming to an end and the Kingdom of God is always arriving. Christians are not simply un-attached therefore, but rather differently attached, and this attachment to God-in-Christ is what makes them unable to occupy a clear space in human society.

Conclusion

What then is freedom? Freedom is the power of love to work with contradiction so as to bring about an intervention which changes the course of events, but with the modification that, in Christianity, this freedom exists *from* the other (God gives this freedom to us as a gift) and and *for* the other (our freedom is not for our own sake, but for the good of others). This interdependence and other-orientation means that freedom also inextricably includes *alienation*. Žižek captures this so well when he describes the highest experience of freedom as the point where liberty and necessity coincide — in the moment of freedom, we cannot *not* be free. We find ourselves with a duty to be free, and we cannot act otherwise than to be free. Counterintuitively then, Žižek helps us see that the reality of freedom is actually freedom coming to actualization *through* us![7] In freedom, we lose ourselves in order that something else can intervene in our circumstances.

But how to do this in an anti-ideological mode which does not succumb to a mysticism of total immersion in the whole? The counter-argument could be raised that what we have just described here — the dual experience of necessity in freedom and freedom in necessity — could also describe the experience of ideology. Does not

---

7. Slavoj Žižek, *Freedom: A Disease without Cure* (London: Bloomsbury, 2023), 8-9.

ideology function such that it becomes the spontaneous standpoint for seeing and acting for the self which has been constituted through an ideology's fundamental fantasy? This is why we must retain the concrete commitment to the scapegoat. Ideology covers over contradiction, reducing it to a mere paradox or simply denying it altogether. The self which comes to exist through the operation of ideology aims to reduce its cognitive dissonance and to assimilate itself to the dominant lifestyle of the group. The one who chooses to love the scapegoat exposes the emptiness of the community's founding myths which it has spun to keep itself in ideological slumber.

Jesus produced a powerful litmus test when he insisted that "you will know them by their fruit. Do men gather grapes from thornbushes or figs from thistles?" (Matthew 7:16), and later he re-iterates this in a different way, saying, "By this everyone will know that you are my disciples, if you love one another." (John 13:35). Judgment may be cast on the basis of fruits, that is, actions and results, not simply the intentions of the heart or the private fictions of the mind. The Pharisees imagined themselves just according to their analytical interpretation of the Law, but the affect of their work was to place an immense burden upon God's people to earn the love which was always already theirs by right.

The Christian experience of freedom then distinguishes itself from this ideological experience of spontaneity by its material and structural effects. The Spirit community which is practicing the freedom of God sides with the contradiction through its commitment to the scapegoat, that rejected and contradictory element in the social body, and thereby it works to achieve a freer and more beautiful communion through attempting to find an answer which supersedes and overcomes this contradiction. The only way this can be done is by a thorough prac-

tice of the highest contradiction at the center of the Christ event —
God-become-man, the dying God, the dead God alive.

We can see how Fr. Rodriguez experiences this visceral burden
throughout *Silence* as he grapples with his responsibility to love and
care for the vulnerable Christians who he realizes are utterly precious
in the sight of God. He intercedes on their behalf with God, and he
is torn apart by their sufferings. In his desire to serve them as Christ
would, he pushes himself to the limits of his courage and spiritual
capacity. He is also forced to die to himself as he continually receives
Kichijiro back to confession, thereby coming to a deeper understanding of the heart of God through these cycles of sin and reconciliation.
The wretched Kichijiro, haunted by traumatic visions of his family
being burned alive and tortured by his own cowardice which he enacts
again and again, confronts us with the brutal difficulty of working
out our freedom both for ourselves and in communion with others.
Rodriguez truly grapples with this problem of God's special love for
the despised and the rejected, how they constitute a core part of who
He is and the message which followers of Christ carry with them into
all the world.

However, I have also come to believe that Rodriguez betrays this
message by turning away from the contradiction. In stepping on the
fumi-e, he betrays the scapegoats of Japanese society — the Japanese-Christians — and sides with power, accepting the regime's ideological framing and conforming himself to their cruel demands. In
becoming complicit with their cold and calculated social control,
Rodriguez looks on as the scapegoat is slaughtered, thus lending his
tacit support to the communal fiction which this murder serves to
establish. Against what the practice of Christian freedom demands,
Rodriguez flees the site of the contradiction to find solace in an interior and ineffectual faith. He forgets that Christ does not demand

sincerity, but rather a costly sacrifice. Christianity is not a religion of authenticity, but something far more terrifying — becoming a vessel in which God's freedom becomes concrete in the world through love.

6

RODRIGUEZ CHOOSES WESTERN BUDDHISM

Introduction

What do the experiences of a Portuguese-Catholic priest in 17th century Japan have to do with being a modern person who lives within the global neo-liberal capitalist order? Quite a lot, in fact, as I argue in this chapter. Not only do we confront some of the same core conflicts in ourselves which we see in Rodriguez, but Rodriguez is also an inescapably modern subject. From his psychological formation in the Jesuit spiritual exercises[1] to his entanglement with the colonial agendas of European kingdoms, he lives on the cusp of modern world which inhabit today in which the individual is emerging as the primary site of meaning-making and total sovereignty, even

---

1. Michel Foucault spoke of the techniques of Christianity, such as confession and absolution, as the precursors of the techniques of the modern state, such as in the realm of law, medicine, and governance. He called them the exercise of "pastoral power."

as the world itself becomes increasingly interconnected economically, politically, and culturally.

However, another reason stands out— Endo, the book's author, was a unique positioned individual whose struggling with the personal and collective conflicts of his times are written all over the pages of his novel. Endo was born during Japan's rush to industrialization and its push for military expansion, and then came of age during the transition to a Western-style capitalist and democratic order overseen by the American military. He also immersed himself in French culture during his studies at the University of Lyon in the early 50's. As a member of a minority religious group in Japan, Endo understood more than most what it was like to feel that they did not fit in where they found themselves.

I take these things to indicate that the contradictions and struggles which Endo confronts through his writing have a special purchase on us today as subjects who also live under the liberal democratic order and the regime of global capital in which we find every form of concrete attachment being dissolved into thin air. What does it take to reconcile the experience of being a free subject with our seemingly contradictory everyday experience of immersion in the immediate particular relations which seem to compose our world? In this chapter, we will turn to consider the way that Rodriguez attempts to resolve the dilemma in which he finds himself. We will interrogate his decision to step on the *fumi-e*, but we will do so as we also ask how Rodriguez's experiences encapsulate so many of the temptations and conflicts which define our own experience as modern human beings.

We will characterize the subjective stance which Rodriguez takes up vis-a-vis power as one of "Western Buddhism," a critical label which Slavoj Žižek has used on a number of occasions to describe a peculiar temptation of the modern subject to an act of withdrawal in our interiority in a pursuit of authenticity, wholeness, and identity. This notion of 'Western Buddhism" contrasts with a form of engaged political action which prioritizes structural and material changes, solidarity and collective emancipation, and which has a universalizing bent which seeks to overcome old divisions. In this way, the 'Western Buddhist' orientation betrays the mission and proclamation of Jesus as we outlined in the previous chapter — the good news of God's salvation in Christ liberates us collectively and individually by the way that God identifies with the lowest and the excluded, thus radically transforming us and our world. In the end, Rodriguez fails to side with the contradiction in the situation in which he finds himself, instead choosing to sacrifice the Japanese-Christians in order to obtain some inner ineffectual faith which he harbors until his death.

The enlightened cynicism of the Western Buddhist

Diogenes, the first Cynic

This tendency which we observe towards a Western Buddhism can also be described as a general reign of cynicism. In fact, we might characterize the fundamental orientation today of the modern Western person as that of "a universal, diffuse cynicism."[2] Cynic-ism comes from the Greek word *kynikos*, meaning 'dog-like,' and was aptly used to describe the mythical father of this movement (which is totally not a movement, man) — Diogenes of Sinope. We have none of his writings,

---

2. Peter Sloterdijk, *Critique of Cynical Reason* (Minneapolis, MN: University of Minnesota Press, 1988), 3.

but we do have a few apocryphal anecdotes about him which might explain the 'dog' moniker which his teachings eventually garnered. Diogenes was said to have slept outside in the marketplace, having only a large piece of pottery as his shelter, and was notorious for being aggressively anti-social. He seems to have primarily taught his philosophy through public demonstration, such as by walking around in the daytime with a lantern, claiming that he was "looking for a man." Legend says that he would also attend Socrates' lectures, but made himself a distraction by bringing food and drink to loudly consume.

The byword which defined him and his followers the most — and which seemed most dog-like to observers — was their shamelessness. They did not care what anyone thought about their actions. They would eat food wherever they were, and would even masturbate in public. They would sleep outside, and they showed no honor to dead bodies. Diogenes praised the dog for its shamelessness in doing what it pleased without hypocrisy or dissimulation, as well as its clear intuition who for who its friends and enemies were — treating friends with boundless affection, but giving no time or attention to its enemies, simply barking at them until they leave.

In some crucial ways, Diogenes serves as a prophetic fore-runner of modernity. Not only did he rigorously apply the corrosive acid of radical individualism to everything he did, but he also first coined for himself the term "cosmo-politan" — a citizen of the world, not simply of Greece or Athens. In this phrase *cosmopolitan*, Diogenes swore off any national or familial attachments, inaugurating the modern subject's flight from any form of attachment. In an ironic twist of fate, as legend would have it, this cosmo-politan Diogenes was enslaved by pirates and shipped off to a foreign land where he died. Although, true to form, we have no indication that Diogenes ever felt perturbed by this turn of events.

This Diogenes of Sinope, this father of Cynicism and practitioner of shamelessness, certainly dared to think a form of the universality with which we are grappling in this book — the power to abstract one's self from their context to ask whether this state of affairs was good or true or beautiful. His lifestyle springs from the in-eliminable experience of stepping back to say, "yes, that's all well and good, but what am *I* to do?" The sense that your conscience addresses you with the voice of the gods, calling you to account, demanding that you don't look away. The life of Diogenes testifies for us how the universal subject experiences this point of decision where givens cannot simply be givens — there are no excuses that "I was just following orders" or "I couldn't help it; it was natural." In response to Kant's injunction that you must do your duty, Žižek adds that you cannot escape the responsibility to choose what is your duty.

However, against the world-less-ness of the contemporary cosmo-politan person who attempts to achieve universality through ceaseless abstraction, does not the cynicism of Diogenes, in maintaining the distinction between friend and foe, still retain some notion of the attachments which would appear to be repudiated in this modern subjective stance of cynicism which distances itself from all the particulars of its circumstances? Diogenes' cosmopolitanism at least retains its loyalty to friends and disdain for its foes, which seems to indicate that universality does not eliminate attachments so much as it can obscure which ones we truly have. The modern cynic is certainly the same in this respect — they have exchanged one set of loyalties for another.

Modern cynicism and the attachment to the ego

Attachment has by no means disappeared among us modern people — human beings seek attachment instinctually. Our lives literally depend on connection with others. We can see this drive for attachment even in the infant's desperate attempts to connect with their caretaker.[3] It must be the case that the one who thinks themselves unattached from family, ethics, nation, or place has not actually become un-attached, but rather must have performed this abstraction by attaching themselves to a *different* object. The only way to be free is to possess an attachment — a love! — which supersedes the particulars of one's circumstances, for only in this relativization of all other phenomena do we create enough distance such that we can gain a universal perspective.

Slavoj Žižek describes this as the introduction of a new and higher division in reality, and he argues that it's precisely the introduction of a higher division which creates new unities, not the elimination of divisions.[4] Žižek uses this concept to describe the genius of St. Paul's theology, for Žižek argues, that St. Paul united the Jew and the Gentile through creating a higher division, that of the divide between 'in Christ' and 'not in Christ.' This new line cuts across all the old divisions, forcing everyone to pick new sides, and relativizing all the conflicts which had appeared so pressing up to that point. In light of

---

3. Harry Harlow conducted some famous experiments with baby Rhesus monkeys which seem to demonstrate that mammals seek connection even more than they do sustenance. For more about Harlow's experiments, see https://www.samsara.clinic/harry-harlow-baby-monkeys-experiments/

4. Slavoj Žižek, *The Puppet and the Dwarf* (Cambridge, MA: The MIT Press, 2003), 108.

the new division between being in Christ or not, the Jew and Gentile distinction is not so much abolished as radically transformed in its meaning whilst also being significantly downgraded in its intensity. I originally considered calling this book "A Higher Division" because this gesture of introducing a new division into the contested social field viscerally describes how the universal subject emerges and intervenes in their context.

What then has the modern cynic raised to level of supreme attachment? What division does the cynic rely upon to constitute themselves in our age? The *ego* serves today for the cynical modern subject as the highest object of worship and the dividing line which slices up their world into 'me' and 'not-me.' The ego or self is what the atomized individual carries with them everywhere they go, and it provides the binding thread for all of the modern person's experiences. This object, which we can pick up like a suitcase when we want to move on from a situation, travels with us in every particular state of affairs, allowing us to remain abstracted from our circumstances through our attachment to this particular cluster of images which we take to be ourselves.

The French psychoanalyst Jacques Lacan emphasized in his work how the ego is an *object* to which we have become attached. It's crucial to remember that you are not a self. Your self is not you. The ego is an object in your mind, almost like an avatar in a video game. In order to cope with the chaos of infantile experience, Lacan contends, each of us mistakes an *image* of ourselves as *being* ourselves. This is the meaning of Lacan's famous "mirror stage" of infantile development in which the child sees an image of themselves in the mirror, hears mommy or daddy coo and point "look, that's you, dear," and in that moment comes to perform a mental operation where they *identify* with an image.

The infant's body is wracked by wave after wave of drives and unsettling experiences which leave us unmoored in our own bodies, and consequently the infant must cling to the mother to provide the physical and emotional regulation it cannot create for itself. Early on, the child is entirely dependent on another, unable to control the powerful urges which well up in their body, and also completely helpless when it comes to the basics of getting food, passing gas, or cleaning themselves. In order to overcome this state of intense helplessness, the child must find a way to lend themselves some coherence, and this happens through "ego formation," which is the process that Lacan describes in which we become attached to a mental image of the object which we take ourselves to be.

We can see how efficacious this achievement is for the infant, for in replacing the dynamic assemblage of the body with a clearly defined object the child attains a level of ideal unity which allows them to venture away from the mother and into the world, but we must also notice how this operation involves a corresponding loss. They have reduced themselves, in some sense, from a process to an object. Although they have become an object unto themselves, they have thereby joined the rest of the objects in the world, and with this minimal level of cognitive leverage the child can begin to wander away from the safe harbor of the mother-child dyad in order to discover their world. This object attachment to the ego thus serves an important function early on in the child's development.

Cynicism has its roots in this self-objectifying process of ego formation. Because it involves a process of making of one-self an object, it inherently produces a pacifying effect in the human. We are enthralled by an image, rendered immobile by a narcissistic fixation. The egoic individual may posture as rebellious because they assert their identity, but the cynic can easily continue going through the motions of compliance with any outward forms imposed upon them. All the while, the cynic withholds a part of themselves, that precious core of the ego. Some inner sanctuary of the cynic is cordoned off, and this hidden jewel in the depth of their interiority is prized as the "true self." The cynic is an idealist at heart, seeking a level of purity which can only be attained in the realm of fantasy — they imagine an un-stained core to their being, and this they worship. Everything else be damned.

The cynic believes that they can maintain their purity of heart and freedom of spirit by retreating so deep into themselves that their actions and surroundings could never penetrate to the core of who they really are. This can be an effective survival method for modern workers who finds themselves locked in the iron cage of capitalism — commuting, paying bills, working mindlessly, sitting in traffic, bombarded by advertisements, swimming in garish images and inane chatter. One feels that they must grow an exoskeleton to keep the world at bay, just to preserve some shred of sanity.

However, for this reason cynicism also poses no threat to the powerful or their power. Elites and their autocratic systems welcome the cynics with open arms. Cynics are, after all, excellent workers. They make fine accountants, psychiatrists, salesmen, and managers. As long as they are allowed to enjoy their private interior prize, and as long as they are supplied with their outward needs to keep them comfortable enough, they will not bite back. They do not have the teeth or the zeal to bite the hand which feeds them, for they have decided to satisfy themselves with a spiritual bread which their soul consumes alone in its private chamber.

The cynical operation of ideology today

Perhaps the foregoing account of cynicism explains the recent proliferation of a variety of "Pop Stoicisms" — Stoicism had some of its
roots in the thought and practice of Diogenes of Sinope (which we
can trace by one particular lineage from Diogenes to Crates to Zeno
of Citium). Recently, Stoicism has become cool again. With writers
like Ryan Holiday putting out books like *The Ego is the Enemy* and
The Obstacle is the Way, or with music artists like Akira the Don
releasing electronic remixes of readings of Marcus Aurelius' *Medita-
tions,* Stoicism has emerged as an integral part of the contemporary
West's dominant culture of self-optimization, especially in the world
of technology where business and spirituality intersect in surprising
ways.

In some ways, Stoicism represents a Western re-fraction of Buddhism, sharing many theoretical and practical crossovers. The Stoic,
just like the Buddhist, locates the source of suffering in the mind.
The world is a fire — an unending flux of change — and we stand
in the midst of that fire. Indeed, we *are* the fire, as one cannot draw
an ultimate distinction between self and world. For the Stoic, the
greatness of the human is the ability to take this rational stance which
steps back from the body's passions and constant churning, and to be
able to take the perspective of the rational soul of the universe which
does not concern itself with the demands of desire. It sees them for the
illusions they are, and in this way becomes free to live without fear or
anxiety.

Slavoj Žižek has described how ideology in our modern context
increasingly functions more like a fetish than a symptom[5] , and that
Stoicism and Buddhism in the West today much more resemble a

---

5. Slavoj Žižek, *Freedom,* 145.

fetish that we cling to in order to obscure for ourselves the true operation of our oppression. Whereas ideology used to be described in symptomatic terms where ideologies were said to "repress" certain truths and that these repressed truths returned in oblique ways as symptoms, today, Žižek notes, ideology operates much more openly. The ideological superstructure of society protects itself by its very openness, taking the form of an "open secret" which loses nothing by its being noticed, thus avoiding the return of the repressed which plagued older forms of ideology.

The concept of a fetish, before it took on its contemporary reference to a sexual obsession with a particular object or body part, developed from anthropological work done by Europeans amongst African cultures where the researchers found people making and revering objects which they took to possess magical powers. Psychoanalytic interpretations of this anthropological finding have argued that the object — the fetish — serves to embody within the physical world a certain conflict or gap in the imagined world of the community. A political antagonism is externalized from the community, and the fetish comes to cover over this gap, and thereby cinches the entire unstable system together. But this only works if the function of the fetish is never acknowledged.

Žižek argues that today the open acknowledgement of how the fetish works has ingeniously come to function as the exact way in which the fetish's function is covered over. "I know that I'm just a cog in a machine working day in and day out for money to pay bills, but..." The frank acknowledgement of the reality is precisely what facilitates passing over this reality, as well as justifying our failure to do anything about it. One professes to believe that they are trapped in a losing game, but their actions continue on as though they do really believe that they can win a modest victory.

This also alerts us to the dangers of the "confessional" nature of so much speech today. The one who confesses seeks absolution, and thus we find ourselves in a society where we compete with each other to confess the cruelty and unfreedom of our lives, to confess the pluriform manifestations of our brokenness, but all this escalation of confessions serves as a temporary salve to the existential guilt which we experience for delivering ourselves over to such an inhuman way of life. The confessional or "tell-all" mood of our society's discourse today testifies to its fundamentally religious nature, and the conflicted spiritual experiences which accompany life within our current material conditions.

This cynical attitude of the modern subject which clings to the fetish of transparent self-knowledge about their oppression serves today as what Žižek calls "Western Buddhism."[6] While Stoicism tends to appeal to a more masculine and right-wing political class, and Buddhism in the West first flourished amongst the hippies who later became Boomer Democrats, both of these philosophical standpoints re-package the same internal maneuver which we have been describing to this point — the retreat from material experience into an internal split from which we can observe ourselves as not truly *involved* in our circumstances.

The tech-bro can breath and quote Marcus Aurelius or he can sit and meditate, but it doesn't ultimately make a difference to the forces which shape our world. In the same way, the Boomer Democrat can post a 'Black Lives Matter' sign on the lawn of their million dollar home in a neighborhood where no black people live. This Western Buddhism which Žižek warns us against is a symptom which speaks

---

6. Žižek, *The Puppet and the Dwarf*, 26.

to a deeper dysfunction in our society, and these practices exemplify the panoply of personal habits which we use to ameliorate the on-going suffering of meaningless work, lack of social connection, and the extreme precarity we experience at the hands of a chaotic and interconnected global society.

Friedrich Nietzsche described Buddhism as a system of hygiene for people who were highly sensitive to pain , but who were spiritually mature enough to no longer seek a supernatural explanation for their pain.[7] Unlike in Christianity where the realization that 'I suffer' immediately demanded that I identify a malevolent cause or perpetrator which exists "out there" which is responsible for my suffering, the Buddhist turns instead to a regime of diet and lifestyle to ameliorate their suffering. Both are regimes of decadence, Nietzsche contends, and by this he means that they are the maneuvers of an exhausted and sick people who are attempting to manage their own physical and spiritual decline rather than living into an increase of vital life energy which leads to increasing mastery over one's self and one's environment.

Nietzsche's diagnosis of exhaustion also feels especially prescient today for those of us living under the capitalist regime of self-exploitation and infinite optimization. The German-Korean philosopher Byung-chul Han talks about ours as a "burnout society" which is afflicted by physical and mental illnesses which testify to the reflexive and self-imposed nature of our oppression today[8] — from

---

7. Friedrich Nietzsche, *The Antichrist*, quoted at https://www.sto neageherbalist.com/p/nietzsche-on-buddhism-a-system-of

8. See Han's *The Burnout Society* for more on this, especially the first chapter.

auto-immune disorders and cancer to depression and anxiety, these maladies all seem to involve an overactivity of particular bodily systems which produce dysfunction by overshooting the target of their optimal function. These are symptoms of decadence, a general decline in the ability of organisms to metabolize adversity into beneficial adaptations and overcoming. Instead, maladaptations begin to proliferate and propagate themselves in the population, leading to overall lower levels of heartiness and an increase of stressed hyperactivity in all bodily systems.

Peter Sloterdijk in his *Critique of Cynical Reason* characterizes the emergence of cynicism as an essentially urban phenomenon which is intimately connected the bourgeois class and the social types which flourish in cities.[9] This is a funny observation, because while Sloterdijk doesn't note this, Diogenes was not originally from Athens — his family was exiled from Sinope under the accusation of debasing the currency, for his father was the mintmaster in charge of the currency in the city.[10] We might see Diogenes then as something of a rebellious trust fund kid who has turned against his father's professional managerial lifestyle. If nothing else, this young philosopher came from a family of white collar criminals who were dependent upon the political economy of the city.

It's no wonder then that Stoicism and Buddhism have become the preferred religious orientation of the chattering classes, and that yoga, meditation, and running have become the *askesis* of choice for our society's elite. We also cannot pass over the proliferation of psy-

---

9. Sloterdijk, 4-5.

10. See Internet Encyclopedia of Philosophy: https://iep.utm.edu/diogenes-of-sinope/

chotherapy as the dominant therapeutic practice in our society, an expensive and high-status treatment which makes appeals to scientific knowledge as it assures supplicants of its power to restore order to their psyche. All these ideological operations ensnare us deeper in the web of the biopolitical state's infinitely expanding apparatus of care and capitalism's never-ending pursuit of profit and economic growth. Increasingly we are turning inward to find a meaning which surpasses our material circumstances, all with the hope that perhaps we alone can be saved from the catastrophe which is to come (and in whose birth pangs we now live).

Rodriguez chooses Western Buddhism

Two camps of interpretation

A poor fishing village nestled in the coastal crags of southern Kyushu may seem infinitely far away from our modern lives, but they are closer than we might presume. I hope that over the course of this work that I've been able to communicate a sense of how many of the changes that we are undergoing today were making their ways into Japan in a similar fashion at precisely the moment when Endo sets his story. As the Tokugawa regime was bringing sweeping social and political changes, family networks were being filed down, the Japanese people were being objectified as information on a government ledger, they were made to be complicit in their own governance by spying on one another (a proto-social networking app perhaps?), and class structures were becoming increasingly rigid and stratified. If you add on top of this that the people were exhausted from centuries of warfare, suddenly we are not so far apart from their experience as we might have presumed.

Clearly the account I have given here is factually accurate while somewhat cheeky, for I have emphasized the similarities between these situations even though we are aware that profound differences nonetheless still exist. While I don't want to invalidate my own account by completely disfiguring the truth, I have taken these creative liberties to help the reader begin to see how especially unique these moments in Japanese history truly were, and how this period of intense change and struggle offers surprisingly relevant insights for our own period of global tumult. Fr. Rodriguez is a Portuguese Jesuit who dies in 17th century Edo, but in many ways the dilemmas with which he wrestles appear in our experience today, especially for those who shares Rodriguez's faith in Jesus Christ.

However, not only are Rodriguez's conflicts similar to our own, so are his temptations and failures. Lest we forget, this book attempts to build a case that Rodriguez decisively *fails* in his fidelity to the message of liberation in Jesus Christ. In stepping on the *fumi-e*, he betrays the Japanese-Christians who are the despised and rejected remainder which the Tokugawa regime would sacrifice for the sake of forging a new social unity under the aegis of nation, sovereignty, and violence. This view falls into one of the basically two camps of thinking I see concerning Fr. Rodriguez and his actions — one camp argues that Rodriguez failed in his calling as a disciple of Jesus by stepping on the *fumi-e*, whereas the other camp sees his stepping on the *fumi-e* as a paradoxical act of faith. Should we understand Rodriguez's decision as a radically counter-intuitive but nonetheless faithful response to the dilemma in which he found himself, or do we maintain that he made the wrong choice by stepping? It is to this question that we will turn for the remainder of the chapter.

A paradoxical act of faith

I did not always think the way that I do now about Rodriguez's decision. At one point in time, I had embarked on fleshing out an argument for the second position, namely, that Rodriguez's choice to step on the *fumi-e* embodied a profound spiritual insight about God, Christ, and the world. In the fall of 2018, I received the green light for a paper proposal which I had submitted to a Christianity and Literature conference. In that paper I sought to argue that Rodriguez's stepping on the *fumi-e* testified to his realization of the emptiness of the big Other (God) and God's entrance into our pain by his Son Jesus Christ. In the proceeding section, I want to elaborate a little bit of this interpretation which relies on the work of Slavoj Žižek's "Christian atheism." However, I also complement this perspective with Makoto Fujimura's interpretation as given in his essay "The Redemption of Fr. Rodriguez" in *Silence and Beauty,* as I believe that the two paint an even more compelling picture together.

Makoto Fujimura, a Christian artist and cultural theorist, has gained some notoriety for his public engagement with Endo's *Silence* as a part of his own work to encourage Christians towards a more beautiful wrestling with faith and culture through the practice of art. I've drawn on Fujimura's ideas throughout this book so far, but here is where I turn to a critique of Fujimura's reading of *Silence* — I take Fujimura to be advocating for the second approach which I have outlined above, namely, that Rodriguez's stepping on the *fumi-e* confronts the reader with an act of faith in which Rodriguez surrenders to God's long work of breaking down Rodriguez's pride, arrogance, and unforgiving heart. "By stepping on the fumi-e, Rodriguez inverts into his genuine faith, not faith dependent on his religious status or his own merit, but a faith in grace —"[11] Rodriguez must relinquish his grandiose visions of obedience to God in his image of his own martyrdom, and must instead cling to God in faith through an experience of being reduced to total illegibility. In surrendering these things to God, Rodriguez is finally able to enter into the traumatic core of the Japanese experience.

The *fumi-e* plays a central role in Fujimura's interpretation, for, as we looked at in the final section of chapter 2, Fujimura also argues that the *fumi-e* presents in visceral form the very shape of Japanese subjectivity and the trauma which operates at its core. The Japanese person has been expected to step on their deepest held loves and convictions for the sake of a "mere formality." For centuries every Japanese person has had to hide themselves in order to live.[12] The fear of rejection and the violence of conformity possess such a powerful grip that the Japanese person's subjectivity takes on the shape of this daily stepping on the *fumi-e* in their heart, Fujimura contends. He focuses on the role that bullying (*ijime*) plays in Japanese society, such that the outward violence of the collective in its ostracism of the person becomes internalized and auto-reinforcing such that individual steps on their personal *fumi-e* routinely and instinctively.[13]

In Fujimura's interpretation then, Rodriguez's stepping on the *fumi-e* becomes an entrance into the reality of this trauma at the heart of the Japanese person and Japanese society as a whole. To experience the pain of denying the God he worships, and to secretly tend this

---

11. Fujimura, 147.

12. Ibid., 146.

13. Ibid., 125.

precious faith in his heart while outwardly denying it for the rest of his days, in this profoundly humiliating experience Rodriguez truly steps into what it means to live as a Japanese person. He turns his back on the zeal of his youthful and idealistic spirit, and instead traverses the traumatic gap which leads into the dirty mess of living in the world where we are complicit in all manner of betrayals. As he live out his days amongst the Japanese people in Edo, Rodriguez takes up the position of a silent witness to Jesus Christ.

As Fujimura's interpretation implies, this dilemma has an ethnic dimension to it as well. Can not Rodriguez's stepping on the *fumi-e* also embody a relinquishing of his colonial mindset as a European Christian who comes to the backward Japanese people to enlighten them with God's truth? What if Rodriguez is apostatizing from a self-assured and compromised Christianity to a humble and servant-like Christianity which knows not yet what it will become? He makes himself the unknown and disgraced representative of Christ amongst the Japanese people in Edo, just as Christ himself was reviled and mis-recognized by the people to whom he came. Rodriguez enters into a cruciform mode of living which forges the path forward for the process of enculturation — the expression of the Christian truth in new cultures and situations.

We have two elements here then — (1) a surrender of the racist/colonial mindset which arrogates itself above the Japanese people and (2) an entrance into the Japanese consciousness through the experience of a profound trauma in which one betrays what is most precious. But what are the implications for this traumatic surrender when we consider it from a theological perspective? Does this have any ramifications for how we understand God?

We can read this story of Rodriguez's apostasy in a theological way by inflecting it through contemporary psychoanalysis. What if in stepping on the *fumi-e*, Rodriguez recognizes and affirms God's fellowship with us in pain? In the midst of this seemingly senseless violence against Japanese-Christians and the utter failure of the Christian mission in Japan, Rodriguez comes to understand that God also lacks, that is, that God also enters into our pain and suffering as creatures, and that by stepping on the *fumi-e* Rodriguez includes doubt, pain, and lack within even God's own person. The Christ which the reader encounters with Rodriguez in the *fumi-e* presents a God who does not remain far off from the filth of existence, but rather He is found precisely in the moment where the contradictions are heightened to the uttermost.

This last interpretation is especially interesting, for as the philosopher and psychoanalytic theorist Slavoj Žižek frequently points out in his own comments on his "Christian atheism," Christianity holds the odd title of remaining the only religion where God doubted Himself. On the cross, the God-man Jesus Christ cries, "My God, my God, why have you forsaken me?" and in this we get the first glimpse of a true atheism. This need not be an atheism in which God does not exist, but rather God *as we thought we understood Him* does not exist — where we thought there was a fullness of presence and total effulgence of Being, we find instead a lack or a void which opens onto the horizon of a continual process of dialectical becoming. However, this process of becoming does not culminate in some grandiose Whole, but rather finds itself embodied in the brutalized body of a man, Jesus Christ — the rejected, the disgraced, and the suffering. Such an atheism seeks not so much to foster disbelief, for such a conception would remain captured by the idea of whatever God or gods is being rejected, but rather, Žižek contends, we see in Jesus' cry the split within even God Himself. The space which Christianity opens up then allows us to begin to wonder if everything we had thought about God to this point has been wrong, and by extension, how we can re-think the world in light of this stunning revelation.

We are transformed by this encounter, but as we are already starting to sense, God cannot come away unscathed either. We cannot escape the implication that God, in His choice to create, *became* God. No language, no consciousness, no Other — God prior to creation cannot be called God in any sense. What's more is that God seems to agree with this thesis, for we can glimpse in His decision to create a testimony to His desire to, as Karl Barth says, not be God without us. In creating, God entered into the journey of becoming God-with-us, and He released Himself into the pain, suffering, and labor of working with negativity, difference, and otherness to forge a better and higher synthesis in partnership with the world He created. We see the essence of this decision in the face of the dying Christ, the portal through which God entered into the experience of suffering, thereby entering into the ultimate communion with us who are lowly and frail by nature.

Rodriguez chooses Western Buddhism

What the *fumi-e* obscures

These interpretations, both individually and together, are fascinating possibilities which tantalize us with all their generative difficulty. I personally find myself drawn back to them again and again, for they seem to hold an immense power for thinking. Like a tempest, I find myself whisked away. The reader may feel the same or differently, but I do not think that the draw of this family of interpretations can be denied. In their confrontation with Rodriguez's physical and spiritual journey, the reader does sense that perhaps Rodriguez manages to access a different spiritual consciousness which can often remain obscured by the facile notion of the exoteric practice of a religion of rule-following.

Martin Scorsese himself would seem to fall into this same interpretive field in which one tries to see how Rodriguez discovers a new dimension of the practice of faith and who challenges us to wrestle with these same ambiguities for ourselves. I don't think that it's a coincidence that Martin Scorsese's two great religious films are "The Last Temptation of Christ" and "Silence."[14] Interestingly enough, Scorsese has said that it was on a flight to Japan immediately following the premiere of "The Last Temptation of Christ" that he first determined to shoot "Silence."[15] In the first film, Scorsese presents us with a Jesus dragged down into the muck of his humanity, depicting him as feeble, tempted, and unsure of himself, ultimately even flirting with the idea failing at his God-given mission by succumbing to the fear of death and a lust for sexual relations with a wife. "Silence" seems to rehearse a very similar theme, of a man plagued by the sense of the meaninglessness of suffering and tempted to choose "the easy way

---

14. In January 2024, Scorsese announced that he would be shooting a film about Jesus, basing the script off Shusaku Endo's "A Life of Jesus," a short account of Jesus' life which Endo penned to "make Jesus understandable in terms of the religious psychology of my non-Christian countrymen and thus to demonstrate that Jesus is not alien to their religious sensibilities." https://thefilmstage.com/martin-scorsese-to-adapt-shusaku-endos-a-life-of-jesus-this-year/

15. Fujimura, 162.

out" by renouncing the faith in this suffering God. Both grapple with this theme of God's absence and silence within suffering, and both portray faith as a highly personal affair wracked by guilt, doubt, and ambiguity.

Martin Scorsese himself is uncomfortably included in his own work[16] (just as Endo appears in his own novel). Scorsese presents a strange type, for while he continues to publicly identify as a Catholic who professes the teachings of the Church, yet he has divorced four different wives over the course of his life and has spent his career shooting films which primarily depict conflicted individuals performing acts of evil and cruelty in a dark world. Many Christians have also accused Scorsese of blasphemy in portraying Jesus, not only in daring to portray him at all, but in shooting a film in which Jesus is depicting engaging in sin. In his creative and artistic practice, Scorsese confronts us with a series of seeming contradictions and provocations.

We get a glimpse into Scorsese's own self-conception, I think, in the last scene and the final frames of the film adaptation of *Silence*. This scene is Scorsese's own addition, for it does not appear in Endo's novel. At the end of "Silence," we watch the man Okamoto San'emon (ex-Fr. Rodriguez) dead from old age, being carried through the streets of Edo in a funeral procession lead by a Buddhist monk. However, before his body is enclosed in the barrel in which it will be ritually burned, Scorsese shows us Rodriguez's wife slipping something into his dead hands. As the barrel containing Rodriguez's body burns in the final frames of the movie, the camera zooms inside the barrel to

---

16. Scorsese has said that he will appear in his upcoming film about Jesus which adapts Endo's "A Life of Jesus."

reveal a small and crudely hand-carved crucifix clutched tightly in the hands of Rodriguez's burning corpse. Here, the movie ends.

This scene stages for us the precise image of the modern cynical subject which we have been investigating in this chapter — the regime collaborator who outwardly complies with the suppression of Christians in Japan has nonetheless secretly retained the faith in his heart, crystalized into this crude object which he clutches in his dead hands. This barely legible crucifix embodies both the ego and the void which serves as its center, the impossible core around which all the self-images coalesce to form the fantasy with which the Western Buddhist identifies to bring them meaning, structure, and coherence. The camera now, like the gaze of the big Other, sees and acknowledges the hidden core of who Rodriguez truly is, registering his identity with the viewers who confirm its reality through their visual witness.

What is obscured in this excessive emphasis on the psychological state of Rodriguez? These interpretations which place the drama of the narrative in the mind of Rodriguez, do they not use the Japanese-Christians' persecution and the horror of the *fumi-e* as a stage for playing out Rodriguez's singular antagonisms and personal development? The contention of this book is not that these interpretations have *no* value at all, for certainly we have already seen how tempting they are, but rather that they should be *de*-prioritized and relativized in relation to a *structural* reading of Rodriguez and his situation. Is it not precisely that this psychological drama obscures what is *really* going on?

We modern folk excessively idolize the world of interiority, which we take to be the realm of authenticity, meaning-making, and even truth. We easily fall prey to hermeneutical theories which contend that the meaning of words is derived primarily from the speaker's mental act of *intending*. In both our everyday discourse and our legal discourse we also perpetuate theories which interpret the significance of a person's actions primarily through their *intention* about what those actions mean. These principles seem inviolable to us. "She didn't mean to." "He was insane." "They didn't know what they were doing." "I was only following orders." Our modern theory of mind attributes an absolute creative force to the person's power of intention, up to even positing today that one can be a different person, gender, or thing on the basis of this internal movement of the will.

Against this modern tendency to understand meaning primarily through human intention, the interpretation I have been trying to advance in this book challenges us to see how meaning operates through the relations of non-human objects (signs) and their material networks (structure). Rodriguez does not get to determine for himself what stepping on the *fumi-e* means, for the *fumi-e* and the act of stepping derive their meaning from the larger structure of cultural signs and political structures in which it is situated and in which it finds its role. The *fumi-e* as a sign possesses its reality and its significance from within a material network of other objects in which it stands.

Thus, regardless of which side one falls on in the debate about whether Rodriguez should have stepped or not, to place Rodriguez's experience as the primary meaning-making operation in the novel commits an important mistake — in this move, the *fumi-e* is radically de-contextualized and de-materialized. Fujimura's move from the historical *fumi-e* to the immaterial *fumi-e* of the heart is highly illuminating, for it mirrors the modern move which retreats from the objectivity of the world's structure into the phantasmic world of interiority. The *fumi-e* in its materiality confronts us, but the sharp edges and resistances of reality recede into a distant roar through the mystical maneuver of re-narrativizing the self and re-making the world through our own eyes. The futility and impotence we experience in the face of the inhuman forces of reality tempt us to run to the highly malleable world of interiority which bends much more readily to our whim.

The *fumi-e* as a physical object exists as a node in a broader material network of meanings and practices, all of which exist as a totality of meanings determined by their use and social location. While these meanings are certainly being contested in Endo's novel, for the Japanese-Christians have labored to negotiate their own relationship with the *fumi-e* in a way which differs from the aims of the Tokugawa regime and its Buddhist inquisitors, this does not make it such that Rodriguez's act of stepping can be abstracted from the totality in which he acts. In his stepping, Rodriguez *gives* Inoue something, regardless of his personal interpretation of the meaning. Far and beyond any sort of meaning which Rodriguez experiences, the structures in which he acts determine the meaning and the reality of what he gives Inoue — the apostasy which Inoue needs to break up and destroy the Japanese-Christian church.

A betrayal of God's people

We must risk appearing brutish in our stupidity — as we see Rodriguez in the act of apostatizing, we stare and blink and stupidly point out that a man is stepping on a picture of Jesus. *What* is happening? As he hears the sound of Japanese-Christians enduring unspeakable torture, Rodriguez is instructed by the apostate Ferreira to join him in apostasy by stepping on the image of Christ. We can picture the entire prison compound as an apostasy-producing machine, for all the events which have lead up to this moment have been carefully crafted by Inoue to manufacture apostate priests who will collaborate with the Tokugawa regime in exchange for the cessation of the violent persecution of the Japanese-Christians. The regime creates suffering by committing violence, and then they extract apostasy from priests by dangling the promise of solving the very problem which they themselves created in the first place. Priests, duped by compassion, think they are courageously trading their souls for the lives of their parishioners.

However, at every turn the Japanese-Christians remain the despised, the rejected, and the abandoned. We turned our attention in the previous chapter to a consideration of how Jesus Christ in his message of freedom identifies with the lowest. This figure of the lowest has a concrete manifestation in the pockmarked face of the poor, but this concrete manifestation also typifies a more general structure, which is that of the remainder which must be excluded in the process of forging a Unity or a Whole. The scapegoats are the ones who are hung over the pit, made to groan in Rodriguez's ears, and whose private tortured dramas provide the background to Rodriguez's spiritual experience. Whose groaning sets the context for our own internal conflicts? On whom do we tread as we supposedly forge new spiritual paths?

Endo does a masterful job of portraying the complex relationship which Rodriguez experience towards the Japanese-Christians. He finds himself in utter awe of their faith, in despair about their situation, full of pity at their miserable existence, and horrified by the torture which they must endure. The figure of Mokichi who is martyred by being battered endlessly by the sea early in Rodriguez's time in Japan typifies the resolute faith and Christian hope to which Rodriguez so desperately aspires. Mokichi is a humble person who simply believes. There is nothing dramatic or showy about him. He merely steps forward when the moment calls for it, and he follows through with his decision once he has made it.

However, I find myself wondering in bafflement at why Rodriguez never asks the Japanese-Christians whether *they* want him to apostatize or not. I'm confident that the answer would be NO. The Christians in the prison know that they could make it all end by simply stepping on the *fumi-e* and walking away, just like Kichijiro did countless times, but they continue resolutely, never complaining. They are hung in the pit for hours, and they endure because of their faithful spirit. Doesn't Rodriguez disgrace their resolute persistence when he steps on the *fumi-e* to make it all go away? Doesn't he hasten to a decision? To fix and solve it, rather than to watch and struggle? The Japanese-Christians have decided that they will endure whatever it takes to remain faithful to their confession, and Rodriguez would take that away from them? If he had asked any one of his parishioners, even as they themselves hung in the pit, none of them would ever counsel him to apostatize. It would be unthinkable.

The hardest thing about disagreeing with Rodriguez's decision is the question which inevitably ricochets back — "okay then, what would *you* do?" Sitting with that question, wavering, and being unable to answer... this is the labor which we must undertake. It's painful and deeply uncomfortable. I don't presume to have the answers to any of this, but my instincts are screaming at me that we have to listen to the Japanese-Christians, not Rodriguez. We have to watch Mokichi, listen to the kind words of Monica, and sit with the tortured struggles of Kichijiro. The Japanese-Christians have already been working on this problem! This is their life, this is their people, and this is their future. In his haste to make the problem go away, Rodriguez betrayed the people most precious in the sight of God, and in the process, he foreclosed the answer which they were trying to arrive at.

According to the official ideology of the time, the Christians were the impurity which had to be eradicated for the sake of the group. Where then would we expect Christ to be at work? Where would we expect to find the subterranean labor which eats like a worm through the foundations of a society's ancient wounds and dysfunctions? Like sheep lead to the slaughter, they walked in the footsteps of their Lord. Who are we to say what they might have discovered? Who are we to cut short the wrestling of those Christians who came to believe on Christ in an alien land so far away from the dust of Palestine?

Of this I am convinced — we are *profoundly* impoverished as the Christian Church because an authentically Japanese Christianity was smothered in its cradle. I consider it a punishment from God for our great wickedness as pompous colonizers, internecine squabblers, and greedy merchants who stained and abused the message of freedom which Jesus entrusted to us to share with others. What an abject failure, what an utter loss! I bow my head in shame and *weep*.

This then is Rodriguez's failure. Rodriguez succumbs to the ideology of the times, rationalizes his complicity in the regime's oppression, and betrays the Japanese-Christians who are Christ's treasure and the site where his freedom is struggling to be born in the world. The psychological experience of profound spiritual insight covers over our participation in material networks of oppression, all while we are ensnared in our imagined identities and fictional communities. Even more importantly though, we can cast judgment on the veracity of Rodriguez's insight because we can see and evaluate what things these supposed insights worked in him — what was his fruit? How can we take Rodriguez seriously when he seems to have grasped the heart of God and yet has missed the very people who have captured God's heart? How can the one who has plumbed the depth of God's grace turn around and become an agent of oppression? Has such a one known grace at all?

Conclusion

Just like Rodriguez, we also find ourselves awash in an ocean of guilt. We are already complicit in the suffering of others, for to live is to be impure. Other things must die so that we might live, our mothers give birth to us in travail, we breath air that was meant for someone else, and daily our desires confront the others in our lives, complicating and confounding existence with our every move. Not only this, but we find ourselves situated in an economic state of affairs where we must prey upon one another for our most basic needs. If you're an owner, you subsist from the surplus-value produced by your laborers. If you're a manager, your boss enriches himself from your labor while you take a cut of the labor of your subordinates. As a laborer, you must sell your labor to another in order to receive a fraction of its value in return, and then you must take those proceeds to the store to purchase goods and services from others. We see people going through the repetitive and soul-crushing motions of work stocking shelves, swiping items, and wiping floors, all while becoming the regular target of abuse from customers and from each other. Not to mention the thousands of other jobs we never see — the mother wearing a headset while being screamed at by an angry customer on a support line, the old man manually typing data into a spreadsheet over and over, and the mindless shuffling of papers and emails which provide the silent backdrop for our entire society.

What we would give to simply make it go away. What we would do to not carry this burden. But our society's brutality is thrown in our face whenever we walk by a homeless person ranting in the street or the exhausted nurse standing alone at the bus stop. The rich can pay to take a detour around such sights — taxi, Uber, private jet, helicopter, high-rise apartment, you name it — but we of lesser means must wade in the squalor everyday. It wears on you, to step onto the public train and immediately be hit with the smell of warm piss. Just like last week. And the week before that. You can't avoid it when society's dysfunction is strewn all over the place with nowhere to go and nowhere to hide. We must not underestimate how much this experience profoundly warps us as people. Eventually, we start to feel like it might be our fault.

Compassion is the most dangerous emotion we can experience today. What an awful thing to think, but I see no way to avoid this realization. As we victimize and are victimized, like crabs clawing at each other in a bucket, we begin to think that something, anything must be done. The itch becomes so bad that we absolutely have to scratch it. But can one person change the world? These structural problems can't be solved through internal tinkering and small adjustments, even where those possible (the tiniest of changes are now becoming Herculean). There is a saying which goes "the purpose of a system is what it does" — instead of saying that a system is designed to achieve an objective which is constantly fails at, perhaps we ought to understand systems as doing precisely what they are engineered to do? If we find ourselves in a system which seems to exacerbate mental anguish and dysfunction, broken families, misery, depression, meaningless work, drug and alcohol abuse, and suicide... well, what do we think the system is really *for*? Perhaps it has already told us.

Orwell's image of a boot stamping on a human face forever comes to mind here as we stare into the abyss of the absolutely colossal mess we've put ourselves in, and it seems like this massively multi-player slow-motion catastrophe has taken on a life of its own — no human or even group of humans can stop this machine anymore. In such a profoundly dark situation what could be more tempting than to apostatize? At any moment we can choose to walk away from the faith which believes that somehow God is at work bringing His kingdom into *this* world. What sort of a God would want to enter *this* world?

It's easier to step on the *fumi-e*, become a collaborator, and console ourselves with the private meaning-making mechanism of our choice — I give to charity, I meditate, I just like to fish, I go on mission trips, I read philosophy, I go to raves, I take LSD, and so on and so forth. Never mind the groaning of the others. They've probably apostatized already too, right? Best to get it over with, and try to mitigate the suffering as much as we can.

Making the suffering go away... that's always what it's about, isn't it? When you strip it all away, we're all dealing with suffering here. Buddhism has as its core a technique for release from suffering. Christianity has as its core God's redemption of our suffering through His own suffering. Transhumanism prophecies an end of suffering through the limitless ingenuity of human technological advancement. Capitalism holds out the elimination of want through a perpetual abundance machine. The State promises an end of suffering through the continual provision of care and security. At bottom, we're all secretly hoping that we can get back to the Womb, where we didn't need or want for anything, perfectly submerged in warmth, bliss, and comfort. But because we traversed those few inches through our mother's birth canal, emerging into a cold hospital room under a bright line, now we've been thrown into the terror of existence against our will. How can we just make the suffering stop? Why not just step on the *fumi-e*?

The first step in spiritual life is refusing to make the suffering stop. Without the joy to confront suffering and the love to resist the temptation to foreclose the Other's suffering too, we will never get anywhere. The drive to eliminate suffering will devour us if we give ourselves over to it. As long as we continue to opt out of the struggle by instead stepping on the *fumi-e*, we miss out on something vital which makes us the strangest animals on God's green earth. Today we must choose to press into the contradiction. What could we find further up and further in?

7

— · —

Conclusion

Speaking to our time

No piece of writing can be divorced from its time, although it can certainly be abstracted such that it speaks beyond its context. This book focuses on Endo's novel *Silence*, a work which possesses the vitality to challenge and speak afresh to every age. However, we would be remiss if we did not ask ourselves what new conversations or avenues for thought this book could open for us in the present. This is a fitting task for a conclusion.

I think it's inevitable to some extent that working with a text to help it speak to our moment will inexorably date our work in some way. Fads come and go; conversations shift and change. The discourse moves on. We run the risk of finding our writing riddled with the detritus of the crowd's chattering, but I don't see a way to completely avoid this without falling into a cowardly abdication which pulls away precisely at the moment when it must speak. That's why in this conclusion I speak directly about conversations that are happening our moment, but I bring them up with the aim of connecting them to larger problems which continually plague human individuals and their communities across time, space, and culture.

This book came from somewhere — it has a context. While I don't know what context you're necessarily bringing to this text, this conclusion serves to share some of my own context which inevitably shapes the words I have written here. This book, with its admittedly odd mixture of historical data, psychoanalytic theory, and theological speculation, provides an insight into who I am, how I think, and my orientation to my present circumstances. The marks of my idiosyncrasies are all over it.

In this concluding section then, I'd like to clearly articulate the problem I had in mind as I wrote this book, a problem to which I believe the insights and challenges of Endo's book address themselves even today — the question of nationalisms in general, but also the renewal of a Christian nationalism in the United States in particular. In this, we also return to the ancient question of how the universal relates to the particular, how the individual should live in community, and what it means to live as a creature in a world which we did not make.

The return of a multi-polar world

We live in an age where opposites seem to coincide and accelerate at a dizzying rate — we are witnessing an increasing fragmentation of our world into a milieu where individual nations exert more gravitational pull in their regions, thus reviving an older and more multi-polar arrangement in which different regions act as countervailing powers to check each by building alliances and jockeying for their self-interests. With the military and financial ascension of the United States in the wake of the devastation wrought by WW1 and WW2, the world underwent a dissolution of this multi-polar arrangement, and in its place there arose a universal international order which folks like Woodrow Wilson had envisioned. Organizations like the UN were constructed during this time, NATO sprang into existence to contain Communism, the only serious rival to this nascent universal order, and increasing coordination between state banks and international corporations created trans-national networks of bureaucratic policy-makers and un-elected decision-makers.

Those who found themselves on the "wrong side" of this ascendant order, which emphasized open borders, participation in international financial institutions, and adherence to human rights agreements, were brutally punished through a variety of procedural mechanisms, such as economic sanctions, cultural ostracization, CIA-backed coups, and even up to military invasion. We can think about examples of large actors like the USSR (then later, Russia) and China who had the resources and ambition to develop their own parallel institutions and seek prosperity in the way they saw fit, but there also sprang up a whole global underbelly of smaller nations run by strong-man dictators or military governments, typically heavily dependent on oil or natural resources to maintain their strategic independence. Since these nations were kept out of international markets where they could freely trade in dollars, wire money internationally, or participate in the explosion of (notional) value on the major stock exchanges, they were forced to devise their own solutions to these problems, often banding together or looking to dissident actors like Russia and China for patronage. These actors have always been here, biding their time, observing the mismatch between what the West says and what it does, and slowly cultivating their own way of life.

Now though, they are re-emerging and re-asserting themselves. When the USSR fell in 1991, there remained no serious challenge to the global order of Neo-liberalism and capitalism. However, the decadence and systemic excess which had begun to infect the United States, and which was spreading to other influential political actors, had already started decades earlier. Post-WWII the United States had cemented itself as the global power which guaranteed safe seas with the world's strongest navy, open borders and economic fair play in the realm of financial networks, providing the underlying world currency for facilitating international trade (especially oil), becoming a powerhouse of industrial production and technological innovation, and also producing arts, culture, and theory which was exported to other countries by way of news media, television, and international student visas. However, the presence of this overwhelming power and influence, and the benefits which it bestowed on all who were willing to maintain their proximity to it through participation in the institutions and norms of the global Neo-liberal order, could not last if these material achievements could not be maintained.

While entire books, indeed, entire academic careers could be devoted to even a single one of the causes for this highly complex state of affairs, I think we can clearly see that this global order has been massively undermined by the increasing inability of the United States to deliver on its promises of a free and prosperous world through the twin ideologies of liberal democracy and free market capitalism. Without the industrial base, the culture, the institutions, or the leaders to build and uphold this planetary vision of prosperity, the United States and the international organizations have become corpses which stagger on blindly while they are hollowed out by opportunistic and cynical bureaucrats or gamed by ruthless businessmen and financiers. For the first time in a century, the pie is starting to shrink, and people are starting to angle for the scraps.

We see the symptoms of this institutional decay and strategic failure everywhere — the advance of China's Belt & Road initiative, Russia's invasion of Ukraine, Houthi attacks on cargo ships in the Gulf of Aden and the Red Sea, undeterred violence amongst religious and ethnic groups throughout the world, cyberattacks from Russia and North Korea, India's refusal to participate in sanctions against Russia, and the uncontrolled flood of migrants into Europe and across the southern border of the US. These are only a few of the many political examples, but they all demonstrate an increasing dis-alignment of more countries from any sort of global consensus, a growing boldness of nations to act in the way they believe is most advantageous for themselves and their allies, and a crippling inability to muster any larger coordination efforts to solve large-scale problems.

We thus find ourselves in a seemingly paradoxical state of affairs where the hold which these un-accountable trans-national institutions have on the world is weakening while these institutional continue to escalate their claims of power and moral superiority to greater levels of grandiosity. The World Bank, the World Health Organization, the UN, NATO, even the EU — these organizations are doubling down even as they are losing their grip. As the old order crumbles, bureaucrats pass stricter laws, demand heightened compliance, increase the complexity of their legal codes, and impose harsher social sanctions for non-comformity. Politicians squabble in the public spotlight while unelected program managers and directors quietly develop and implement policy — the machine keeps turning. The police are defunded and recalled, the borders are left undefended, children and adults are drugged at alarming rates, and the average person must learn to fend for themselves, even as they are put at the mercy of the economic shockwaves caused by the fluctuations of arcane financial instruments. We are living in the nexus of millions of overlapping social experiments conducted by the supposed experts who will, in either case, not suffer the consequences of their actions — that will fall to the rest of us.

Power in the West and its allies continues to concentrate into the hands of elite actors who are not tied to any particular country's people, institutions, or interests — they live in New York City, they hold two passports, they vacation in the Alps, their corporation is incorporated in Delaware but the taxes are handled in the Caymans, and they have appointments on the board of nonprofits sprinkled through the world. Even within nations themselves, the policy decisions which shape everyday life are being made increasingly by a class of people who have concentrated in a few large cities, and who have attained certain pieces of paper or social recognition for mastering the theories and techniques which today make universal claims of validity on the basis of scientific method. At every turn, we sense that particularity is being negated. There is a war on the particular, the parochial, the divergent, the invisible. If it cannot be turned into data for monitoring and modeling, then it's a threat to democracy and security everywhere. Difference must be stamped out, and everything must be made perfectly transparent so that it can be seamlessly manipulated to come into greater conformity with the agenda of policymakers, advocates, lobbyists, and academics.

In this world where the hard and social sciences have claimed the right to speak authoritatively on every aspect of human life, and a whole class of people have arrogated to themselves to speak for Science, it's no wonder then that particularity has begun to re-assert itself. In America, at least, people have grown tired of consuming the nationally shared culture which is produced primarily in LA and New York. This "universal" culture, abstract because it could be consumed by people from rural Kansas to the Bronx alike, supplanted local communities, their stories, their particular concerns, and their ways of life, replacing

them with a collage of images at once vivid in technicolor but ultimately empty in their ethical or communal value. From the upwardly mobile family comedy, to the coming-of-age stories involving sex,
drugs, and rebellion, or the tales of society's criminal underbelly in
which the heroes are just as bad as the bad guys, people have begun
to question in earnest the images which have seeped into our minds
through our televisions and computer screens.

This phrase "ways of life" has become a flash-point in contemporary
discourse, with some deriding it as a dog-whistle for Nazism while
others hail it as a sacred concept which should not be violated under
any circumstances. Regardless of how one interprets, the resurgence of
this concept in political discourses in many different countries speaks
to the way that people have felt de-humanized and dis-connected by
the past century's agenda of globalizing trade and financial networks,
centralizing culture and knowledge in urban hubs, and the application
of scientific technique and policy to everything from child-rearing to
farming to our most intimate experiences of mental anguish. Capital's
drive towards abstraction has begun to produce a world in which we
can no longer recognize ourselves. It at once proclaims an infinity of
diversity, but does not contain space for the actual difference which
makes up the full range of human experience.

While this phenomenon is unmistakably moral, I do not think that
it can be reduced to the crass moralism of the televangelist. We must
see how the convergence of abstract modes of thinking and the moral
values of liberalism have produced institutions and social networks
which are fundamentally ineffective at their primary mission of delivering a free and just existence to our communities, and this daily
experience of living under the constant economic and moral demands
of capitalist society whilst navigating an ever-expanding regulating
state has warped us all, both individually and collectively. There is a

lack of physical and spiritual vitality which saps away at our ability to courageously do big things or to boldly experiment with small things. Instead, we find our own desires corralled into the images and fantasies which are produced and circulated throughout our nation by various social networks, media outlets, and products. We've lived so deep in the ideology for so long that, as we've started to rouse from our slumber, we have come to discover that we really are not quite ourselves anymore.

The revival of Christian Nationalism

How did we start to rouse from our ideological slumber? The election of Donald Trump in 2016 was a watershed moment for this awakening, because it represented a concrete act in which many people who felt left behind by American society successfully asserted their will against the judgment of the chattering classes which govern from their media outlets, government agencies, and ivory towers.[1] We must read Trump in all his garishness and bombast as a middle finger which the people gave to the international elite who populate our coastal cities and who fly to and fro on their breathlessly important mission to save democracy. Only retrospectively have many Republican commenta-

---

1. As a personal note, I have never voted in an American presidential election. I find it interesting to understand why people vote the way that they do, because it's symptomatic of what is shifting at the most fundamental levels of our society, but I cannot bring myself to participate in the dog and pony show. Real political power in this country does not reside at the top, but is diffuse throughout the entire governmental apparatus.

tors attempted to construct a coherent policy agenda from Trump's utterances, but he fundamentally represents the people's simmering rage, not a well-thought out plan for effective governance. So far though, our society's elite purveyors of scientific abstraction and vapid liberal anti-values have not really listened too closely to this rage. Since Trump's election, they have focused their energy on pathologizing those who critique or oppose them, steadfastly refusing to wonder whether it might be *they* who are the problem, and not necessarily the rural working class who voted for Trump. The explanation that the yokels are angry because they are racist tickles the heart strings of the liberal too much to relinquish it so easily, especially when the alternative line of thought holds the potential to undermine their upwardly mobile and affluent lifestyle.

However, I think that the Covid pandemic brought much of this fragmentation out into the light, making it hit home personally for many Americans. In particular though, the Covid era generated a new consciousness about the Christian Church's relation to the State — Do we keep churches open or do we close them? Can Christians agree or disagree about whether to get vaccinated? Should Christians in government roles enforce policies they believe are unjust? In what concrete situations should Christians engage in civil disobedience? Other religious communities had to wrestle with similar questions, for these problems inevitably arise in any community which pledges an allegiance to an ethical standard which is higher than the human law of any particular kingdom. The antagonism and struggle which came out of the Christian Church's attempt to navigate the Covid pandemic in America served to renew and radicalize a new discourse of Christian Nationalism, a movement which called for a return to civil disobedience and political action aimed at bringing about a government which is explicitly Christian in its principles, laws, actions, and ceremonial symbols.

I have witnessed and participated in many discussions of Christian nationalism, both online and in-person, especially amongst Christian men from the Anglican, Reformed, and Baptist traditions (broadly Protestant) (there is also a robust discourse of "Catholic integralism" within the Roman Catholic Church, which I will not be touching on, but which is certainly relevant to this conversation). Like many others, I read Stephen Wolfe's book *The Case for Christian National-ism* when it came out, a controversial monograph which functionally breathed new life into a concept which had been previously regarded as outmoded. There are scholars and leaders in the Christian Church right now who believe more than ever we need a robust and pragmatic account of Christian nationalism. There are more of them than we think (not all of them are ready or willing to speak up for fear of the repercussions), but their influence is growing in many circles. Since they are also extremely active and vocal online, their perspective has an out-sized reach, forcing itself into the conversation and re-organizing the coordinates of public discourse.

The idea of Christian nationalism is not new (as its proponents would be quick to point out) — I was educated in a private Christian school where we were made to watch all of Francis Schaeffer's "How shall we then live?" series which put forward what postured itself as a distinctly Christian account of philosophy, art, politics, and Western culture generally. Our Bible teacher (who was also our literature teacher, and chemistry teacher, and theater teacher...) made us read books by obscure Reformed theologians such as R. J. Rushdoony, Cornelius Van Til, Gary North, Gary Demar, and many others who were either Christian Reconstructionists or Theonomy adjacent. This was the air which I breathed as a budding young intellectual trying to understand the world.

Not everyone is familiar with Theonomy or the Christian reconstruction movement, and that's okay. Candidly, you don't need to know all the names from that last paragraph to appreciate the points I want to make in this conclusion. Figures like Rushdoony, Van Til, and Schaeffer emphasized that Christianity necessarily touches every aspect of life — including art, politics, and philosophy. As a comprehensive story about the world, its meaning, and our place in it, Christianity cannot be restricted to one cordoned off area in the interior of a person. In this way, the account I've given in this book resonates with their critique of a purely private religious life. Rodriguez's Western Buddhism and the cynicism of the modern self typify this orientation. Schaeffer talks about how our culture is defined by the idols of "personal peace and affluence," and all these theologians I've mentioned were firmly convinced that any Christianity which brokered a truce with these gods of personal peace and affluence was no Christianity at all.

By no means though was the Theonomy/Christian Reconstruction movement the first theological discourse about the Church and the State (it was simply the most influential one on me) — Christians have been debating the relationship between the Church and state power for as long as the Spirit community has existed. The idea of "the Christian prince" played an important role in political theology during the Reformation, and some notion of a "natural law" which contains the seeds of God's law has been a consistent talking point in various Christian discourses throughout Church history. Christians have frequently called kings and emperors to account throughout history by appealing to God's law, although some have also argued for a more permissive framework which emphasizes a divide between the "sacred" realm of the church and the "secular" realm of politics. This rhetoric of religious toleration emerged especially in the wake of the religious wars in Europe, and it even laid the groundwork for the values of liberal societies today.

While this history is long and complicated, where the Christian Reconstruction movement differed from prior manifestations of Christian Nationalism was its intense commitment to a Biblical literalism. However, this latest return of Christian Nationalism closely coincides with a recovery of natural law theory in Protestant circles. These more recent iterations, as developed by theorists like Wolfe and others, diverges from these older forms of Christian political thought in that the political science of nation building for these new Christian nationalists has become uncoupled from the biblical literalism of the Theonomists. Whereas Gary North would have looked to the case laws in Exodus as a divine blueprint for building a Christian nation, Wolfe looks more readily to concepts such as "the laws of the nations," "natural reason," and the empirical politics of figures like Machiavelli and Schmitt. This would have been anathema to Rushdoony and Van till, but this is the state of play in which we find ourselves today. Natural law is back with a vengeance after being maligned in evangelical circles for decades.

Why is this difference important? Isn't it better that we have people looking to arrive at ethics by reasoned debate rather than through some good old-fashioned Bible thumping? The resurgence of natural law ethics in Christian political discourse also brings with it certain conceptions of what nature is, what is natural, and what human beings are. Since these questions are highly contested, and they carry with them a host of conceptual traps, we have moved from the realm of divine law which makes universal claims transcending human reason (as in the case of the Theonomist who looks to Scripture) to the realm of rationality which justifies itself with respect to the particulars of a certain people, place, or culture (in the case of the natural law theorist). Thus, we find ourselves once again mired in the question of how the particular must be situated in relation to the universal. Rather than a clash between two universals, the theorizing of the Christian nationalist attempts to defer answering this question by instead simply respecting the particulars of specific people groups and their cultures, but in doing so they risk smuggling into politics many cultural assumptions or practices which may be contrary to the message of God in Jesus Christ. The journey of how a people can be themselves under the lordship of Christ must be worked out by the people themselves, and involves a painful struggle of examination, repentance, and change, and this is precisely the process which the Tokugawa regime foreclosed in its ultimate rejection of Christianity in Japan.

The problem of particularity

This problem of "particularity" unites all the phenomena we have been discussing thus far, from the Russia-China alliance to many Christians' resistance to Covid policies. Unfortunately, many on the Left has chosen to frame this problem as one of a revival of fascism, which serves to shut down the conversation before it can be genuinely understood. To even platform a supposed fascist is to commit violence against the protected groups, and thus no dialogue can even get off the ground to discuss questions like immigration policy, Covid school-closures, and much much more. The liberal ideology of abstract universality which animates Capital and the state must characterize any claims of particularity as fascist, regressive, nativist, jingoist, nationalist, xenophobic, racist, the list goes on, because any discussion of concrete difference serves as a threat to a homogenous international order in which those differences must be dissolved.

While the differences of certain protected racial and ethnic classes must be celebrated at the regime's behest, this happens only in so far as they do not threaten the ruling ideology, whereas intractable differences (such as biological differences between men and women) must be erased through a mixture of scientific procedures and institutional policy so as to "liberate" people from the constraints of a recalcitrant reality. Women are liberated from their bodies so that they can become entrepreneurs for Capital, and men are liberated from being men so that they can become women if they so choose. The liberation proclaimed by the clerics of liberalism is thus highly selective, and all the while the actual relations of power and the ruling ideology remain unchanged, now simply appearing with a more colorful cast of characters to staff the legacy institutions.

There are certainly some genuine fascists and some very real racists lurking on 4chan (and yes, even in some churches), but we cede far too much ground to the de-humanizing forces of capitalism when we allow any claims of particularity to be automatically deemed as fascist or racist. This reflexive move carries water for the regime by silencing critics and creating massive blindspots in our theoretical paradigms. When we reduce the plurality of voices in society, we close off the internal mechanism of critique which society needs in order to continually renew itself moment by moment. This is, I think, what free speech absolutists are trying to preserve — they realize that the power to suppress speech is the primary prerequisite to creating and sustaining an ideological thought regime in society, and thus a radical commitment to protecting any and all speech is the only real mechanism for sustaining this possibility of internal critique through the potential irruption of alternative ideas. There are other complications with this position (what do we make of libel or incitement to violence?), but I think that what makes free speech so compelling as a position is precisely the way it maintains society's openness to an Outside which can unsettle its most basic assumptions and rigid structures.

The alternative to free speech which is pushed by the alliance of politicians, scientists, and activists embodies a paternalistic regime of censorship in which we must be protected from ideas which are harmful or dangerous for us, and that we should instead outsource our own thoughts to the individuals and institutions which claim to speak for "the facts" as conceived and analyzed according to the universally valid technique of science. We must simply trust them, no matter what else we might hear to the contrary. But in so doing we reduce ourselves to objects, denying the responsibility which comes with being a subject, and foreclose the possibility of achieving collective emancipation with our own hands. The problem of particularity must be engaged today more than ever, but those who are supposedly the best and the brightest among us have constructed an echo chamber for themselves wherein this problem has already been solved — everyone just has to get on board with their solution, and they will use the state to force anyone who does not comply (for the sake of protecting others, of course).

Both fascism and the ideological uniformity under which we live in the West represent modes of totalitarianism. Both are authoritarian in their own way, and James Burnham's analysis of "managerialism" in his *The Managerial Revolution* is illuminating on this front — both fascism and communism represent different historical attempts of the managers to wrest control of the means of production away from the capitalists. Burnham predicted a shift of power away from the owners of corporations to the managers who actually ran the day to day operations ("personnel is policy"), and that ultimately the managers would re-write the rules to make those who control the means of production more powerful than those who owned the means of production on paper. This can be done through external regulation, but also through internal policy-making and activism within the organizations themselves.

A cursory study of 20th century history reveals that fascism and communism differed only in how they treated the capitalist class after the takeover was complete — did they de-fang them, making them their dogs (fascism), or did they make them disappear into either a gulag or a grave (communism)? In either case, unsurprisingly, the means of production never found their way back into the hands of the workers themselves. Power seems only to have continually accrued to the managers who observe, analyze, and proscribe in accordance with the universal discourse of science, and the world we live in today bears all the marks of being run by managers rather than owners.

You'll notice that I slid from speaking of the reigning ideology to speaking about communism, so I want to simply note that although the liberal capitalist order which we live under today may have defeated the communist USSR, I would still characterize our current arrangement as originating within the stream of communist thought. I'm not here referencing the "cultural marxism" phenomenon pushed by some on the Right, which I think is actually a gross simplification of what is going on, as well as an unsympathetic reading of the valuable social and economic analysis which Marx performs. Rather, I'm arguing that the core Leftist values of the French Revolution — liberty, equality, fraternity — which the Communist vision attempts to embody today seem to also be the ostensive values of our contemporary international order.

The push for egalitarianism and equality, as well as the total liberation of the individual from all constraints, underwrites so much of the policy-making taking place at the highest levels of Western societies today. The fraternity of all peoples has drawn us into one big Oedipalized planetary family which triangulates our identity through Daddy Capital and Mommy State. The international order has as its vision a massively coordinated and interconnected network of open-border nations in which everyone has what they need because of the abundant power of human technology to eradicate need, and in this respect it closely mirrors what communism hoped to achieve (fully automated luxury communism, anyone?).

This book tries to be critical of both the Right and the Left, because both in their own ways are inadequate to the task of living in the freedom of God. However, at the risk of being untimely in my intervention, I'm also deeply concerned that this problem of particularity which so desperately needs to be addressed and worked out in our contemporary moment will enable a return to various forms of oppression through nationalistic projects and highly striated societies. I see this clash between the re-assertion of particularities against the leviathan of universality as the fundamental conflict of our time, and while it looks like the leviathan may have the upper hand, there are all kinds of economic and social factors pointing towards a violent return of particularity. We humans delude ourselves if we ever think that have strayed terribly far from a relapse into barbarism.

As we continue to witness falling birth rates, progressive declines in industrial output, and the depletion of natural resources, the capitalist machine must begin to sputter at some point. When that is, I cannot say. It's dangerous to bet against capitalism because the system itself is built on its own continual self-revolution, but we can also see that the historical and material conditions for the capitalist economic system likely cannot be sustained into the medium-term future without significant advancements in the realm of robotics, artificial intelligence, and energy production to replace human labor. This is why so many industrialized nations are racing to develop these technologies — they realize they won't have enough humans to sustain the growth which the system needs to stay afloat.

Every financial mechanism depends on "line go up" to continue because today's financial wealth only exists by pulling tomorrow's projected value forward in time. Ultimately, the entire financial infra-structure which drives our economies composes an elaborate game of trading bets on positive future outcomes. However, the hegemony of this alliance between the capitalist machine and the global neo-liberal order faces a severe crisis as we are heading into a decades long decline in the world's population. As finite resources like oil, coal, and rare earth metals are mined at ever increasing rates, how will the economic engine sustain itself? Capitalism will need to make an end-run around human beings if it has any hope of propagating itself much further into history, although this was likely the goal all along anyways — as capitalism is ultimately in-human, it preaches a cyborg eschatology in which human beings and machines must fuse and mutate to produce a superior being which will surpass natural man's capabilities.[2] Will this epoch arrive in which human beings are gathered up into a techno-singularity, or will the wheels fall off the machine as we revert to a more primitive level of existence?

For fearing of losing our greatest gift

---

2. Nick Land is the theorist to pay attention to in this respect. I recommend grappling with his vision as advanced in his essay "Meltdown."

In the chaos created by the precarious collapse of the capitalist order, Christian nationalists of both Protestant and Catholic varieties seem to be proposing a return to societies like the one which the Tokugawa regime was trying to establish in Japan during the early decades of the 1600's. We can characterize these societies as having a high level of ethnic, cultural, religious, and ideological uniformity which positions itself over and against an "outside." They sustain their national character through their citizens' imaginary identification with the fictitious whole of "the nation," fundamentally remaking people's experience through various mechanisms of psychological and social control. Further, this entire arrangement rests on violence against a particular rejected part of the community which represents the outside or alien element which must be expelled from the society to maintain its purity. To live in such a society requires one to live "as if" the reigning ideology is true. The reactionary claims to want a return to monarchy, but they are already too enlightened to truly submit to a monarch who claims the divine right of kings. There is no returning to our first innocence (if such a thing ever existed). The best one could do would be to simply LARP, but how can a vital, structured, disciplined society rest on such play-acting unless a powerful deception is perpetrated on the masses by a cynical elite?

We cannot escape the fact that Christianity inherently militates against any such project in which the powerful of a society attempt to construct a coherent and stable national identity in which all can recognize themselves, whether that be racial, ethnic, linguistic, or otherwise, with the goal of producing a unified and mobilized nation. Not only should we reject nationalism on the grounds that "the nation" is imaginary and thus technically impossible to achieve, but we must also vigorously maintain that the cost of attempting to construct such an imaginary object is too high — we must refuse to join in the sacrifice of the scapegoat, whatever and whoever that may happen to be. The nationalist project of a hierarchical world in which everyone and everything finds its place through a collective imaginary necessarily involves this violent sacrifice of the disturbing element within the body politic, for the only thing which a fantasy cannot tolerate is the harsh edges of reality.

Not only does this violence happen at the communal level, but it must also take place at the individual level. The subject is the disturbing element which cracks up the sediment of all our experiences, desires, and imaginary identifications, breaking into our world to turn it upside down. The subject appears as the violent insistence of love, which supersedes every particular in our life-world and posits its own values and objects, radically overturning the smooth operation of ideology in which we have secure answers about what we are, where we are, and what we should do. The subject unsettles those things which seemed so certain before, revealing them as so many contingencies which merely arrogate to themselves a false universality and the deceptive appearance of necessity. We are creatures out of joint, tortured by an infinity within us which cannot be suppressed. To deny this is to play a losing game, but how to embrace this infinity without devouring the world? The subject is burdened with the other-worldly power of being able to create a whole new world by enacting an intervention in the seemingly necessary chain of events which made up the world to that point in time.

The human power to touch the universal constitutes both our blessing and our curse, the terrifying power of the understanding. However, as I have tried to argue in this book, we touch the universal not through a mystical spiritual experience but through the contradictions which make up our lives. The contradiction which founds the imaginary relationship between whole and part, this is the true universal, and this is also where we encounter God's work through His son Jesus Christ. We become like God in His freedom as we side with the contradiction, take it up, and allow it to propel us on a journey of becoming. Only as we work with the contradictions can we begin to struggle towards an achievement of a new and higher synthesis (which is itself only another step towards another synthetic process), but to do this we must refuse to turn away from these painful contradictions by retreating into private meaning-making which cannot satisfy us.

I'm persuaded that the contemporary longing for a hierarchical society with a defined culture, distinctive national character, broad religious unity, and expresses a longing for the type of community which we find in God's kingdom which He is even now working on earth, but this burning desire is misplaced when it becomes identified with these human, all too human, projects which rely on all the structures of violence and control which we are so familiar with as humans. We have lived in our own wickedness so long that we've become addicted to it — violence is the only thing we know. The work of reconciliation, forgiveness, and love demands far too much in terms of being vulnerable with one another, compromising, and painfully struggling towards an unknown outcome, and thus we choose to short circuit that process by using hierarchy, fantasy, and violence to forge our communities in the fire of violence instead of the fire of the Holy Spirit.

The Church is a place where this should not be the case though, like a laboratory where we are experimenting in partnership with God on the road towards the appearance of His Kingdom. This is also why the Church is inescapably political — in the Spirit community, humans and God are learning how to be with one another in a brand new way. St. Paul says that there is now neither Jew nor Greek, slave nor free, rich nor poor in Christ. The Christian Left today reads this as a total abolition of these categories such that we can all be absorbed into an abstract identity of "human," an identity which somehow ends up being a very particular interpretation of what it means to be human, namely, an unattached and sovereign self floating free of attachment. However, projects of Christian nationalism do not take this verse seriously enough, for they put at risk Christianity's incredible innovation, which is its introduction of a radical division which ultimately relativizes every form of loyalty or material bond — be that blood, family, clan, language, people, or nation. Only by negating each of these attachments can we attain a new level of solidarity and flourishing as humans, for the claims which blood, clan, and nation lay upon us demand acts of violence and sacrifice which will ultimately lead us down to the pit.

As Hegel's dialectics demonstrates though, the negation of a particular does not constitute an annihilation or total abolition, but rather a process of becoming in which its truth comes to full self-appearance through a journey in which it others itself and travels through its constitutive moments. The notion or concept which emerges through this dialectical becoming includes both the original object but also those contradictions and negations through which it traveled on the conceptual journey towards becoming actual in time and space. This movement from the indefiniteness of Being to the abstraction of Essence to the actuality of Notion is what Hegel traces for us in his *Science of Logic*, and also charts a path for how we as finite creatures make a transition from object to subject, from pure inert substance to active agency which works and creates new worlds out of the nothingness of pure possibility.

This exact problem faced the Jesuits who first brought Christianity to Japan, and it also confronted those Japanese who embraced the good news of Jesus Christ as it was preached to them. The Jesuits who brought the story of God's death and resurrection to the Japan people were forced to wrestle with what it meant to proclaim God in a place which did not share the same cultural or metaphysical assumptions. How to refer to God in a world that had never known monotheism? No, not a god, not a spirit, not a Buddha... ex-Fr. Ferreira references this problem when he despairs that the Japanese just believe that God is the primordial Sun Buddha ("Dainichi"). He sees this as fundamental limitation rather than the embarkment on a journey whereby the fullness of God-in-Christ may other itself through a radical negation, producing a new understanding of God with us through this experience of wrestling. The Jesuits had to learn to negate their own theological assumptions, and it took courage to see this as an opportunity rather than imposition. It required one to release themselves into a process which cannot be controlled at the outset, a process which Europeans and Japanese could undertake together to understand what it could look like for different peoples to live as one in Christ.

Fr. Rodriguez's life embodies one such attempt to meet this challenge of forging a Japanese experience of God, but I believe that the answer he gives fails in crucial respects. There is an element of fate to this as well, for Rodriguez surely would have chosen the path of martyrdom if it was offered, but by God's providence it never was. Nonetheless, it's still not clear though whether martyrdom is the right answer either. Is Fr. Garrpe's choice to die in his desperate attempts to save the other drowning Japanese-Christians really a better decision? The novel does not cast judgment, and the question remains decisively open. At least Fr. Garrpe avoided becoming complicit with the oppression of the Japanese-Christians like Rodriguez eventually did, but this is as much as we can say, I think. Did the Japanese people need more martyrs, or did they need something else? At a certain point, individual solutions are insufficient to bring to bear on a collective event of struggle.

The emancipation which God achieves on the cross and unveils in His resurrection must be collective first and foremost if it is to mean anything, so the attempt to short circuit the group in order to achieve individual salvation as Fr. Rodriguez did fundamentally misses the point of what God is doing in the world. Endo's novel *Silence* forces us to ask again and again — where is Jesus Christ working in this great darkness, and how do we align ourselves with what he is doing? Certainly what Rodriguez undergoes is a de-centering where he realizes that he is not the hero of his own story, that the story of the Church, and Japan, and the world are not *about* him. We must also come to the threshold of this experience wherein we glimpse our own profound smallness in the open and unfolding process of God and His relation to the world. However, the cross of Christ does not leave us with a sense of futility or paralysis at this seemingly all encompassing mystical vision of a grander Story, but rather it throws us back into the process to engage all the more. Having heard, we must now speak. Having received, we must now give. As we walk drenched in grace, we are free to risk ourselves for others, and to boldly make our minor contribution which we release into a world which we cannot control.

8

—·—

BIBLIOGRAPHY

Bibliography

- Anderson, Benedict. *Imagined Communities: Reflections on the Origin and Spread of Nationalism*. New York: Verso, 2016.

- Barnes, Gina L. *Protohistoric Yamato: Archaeology of the First Japanese State*. Ann Arbor, MI: The University of Michigan Center for Japanese Studies, 1988.

- Baskind, James. "The Matter of the Zen School: Fukansai Habian's *Myotei Mondo* and His Christian Polemic on Buddhism." *Japanese Journal of Religious Studies* 39, no. 2 (2012): 307-331.

- Bowring, Richard *The Religious Traditions of Japan 500-1600*. Cambridge: Cambridge University Press, 2005.

- Boxer, C.R. *The Christian Century in Japan 1549-1650*. Berkeley: University of California Press,1967.

- Cary, Otis. *A History of Christianity in Japan: Roman Catholic, Orthodox, and Protesant Missions.* Tokyo: Charles E. Tuttle Company, 1976.

- Cieslik, Hubert. "The Case of Cristovão Ferreira." Monumenta Nipponica 29, no. 1 (Spring 1974): 1–54.

- Clements, Jonathan. *Christ's Samurai: The True Story of the Shimabara Rebellion.* London: Robinson, 2016.

- Cobbing, Andrew. *Kyushu: Gateway to Japan - A Concise History.* Kent, UK: Global Oriental LTD, 2009.

- Coleridge, Henry James. *The Life and Letters of Francis Xavier.* London: Burns and Oates, 1872.

- Deal, William, and Brian Ruppert. *A Cultural History of Japanese Buddhism.* West Sussex, UK: Wiley Blackwell, 2015.

- Drummond, Richard Henry. *The History of Christianity in Japan.* Grand Rapids, MI: W. B. Eerdmans Publishing Company, 1971.

- Ellison, George. *Deus Destroyed.* Cambridge, MA: Harvard University Press, 1973.

- Endo, Shusaku. *Silence.* New York: Picador, 1969.

- Farris, William Wayne. *Japan to 1600: A Social and Economic History.* Honolulu: University of Hawai'i, 2009.

- Fukansai Habian. *The Myōtei Dialogues: A Japanese Christian Critique of Native Traditions.* Translated by James

Baskind and Richard Bowring, Leiden: Brill, 2015.

- Fujimura, Makoto. *Silence and Beauty*. Downers Grove, IL: IVP Books, 2016.

- Han, Byung-Chul. *The Burnout Society*. Redwood City, CA: Stanford University Press, 2009.

- Hoey III, Jack. "Alessandro Valignano and the Restructuring of the Jesuit Mission in Japan, 1579-1582." *Eleutheria* 1, no. 1 (October 2001).

- Hudson, Mark J. *Ruins of Identity: Ethnogenesis in the Japanese Islands*. Honolulu: University of Hawaii Press, 1999.

- Jennes, Joseph. *History of the Catholic Church in Japan, from its beginnings to the early Meiji period (1549-1873) ; a short handbook*. Tokyo: Committee of the Apostolate, 1959.

- Kasahara, Kazuo. *A History of Japanese Religion*: Tokyo: Kosei Publishing Co., 2001.

- Kitagawa, Joseph M. *Religion in Japanese History*. New York: Columbia University Press, 1990.

- McMullin, Neil. *Buddhism and the State in Sixteenth-Century Japan*. Princeton, NJ: Princeton University Press, 1984.

- Moltmann, Jürgen. *The Crucified God*. Minneapolis, MN: Fortress Press, 1993.

- Oliveira e Costa, João Paulo. "Tokugawa Ieyasu and the Christian Daimyō in the crisis of 1600." *Bulletin for Por-*

tuguese Japanese Studies no. 7 (December 2003), 45-71.

- Sansom, George. *A History of Japan: 1334-1615*: Tokyo: Charles E. Tuttle Company, 1963.

- Sansom, George. *A History of Japan: 1615-1867*: Tokyo: Charles E. Tuttle Company, 1963.

- Sloterdijk, Peter. *Critique of Cynical Reason.* Minneapolis, MN: University of Minnesota Press, 1988.

- Žižek, Slavoj. *Freedom: A Disease without Cure.* London: Bloomsbury, 2023.

- Žižek, Slavoj. *The Puppet and the Dwarf.* Cambridge, MA: The MIT Press, 2003.

- Žizek, Slavoj and John Milbank. *The Monstrosity of Christ.* Cambridge, MA: the MIT Press, 2009.

- Žižek, Slavoj. *Sex and the Failed Absolute.* London: Bloomsbury Academic, 2021.

ABOUT THE AUTHOR

Matthew A. Stanley is an independent scholar who writes about religion, philosophy, and psychoanalysis at Samsara Diagnostics. He has published on a number of topics, including Martin Heidegger, the Kyoto School, and Hegel, and he serves on the board of the Sacramento Psychoanalytic Society. Matthew produces the podcast Samsara Audio where he hosts conversations with thinkers and researchers making interesting contributions in contemporary religion and philosophy. He lives in Sacramento, CA with his wife and son, where they are active in their local Presbyterian church.

Subscribe to the Samsara Diagnostics newsletter free at https://samsara.clinic

You can purchase the ebook and audiobook versions of this book at https://ko-fi.com/samsaradiagnostics

Listen to Samsara Audio on any major podcasting platform, or visit Substack for more.